ONE NATION UNDER CONTRACT

ONE NATION UNDER CONTRACT

*The Outsourcing of American Power
and the Future of Foreign Policy*

Allison Stanger

YALE UNIVERSITY PRESS   NEW HAVEN AND LONDON

Designed by James J. Johnson
Set in Baskerville and Bulmer types by Technologies 'N Typography.

Printed in the United States of America.

Library of Congress Cataloging-in-Publication Data

Stanger, Allison.
One nation under contract: the outsourcing of American power and the future of foreign
policy / Allison Stanger.
    p.   cm.
Includes bibliographical references and index.
ISBN 978-0-300-15265-4 (hardcover: alk. paper)

1. United States—Foreign relations—21st century.   2. National security—United States.
3. Privatization—United States.   4. Contracting out—United States.   5. Government
contractors—United States.   I. Title.
JZ1480.S77 2009
327.73—dc22
2009017133

A catalogue record for this book is available from the British Library.

This paper meets the requirements of ANSI/NISO Z39.48–1992 (Permanence of Paper).

10 9 8 7 6 5 4 3 2 1

Contents

Preface   vii

Acknowledgments   xi

CHAPTER ONE. The New World   1

CHAPTER TWO. The United States of Market Values   12

CHAPTER THREE. State Power in a Privatized World   34

CHAPTER FOUR. The End of Statesmanship   56

CHAPTER FIVE. The Privatization of Defense   84

CHAPTER SIX. The Slow Death of USAID   109

CHAPTER SEVEN. Laissez-Faire Homeland Security   136

CHAPTER EIGHT. A Postindustrial Foreign Policy   162

Notes   185

Bibliography   213

Index   231

Preface

When I began writing this book, Americans were in the era of getting government out of the way so that markets could work their magic. When I finished writing, the pendulum had swung entirely the other way, and we were talking about trillion-dollar bailouts to contain the fallout from market failure. Our collective celebration of free markets after the Cold War's end made many of us lose our sense of the things that only government can do well. That sense is what this book aims to restore.

A good place to begin is by asking a simple question: When Washington transferred billions of dollars to banks in late 2008, who was really in charge? Something fundamental has changed about government when the answer is not obvious. After decades of privatization, the U.S. federal government is today but a shadow of its former self. Democrats and Republicans alike embraced outsourcing the work of government to the private sector whenever possible, both as a perceived cost-savings measure and as a mechanism for getting things done more efficiently. When the Bush administration began to privatize oversight of its programs as well, government played a central role in its own disempowerment. Wholly dependent on contractors, it had no choice but to ask the very forces that had taken excessive risks to get us out of the financial catastrophe that excessive risk-taking had created.

This book is focused on the implications of privatizing foreign policy, a smaller but revealing slice of a larger problem. It argues that outsourcing as presently practiced is scandalous, but turning the clock back and reasserting top-down government control, tempting though it may be, is no solution. Globalization and our penchant for privatization have transformed power itself, expanding the range of options for individuals to make a difference. When Washington outsources so much of its work to the private sector, the old debate about the size of government is rendered moot. We don't need big government or small government. We need good government. And good government in the information age will harness all the networks at its disposal to advance the public interest.

In turn, the threats of the twenty-first century differ radically from those of the Cold War. Our principal enemy is no longer another country but a network of malevolent forces bent on subverting the existing international order. When so much has changed, deploying twentieth century strategies to confront twenty-first century problems can only put us on a road to irreversible decline. In the foreign policy realm, that will inevitably mean greater collaboration, both with other countries and with those transnational networks and individuals that have a shared stake in sustainable globalization. It will mean more public-private cooperation rather than less, and these ventures must be fully transparent to the general public. It will require a reinvention of foreign policy from the bottom-up, a transformation of business as usual—innovation, not renovation.

In the chapters ahead, I explore the impact of outsourcing across the so-called three Ds—diplomacy, defense, and development—as well as homeland security. The sweeping approach is novel for two reasons. First, policy specialists typically focus on one of the three Ds, and a discourse develops that can be hard for the nonspecialist to digest. This language presents a significant impediment to comparison across specialties as well as to public understanding. A focus on one issue area cannot reveal the unprecedented reach of privatization. Second, the enormous technical complexity of contracting and procurement means that it is typically seen inside the beltway as a specialization in itself, divorced from any actual policy. That policymakers frame the issue in this way is itself part of the problem. The impulse to outsource has everything to do with the substantive aims of policy. What at first glance seems like an esoteric concern in fact raises very big questions about both the means and ends of government.

Our revulsion at the tales of corruption, waste, and hypocrisy to be found in the pages that follow should not blind us to the transformative potential of capitalism itself. As Marx himself was keenly aware, capitalism is a revolutionary force, slowly enabling money rather than birth to be the arbiter of prestige and power. It may seem like it is all about profits and self-interest—and it is—but meritocratic values are capitalism's DNA. Capitalism rewards those who generate wealth, regardless of race, class, religion, gender, or national origin. For American-style equality of opportunity to take root, the tyranny of birth and breeding has to be unseated by money. There is a virtue in that reordering that the previously excluded should not undervalue.

To be sure, gross wealth disparities both at home and abroad suggest that the system itself is no longer aligned. The challenge for the developed world will be to narrow the gap between the haves and the have-nots of the planet without maligning the values that have been the engine of global growth and broadening equality. What we need is capitalism with a human face, and capitalism with a human face is all about fairness and choice, not privilege and coercion. But we will never have capitalism with a human face while laissez-faire government outsourcing drives our foreign policy. Unless government provides the appropriate incentives, business will always choose short-term profitability over the common good. And so long as their reelection demands perpetual fundraising, our elected officials will always favor the wealthiest individuals and companies.

Money's conquest of American politics has therefore rendered impotent the well-worn prescriptions of the left and the right, which now deliver only scapegoats rather than solutions. That is because the terms of political engagement have shifted dramatically over the past two decades. In the twentieth century big government was, by definition, bureaucratic government. Today, government can be "big" in terms of spending while handing all its work over to contractors. In the twentieth century, business and government were adversaries. Today, the wall between the two that may have once existed has become a revolving door, and both share common interests. Neither liberal nor conservative visions of good government can be realized so long as government itself is for sale.

While national security is my principal concern, the larger lessons don't stop there. The privatization of American power means we need a brand new template for thinking about how government and the private sector should interact in the digital age. We must restore the American people's trust in government by reaffirming government's irreplaceable role as chief custodian of the public interest. Only government can secure its citizens against threats from within and without; laissez-faire strategies have only failed to deliver what we should never have expected of them. But frustration and moral outrage must not lead us to throw the baby out with the bathwater. We can't be against the private sector, because the private sector is us. That American power has been privatized ultimately means that each of us has potential power that individuals of another generation did not. Coming to terms with the new world is the key to wielding that power for the good.

Acknowledgments

The book you have in your hands is the product of so many acts of human kindness and generosity. My enduring optimism, I realize, is in part a measure of good fortune.

The ideas for this book began to take shape at an October 2004 conference at the Rohatyn Center for International Affairs on the Privatization of National Security, which was co-sponsored by the Princeton Project on National Security. Anne-Marie Slaughter's and John Ikenberry's early enthusiasm and support reinforced my sense that there was a much larger issue to explore. At that conference John Hamre made me see that the outsourcing epidemic was not a phenomenon confined to the Pentagon alone. I subsequently coauthored an article with my colleague Mark Williams on private military companies. I learned important things through that collaboration and was thereafter convinced that security contractors were just a small part of a much larger story. I am indebted to David Shipley of the *New York Times*, who pushed me hard at a critical moment to ground my argument in numbers. Bill Germano deserves special thanks for helping me understand what I needed to do to turn a tangled mess of overlapping ideas into a book proposal.

It would have been impossible to write this book without the insights gleaned from over one hundred interviews with former and current government, NGO, and business leaders. They shared their time and thoughts, often on multiple occasions. Some spoke on the record and others did not, and I learned much from all of them. I am thankful for their invaluable contribution, as well as for the many friends and colleagues who helped me connect with such interesting and committed people.

The staffs at Café Ebel and the Statní Technická Knihovná (State

Technical Library) in Prague and the Middlebury College Library in Vermont were staunch supporters of the project right from the start, creating wonderful work environments through multiple favors and gifts of home-gathered honey—even routinely letting me in before official opening hours. The staff of the Rohatyn Center—Martha Baldwin, Carolann Davis, and Charlotte Tate—provided extraordinary assistance routinely and above all, made work fun. For critical financial support, I am grateful to Middlebury College, which funded my sabbatical in 2006–7, when the first draft of this book was born, and to the James Jermain Professorship in Political Economy and the Russell Leng '60 Professorship in International Politics and Economics.

Books don't get written without loyal friends who listen to your laments and gently suggest remedies when you hit the inevitable bumps in the road. Andrew Moravcsik, Gideon Rose, Anne-Marie Slaughter, and Fareed Zakaria have helped me in countless ways over the years to refine my thoughts and have lifted my spirits when I needed it most. Debora Spar is a wonderful sounding board and perfect ski buddy. Felix and Elizabeth Rohatyn have been an unfailing source of support and friendship. The LSE ladies (Deborah Jospin, C. Nell Henderson, Sally Rand, and Kim Burnett) and Cathy Lee and Darius Nassiry were there when it mattered and made my interview trips to Washington, D.C., guaranteed fun, even when things did not quite go as planned. Tom Friedman's ideas have shaped my thinking in so many ways, and his unrelenting pursuit of the truth is an inspiration to me. David Rothkopf made me laugh aloud, and our conversations always make me think about the world in new ways.

Every step of the way I had outstanding research assistance from Middlebury's students. For their dedication to the cause, I would like to thank Fernando Aragon, Caitlin Arnold, Molly Eberhardt, Andrew Fuller, Brian Fung, David Haglund, Eric Harvey, Courtney Hillebrecht, Haseeb Humayoon, Phil Kehl, Patrick Mott, Scott Robinson, Bilal Sarwary, Ria Shroff, Nicholas Spencer, Colette van der Ven, Rachel Wold, and Allie Widas.

I owe an enormous debt to all those who commented on earlier drafts of the manuscript or portions thereof: John Patrick Allen, Paul Applegarth, Caitlin Arnold, Nathan Bruggeman, Kateri Carmola, Jeff Carpenter, Maria Sartori Clayton, Matt Dickinson, Will Dobson, Stephen Donadio, Murray Dry, Rachel Dry, John Hewko, Bertram Johnson, Charles Tucker Johnson, Michael Kraus, Cathy Lee, Jeffrey Legro, Russell Leng, Ioana Literat, Christopher McGrory Klyza, Michael McKenna, Quinn Mecham, Andrew Moravcsik, Patrick Mott, Darius Nassiry, Andrew Natsios, Keith Reinhard, Elizabeth Robinson, James Robinson, Pathik Root, Anne-Marie

Slaughter, Debora Spar, Jeff Stauch, Max Stier, Charlotte Tate, Thierry Warin, Allie Widas, and five anonymous reviewers for Yale University Press. Their suggestions and feedback sharpened my argument when I possessed neither the insights nor the energy to push things further on my own. You should attribute what you like to their wise counsel, and what you dislike to my shortcomings.

The Middlebury and Harvard undergraduates in my courses on Empires and on American Foreign Policy over the years have been an incredible sounding board; in many ways, this book is written for them. I am grateful to my much missed friend, the late General William E. Odom, for first making me see that they were one of my biggest assets.

I won the lottery with my publishing team. My agent and friend Will Lippincott has been an extraordinary guide and champion, and I couldn't imagine the journey without him. My remarkable editor, William Frucht, understood what I was trying to accomplish even when my thoughts were still half-formed, and his faith in me from the very start has made all the difference. I have learned much from both of them, for which I am deeply grateful. At Yale University Press, Jeff Schier did an amazing job of whipping my prose and footnotes into shape, and editorial assistant Christina Tucker inspired confidence throughout.

Politics is ephemeral but family endures. Here I have been luckiest of all. My iPod would be impoverished and the soundtrack for this book incomplete without the expertise of my sister, fitness goddess Karen Stanger Davis. My baby brother Robert makes me proud. Much to my constant delight, my Prague-born husband Michael's well-developed sense of the absurd makes daily life an exciting adventure and always cause for laughter. He is my best friend and most valued critic. Our beautiful children, Hannah and Jakub, endured multiple absences and eruptions of grumpiness; they even both attended a remarkable Czech school (Základní škola sv. Voršily) while their mother wrote in a nearby café. My parents, Richard and Joan Stanger, gave me everything I needed and more. If this modest effort makes them happy, I will have succeeded.

Three years ago, I told our then-seven-year-old Jakub that if he could just learn Czech and go to Czech school, Mommy would write a book and dedicate it to him. He was more than successful, and as a book lover like his parents, he has never forgotten that promise. Jakub, this one is for you.

1

The New World

Power is a word the meaning of which we do not understand.
—Leo Tolstoy, *War and Peace*

IN THE TWENTIETH CENTURY, if you wanted social change you demonstrated in the streets, lobbied government, or ran for political office. As the successful strategy of the Obama campaign demonstrated, the engaged activist in the twenty-first century has other options. Technology can be deployed to unleash the force of social networks to do unprecedented things. As a result, nongovernmental organizations (NGOs) have never had greater power and reach. For-profit entities are becoming—or at least claiming to be—agents for social change. They have political platforms and pursue agendas that used to be the exclusive domain of government.

Even some megacorporations increasingly sound like governments. In an unprecedented move, retail giant Wal-Mart in January 2008 issued a social manifesto, pledging to cut the energy use of many of its products by 25 percent, force its suppliers to meet stricter ethical standards, and help other companies deliver better health care for their employees. Wal-Mart CEO H. Lee Scott Jr. said, "We live in a time when people are losing confidence in the ability of government to solve problems," but Wal-Mart "does not wait for someone else to solve problems."[1] The same month, Google got into the global development business, announcing it would fulfill a pledge made to investors when it first went public in 2004. Google would henceforth reserve 1 percent of its profit and equity to "make the world a better place." In an unconventional move, the unit in charge of this fund, Google.org, said it would invest in for-profit as well as traditional philanthropic ventures.[2] To fight the AIDS epidemic in Africa, Project (Red), the brainchild of lead singer Bono of the rock group U2 and Kennedy family member Bobby Shriver, has forged a coalition of iconic companies to manufacture Product (Red) branded products. Companies from Dell to Gap to

Apple have signed up to produce Product (Red) goods, and a percentage of proceeds from their sales automatically goes to the Global Fund to help women and children affected by HIV/AIDS in Africa.

Even as the lines between business, philanthropy, and government have grown ever more difficult to draw, government itself has furthered the cross-dressing craze by outsourcing whatever it can to the private sector. The result is that the U.S. government can now conduct neither its foreign policy nor its wars and reconstruction efforts in Iraq and Afghanistan without the extensive and unprecedented support of contractors. While the American people's attention was focused elsewhere, private companies have become a permanent feature of what used to be called governance, both at home and abroad. They are deployed to run American prisons, collect our taxes, interrogate prisoners of war, and guard American diplomatic personnel.

Since the reach of privatization has been extended gradually, it is not something we often notice. Yet by August 2008 the United States had spent over $100 billion on contractors in Iraq alone.[3] Not surprisingly, outsourcing as presently practiced is scandalous, a common result when the work of government takes place beyond the public eye.

Examples of contracting run amok are not difficult to find, and more come to light each day. For-profit foreign aid is now a booming business, with billions of U.S. government dollars flowing into sketchy projects. Afghanistan is a prime example. In 2004, Afghan finance minister Ashraf Ghani was so angered by the poor performance of U.S. contractor BearingPoint that he had the company thrown out of the country. A 2005 congressional study reported that, of 286 schools that were to be rebuilt with United States Agency for International Development (USAID) funds by the Louis Berger Group, only 8 had been completed and that only 15 of 253 planned health clinics were operational. Since contracts in Afghanistan and elsewhere can pass through as many as five layers of subcontracts, each charging a substantial fee as it passes work down the supply chain, when a project does get completed it is often wildly overpriced. For example, a school that costs USAID $250,000 to build can be built by a local Afghan contractor for just $50,000.[4]

The enormous cost overruns for building the world's biggest American embassy in Baghdad, perhaps as much as $144 million above the projected $592 million, replicate this pattern. The lead contractor on the embassy project was First Kuwaiti General Trade and Contracting, which received permission from the Iraqi government to allow some two thousand non-Iraqi construction workers to extend their stay in the country to complete the project. The biggest construction job in Baghdad imported workers instead of hiring Iraqis. The man who had been charged with overseeing the entire project, James L. Golden, himself a contractor, was banned from Iraq by the U.S. ambassador, Ryan Crocker. After a worker died on the job, Golden allegedly destroyed evidence related to the case. The State Department is still looking for funds to cover the unprecedented cost overrun.[5]

With the web of subcontracting making it difficult to figure out what went wrong with any given project, the prospects for corruption and abuse of power grow ever larger. We are only just beginning to see where Washington's penchant for outsourcing has taken us, since much of it is shrouded in proprietary secrecy. But there are some early clues. In 2004, Darleen A. Druyun, the number two weapons buyer for the air force, was sentenced to nine months in prison for steering electronic controls contracts to Boeing for planes that had originally been built by Lockheed Martin, and then overpaying Boeing to boot.[6] Her replacement, Charles D. Riechers, committed suicide in October 2007 following accusations that he had accepted kickbacks from a private contractor, Commonwealth Research Institute.[7] In 2006, the U.S. attorney general's office unsealed charges that a former employee of Kellogg, Brown, and Root (KBR; the company in charge of logistics in Iraq and Afghanistan) had received $124,000 in kickbacks.[8] In February 2007, the army announced that it would withhold $19.6 million from the oilfield services corporation Halliburton after discovering that its subcontractor, ESS Support Services, had hired the armed security firm Blackwater USA to protect its operations. Contrary to Halliburton's interpretation, the army claimed that its five-year, $16 billion contract with Halliburton barred the company and its subcontractors from hiring armed security.[9] In November 2008, the Pentagon's Defense Contract Management Agency found KBR to be in "serious non-compliance" for shoddy electrical work that caused the deaths of at least eighteen troops. Green Beret Ryan Maseth was electrocuted while taking a shower.[10]

The Pentagon is concurrently investigating another Iraq war contractor, the private military company Custer Battles, for cheating the U.S. government out of tens of millions of dollars. Among other charges, Custer Battles is accused of creating sham companies through which it shuttled subcontracts, double-billing for salaries, and repainting the Iraqi Airlines forklifts its workers found at the Baghdad Airport and then leasing them to the U.S. government. The company was banned from operating in Iraq in 2004. The Bush administration never pressed criminal charges, in part because it did not consider Custer Battles an arm of the U.S. government and therefore not liable under U.S. law. "If urgent steps are not taken," the anti-corruption group Transparency International has warned, "Iraq . . . will become the biggest corruption scandal in history."[11]

In addition to the disturbing potential for corruption when money and instructions change hands multiple times in a foreign country, contractors have created a series of diplomatic disasters for the United States. The 2007 killing of seventeen civilians in Baghdad by Blackwater employees was not an isolated incident. In 2005, Blackwater used CS gas—a riot control substance that the army is forbidden to use—at a crowded Baghdad checkpoint, temporarily blinding Iraqi civilians and at least ten U.S. military personnel. Blackwater's State Department contract did not explicitly forbid using CS gas.[12] Contractors figured prominently in the 2004 Abu Ghraib torture scandal. Twenty-seven of the thirty-seven interrogators at Abu Ghraib prison that year were employees of the private military company CACI International, and twenty-two of the linguists who assisted them were employed by California-based Titan International.[13] None of the contractors to date have been prosecuted. In December 2007, 256 Iraqi prisoners filed suit against CACI for abuses in Abu Ghraib and at Guantánamo Bay. In February 2008, we learned that the CIA's secret interrogation program has made extensive use of contractors, in roles that likely included the waterboarding (simulated drowning) of terrorist suspects.[14] In all of these cases, government silence has perpetuated ambiguities over who has legal jurisdiction.

At the same time, and more benignly, globalization has opened up opportunities for individuals and groups to conduct foreign policy without asking for government's permission. Greg Mortensen, best-selling author of *Three Cups of Tea*, built schools for girls in Afghanistan without a license from Washington. The lending activities in Iraq by the nonprofit organization Kiva are another excellent example of the new opportunities for innovative individuals to make their own diplomacy. Kiva (which means "agreement" in Swahili) uses the Internet to connect aspiring entrepreneurs in developing countries with private citizens willing to lend them money. In May 2007, Kiva began adding Iraqi entrepreneurs to its Web site with the disclaimer, "This entrepreneur is from a volatile region where the security situation remains unsettled. Lenders to this business should be aware that this loan may represent a higher risk and accept this additional risk in making their loan." Despite the warning, all the loans were fully funded within a few hours, largely by American citizens who apparently wanted to lend a personal hand to Iraqi reconstruction.[15]

Then there is the Clinton Global Initiative (CGI), which blurs the boundaries still further. A project of our forty-second president, CGI describes itself on its Web site as "a non-partisan catalyst for action, bringing together a community of global leaders to devise and implement innovative solutions to global problems." It operates "to increase the benefits and reduce the burdens of global interdependence." From one perspective, CGI is a standard charity for the information age; its Web site offers opportunities for individuals to contribute directly to development projects around the world. Yet in terms of how it actually functions, it is another animal entirely. While webcast to the public at large, CGI meetings are by invitation only, "limited to a select and diverse group of heads of state, CEOs, media voices, philanthropists, foundation heads, religious leaders, academics, original thinkers, and those who run highly effective non-governmental and non-profit organizations."

What happens at a CGI meeting is quite extraordinary. The second annual meeting, in September 2006, featured prominent individuals and corporations making 262 public commitments totaling more than $7.3 billion. Forty-two current and former heads of state were in attendance, along with more than six hundred business leaders. Sir Richard Branson of Virgin Group pledged a $3 billion investment over the next ten years in alternative energy sources. Citigroup committed $100 million to microfinance programs in the developing world. Siemens offered $10 million for rural health clinics in China. These pledges will be channeled through more than five hundred organizations in more than one hundred countries. CGI is simultaneously a charity, an engine for market creation, and a platform for public figures. Microsoft founder Bill Gates has called it "a deal-maker between rich world producers and poor world consumers."[16]

Gates certainly understands the unharnessed potential of the private sector. In January 2008, in his last speech as a full time employee of Microsoft, Gates urged attendees at the World Economic Forum in Davos to take innovation to the next level and embrace "creative capitalism." Businesses seek both profits and recognition, Gates argued, so recognizing innovative work that reduces poverty, regardless of what motives inspired the initiative, is in the interests of both the public and private sectors. Creative capitalism is "an approach where governments, businesses, and nonprofits work together to stretch the reach of market forces so that more people can make a profit, or gain recognition, doing work that eases the world's inequities." When this new approach to capitalism prevails, "the highest-leverage work that governments can do is to set policy to create market incentives for business activity that improves the lives of the poor."[17]

Gates cited a U.S. law signed into existence by President Bush giving any company that develops a new treatment for a neglected disease like malaria or tuberculosis a fast-track FDA review for another product it has created. In other words, if you commit some of your company's resources to making the world a better place, you may get your new cholesterol-reduction drug on the market a whole lot earlier. That's a powerful incentive. As Gates put it, "There is a growing understanding around the world that when change is driven by proper incentives, you have a sustainable plan for change, because profits and recognition are renewable resources."[18]

Other individual efforts promise to have transformative impact on the world's most vulnerable interest group—our children—while also creating new markets. The mission of One Laptop Per Child (OLPC) is straightforward: to help the children of developing countries to learn by providing one connected laptop to every school-age child. The virtually indestructible $200 XO laptop runs on Linux, is totally self-contained, and is wildly kid-friendly; it looks like a Fisher-Price toy developed for Kermit the Frog. David Pogue, technology correspondent for the *New York Times,* calls it "a kid magnet." Both the XO and OLPC's mission are the brainchild of Nicholas Negroponte, co-founder and director of the MIT Media Laboratory.[19]

In November 2007 OLPC began its innovative "Give One, Get One" model: you could send in $400 and receive in exchange a tax deduction, an XO for yourself, and one to be shipped to a child in the developing world. OLPC is working in partnership with Amazon.com, eBay, Google, and others to get third-world governments interested in large-scale acquisitions of the XO. The educational content—the software—is to be provided by local initiative. In targeting educational systems in need, OLPC is, in effect, making development policy over the head of the U.S. government.[20]

The International Campaign to Ban Landmines (ICBL) is the same phenomenon seen from a slightly different angle. A broad coalition of prominent individuals, middle-power governments, and more than 1,400 NGOs in 90 countries, ICBL has a twofold purpose. First, it seeks action on removing antipersonnel landmines that had already been deployed around the world. Second, it was instrumental in organizing a ban on the future use of these weapons, which more often than not maim innocent civilians. Led by 1997 Nobel Peace Prize recipient Jody Williams, 122 countries gathered in Ottawa in December 1997 to sign the Convention on the Prohibition of the Use, Stockpiling, Production and Transfer of Anti-Personnel Mines, otherwise known as the Ottawa Convention. The United States has yet to sign the treaty, but it was signed by all members of the European Union. The United Nations supports the Ottawa Convention even though the movement was not a UN initiative.[21]

The Bush White House picked up on these innovations and sought to harness their potential. In December 2007, the Bush administration asked Case Foundation CEO Jean Case, president and CEO of the Aspen Institute Walter Isaacson, Citigroup chairman emeritus Sandy Weill, Material Service Corporation chairman Lester Crown, and American Task Force for Palestine president Ziad Asali to serve as co-chairs of the U.S.-

Palestinian Public-Private Partnership, a new venture dedicated to creating economic opportunity for the Palestinian people. This public-private partnership has the full backing of the State Department and USAID and is to complement the efforts of former British prime minister Tony Blair. Since June 2007, private citizen Blair has been special envoy for the "Quartet," which is diplomatic shorthand for the four major outside players in the Israeli-Palestinian peace process: the United States, Russia, the European Union, and the United Nations.[22] In other words, the U.S.-Palestinian Public-Private Partnership has been tasked by the U.S. government to work in conjunction with a private citizen on behalf of the world and at the behest of no single country.

These seemingly disparate stories reveal an entirely new picture of our world. On the one hand, the U.S. government has embraced outsourcing as a solution for every international problem, with often disastrous consequences. On the other hand, a simultaneous explosion of creative bottom-up initiatives has had real foreign policy impact. Taken together, these two observations lead to an unavoidable conclusion: American power is taking on a different shape.

Consider a third observation, and the general trend becomes obvious. American and European corporations have displayed unprecedented global muscle relative to national governments. Wal-Mart's revenues in 2005 were larger than the total gross domestic product (GDP) of all of sub-Saharan Africa.[23] In 2006, the combined sales of the top five multinational companies—ExxonMobil, Wal-Mart, Royal Dutch Shell, BP, and General Motors—were larger than the GDP of all but thirteen countries. "Exxon Mobil," writes David Rothkopf, who was Clinton administration deputy undersecretary of commerce, "is bigger than Sweden (the world's twentieth largest economy). Wal-Mart ranks between Argentina and Hong Kong, and General Motors tops Peru."[24] In 2007, Rothkopf examined all entities with sales or GDP greater than $50 billion and found that the majority (89 of 172) were private companies.[25]

These three observations represent different aspects of the privatization of American power. In all three instances, privatization transfers responsibilities that were once the exclusive preserve of government to private actors. When government or business chooses to devolve work to others outside their immediate community, this is called outsourcing. Work can be outsourced to NGOs, for-profit entities, or some hybrid of the two (because the line has become so blurred, I will use the term "private sector" to encompass both for-profit and not-for-profit actors). Most Americans are unaware that the large growth in American philanthropic power in recent years is primarily a product of government outsourcing, not increased individual charitable contributions, which have remained roughly steady in the same time period as a percentage of GDP.[26] But privatization also encompasses functions one would never expect to see outsourced as "work," including oversight and even policymaking itself.

With its emphasis on individual initiative, privatization is an expression of core American values. Yet the outsourcing of oversight and the lack of transparency that has accompanied its rise undermine those very values. Public-private partnerships that exploit the information revolution to common advantage can help ensure that government has the necessary capacity to provide for the public good. Since the private sector has already been entrusted by government to do so much, it makes sense to think creatively about the business-government relationship. But the ultimate responsibility for ensuring pursuit of the common good falls to government alone. Unfortunately, a government dependent on contractors to function too easily loses sight of those things that only government can do well.

A member of the antiglobalization movement might protest that "enlightened" business-government collaboration is merely a cover for rapacious capitalist greed. The implicit assumption seems to be that it would be desirable to turn the clock back and reassert traditional government authority in some unclearly specified way. That would be a terrible mistake, for at least two reasons. First, power in the international system has already been transformed. Private actors will continue to make their own foreign policy with or without an overt government response. Second, in pursuing its privatization agenda, the U.S. government has undermined its capacity for independent action. Curtailing outsourcing without simultaneously addressing government's precarious condition is a recipe for a worse disaster than anything contracting has yet brought about.

With the unprecedented privatization of American power, functions that were once exclusively the province of the U.S. government have diffused to corporations, civic groups, and individual social entrepreneurs. Many of these independent actors are American. But even when they are not, they are part of a global coalition that is animated by the universal values first embraced by America's founders. They believe in the power of free markets and equality of opportunity. They strive to promote these values worldwide, just as the American government does, though in countless decentralized and more effective ways.

This vast web of actors can thus be understood as an empire—of a kind the world has never seen before. It is vast in its dominion, controlling untold riches and reaching all corners of the earth. But unlike any previous empire, it has no emperor and no subjects. It is an empire of the willing. It would not exist without the American contribution, but it is not an American empire. Its stakeholders are all those around the world, from the governments of liberal democracies to beleaguered individuals in distant lands, who share its core values.

The empire of the willing advances its interests through the universal appeal of its ideals: economic freedom, equality of opportunity, and sustainability. It unites human beings across borders, inviting the newly enfranchised into its ranks regardless of national origin, race, gender, or creed. In measuring value through economic achievement, it lays waste to all other prestige hierarchies, which is why traditional elites around the world find its core values threatening to their interests. The empire of the willing is a vehicle of change that does not shrink from tearing down the very hierarchies that helped create it.

It is a measure of American confusion that the U.S. presence in Iraq and Afghanistan has to date been a textbook case of traditional imperial intervention. Fitting our three core facts together—hollowed-out government, private-sector innovation, and unprecedented corporate power—and understanding the extent to which American foreign policy has already been privatized provides the flare we need to regain our bearings. Getting the United States back on course requires acknowledging that unenlightened outsourcing—our present standard practice—creates an enormous accountability vacuum that has enabled three dangerous developments: gross fiscal irresponsibility, dangerous apathy among the public at large, and the inadvertent militarization of American foreign policy. Let me take up each of these individually.

First, explosive overseas outsourcing has gone hand in hand with gross fiscal irresponsibility.[27] We are spending huge sums of money without the most basic accounting procedures in place for monitoring and evaluating our expenditures. For example, one Iraqi former chief investigator testified before Congress in September 2008 that $13 billion in reconstruction funds from the United States had gone walking.[28] Subcontracting chains only intensify this effect. What the U.S. government does would never cut it in the private sector. Business has a bottom line, so when a business outsources irresponsibly, people get fired or the company goes out of business—except when they are the beneficiaries of a government handout. The same is not true of government, which can defer the day of reckoning indefinitely, because a country cannot cease to exist. The inflated costs and other consequences are passed on to our children and grandchildren. When the U.S. government borrows and prints money to bail out businesses that have screwed up, we have taken our fiscal irresponsibility to a new level.

Second, when government cedes responsibility to contractors, the general public is one step further removed from the choices its elected officials have made. Without contractors, who supply the vast majority of the support services in Iraq in order to free up military personnel for combat roles, the Bush administration would have had to institute a draft to wage its war there. All of America's sons and daughters would face having to go off and fight, and popular discontent would make our presence in Iraq unsustainable. Instead, the American public has chosen to tolerate a war most of us feel is bad for the nation, provided we don't have to be personally involved. Alexis de Tocqueville warned of the soft despotism that could overtake American democracy should American individualism lose its vital connection to the common good. As he put it, "Citizens quit their state of dependence just long enough to choose their masters and then fall back into it."[29] Tocqueville's antidote was his doctrine of self-interest, properly understood. His enlightened self-interest is the key to reviving civic virtue at home. The sustainability of globalization itself now depends on it.

Third, our addiction to outsourcing has inadvertently facilitated the militarization of American foreign policy. This is not an inevitable consequence of outsourcing but a peculiarity of the American government, where the Pentagon, with by far the largest budget, can vastly outspend all other departments. It can also outspend other countries; Americans spend more on their military than do the defense budgets of the rest of the developed world combined. In part because the Pentagon budget dwarfs all others, the face America presents to the world is increasingly a military one. This alienates our allies in an era when the biggest threats—terrorism, nuclear proliferation, global inequality, and climate change—demand extensive cooperation. These challenges cannot be met with Pentagon muscle alone, and indeed, the rippling muscle may decrease the appetite for collaboration among the potentially like-minded. While Department of Defense's faithful execution of government wishes is admirable, just because the Pentagon is able to do something doesn't mean that it should. Promoting American values through the military, a massive symbol of coercion rather than choice, often undercuts those very values.

In all realms, nonstrategic outsourcing works at cross-purposes with American interests. We have to be more strategic: we have to think creatively about harnessing the formidable power of the private sector to meet the challenges of twenty-first century global leadership. We need to propose ways that government can join forces with business to advance their mutual interest in sustainability. While hard economic times will make it more difficult, private sector aspirations must not solely be seen as a problem for government to police but as a vital part of the solution. The times demand a foreign policy that acknowledges the privatization of American power rather than denying it or endeavoring to undo it.

It is easy to see things gone awry and to scapegoat contractors. But contractors aren't the problem; the problem is the loss of good government. If the contractors in Iraq seem wildly expensive, it is not because corporate greed has dictated outcomes but because government's aspirations there have been far too ambitious and its controls far too few. When private security forces overstep moral bounds, it is ultimately government's responsibility for having deployed them in a conflict zone with too little legal recourse if they misbehaved. The 2007 Blackwater scandal, which hinted at the extent of the federal government's addiction to outsourcing, can have a positive effect if it sparks a national discussion on which functions should never be outsourced and redirects public attention to the proper ends of government. Government cannot properly lead if it refuses to take responsibility for what it has been called into being to do.

The outsourcing of foreign policy matters enormously for America's strategic interaction with the world, but it has yet to be explored in a systematic and comprehensive fashion. If we ever hope to realign our foreign policy to fit the new reality of a privatized world, we have to get outsourcing right: we must manage it in a way that furthers American values and interests and does not, as was the case in Iraq, subvert them. If power has been privatized, the state must not simply issue orders but must actively seek new forms of collaboration. Cooperation among states is, of course, nothing new, but the question of how government should optimally collaborate with the private sector to advance its international interests is a topic that has yet to receive proper attention.

Strategic outsourcing with appropriate oversight can serve American interests, but our foreign policy during the Bush years was anything but strategic. So where do we go from here? Ultimately, detailed reform proposals must come from those closest to particular problems. To argue otherwise would be to contradict a central message of this book: that top-down decrees and large government bureaucracies are obsolete tools for securing legitimacy in the postindustrial era. To tackle global problems, we will need to harness the power of bottom-up innovation and embrace radical transparency to ensure fair play. Washington will not get there on its own. The American people will have to intervene and lead.

2

The United States of Market Values

This, too, is probable, according to that saying of Agathon: It is a part of
probability that many improbable things will happen.
—Aristotle, *Poetics*

The Americans have this great advantage, that they attained democracy
without the suffering of a democratic revolution and that they were born
equal instead of becoming so.
—Alexis de Tocqueville, *Democracy in America*

K NOCK ON THE DOOR of the federal government in 2009, and
chances are that you will find nobody home. The U.S. government's impulse to exploit the comparative advantage of the private sector, and the private sector's responsiveness to demand for its services, have combined to replace big government with a staggeringly large
shadow government. In this new world, the private sector increasingly han-
dles the everyday business of governing.

It is hard to grasp the scale of this shadow government. The biggest
federal contractor, Lockheed Martin, which spent $53 million on lobbying
and $6 million on donations from 2000 to 2006, gets more federal money
each year than the Departments of Justice or Energy.[1] Lockheed Martin
sorts your mail, tallies up your taxes, cuts social security checks, counts
people for the U.S. census, runs space flights, and monitors air traffic. Almost 80 percent of its revenues come directly from the U.S. government.[2]
And Lockheed is just one such beneficiary. The top five U.S. contractors—
Lockheed Martin, Boeing, Northrop, General Dynamics, and Raytheon—
reaped *profits* totaling $12.94 billion in 2005.[3] For a sense of just how lu-
crative government contracts can be, consider that former Wall Street
juggernaut Goldman Sachs at the height of its powers reported profits of
$5.6 billion that same year.

Federal government reliance on contractors accelerated rapidly in the
George W. Bush years. Contract spending more than doubled during Presi-

dent Bush's time in office, having grown from $201.3 billion in 2000 to $377.5 billion by 2005 alone, an 86 percent increase. In 2007, Washington spent $439.5 billion on contracts. By that time, the federal government was spending more than 40 cents of every discretionary dollar on contracts with private companies.[4]

Conventional wisdom would point to the ideology of the Bush administration as the driving force in this trend. While blind faith in the free market and a contempt for government is certainly part of the picture, blaming the explosion of outsourcing on Bush alone, or even on the Republican Party, is to miss a much larger story.

That story has two major threads. The first involves choices made by both Democrats and Republicans regarding how foreign policy is pursued. The second follows from the opportunities globalization presented to both parties. With respect to partisan choices, the Democratic Party slowly came to wholly embrace what was once a largely Republican faith in the potential of the private sector to outperform government. As a result, a twenty-first century stimulus package will of necessity be different in kind from its twentieth century predecessors. Calls for increased government spending might sound like a return to big government, but we are a far cry from the New Deal when contractors lead the charge. Since outsourcing is now a bipartisan venture, big spending need no longer mean big government bureaucracy.

When most people hear the term "outsourcing," they think about what globalization might mean for employment opportunities in America. To the government, however, outsourcing is a matter of how taxpayer money is spent; in budgetary terms, it is simply the total of government contracts plus grants. Government outsourcing involves the transfer of jobs from the public to private sectors, but the work itself may be done by nonprofit organizations, for-profit organizations, or some hybrid entity.

While privatization was at first primarily focused on activities on American soil, overseas outsourcing has now turned the choices of American policymakers into a genuinely global concern. The complexity and geographic scope of the web of contracts and subcontracts has remade the character of Washington's relationship with American citizens and with the world.

The Shadow Government

The shadow government can trace its founding moment to the Eisenhower administration, when concerns about government bloat and the associated fiscal challenges led the president to instruct government agencies to pur-

chase as much as possible from private sources. He issued an executive order prohibiting the federal government from engaging in "any commercial
activity to provide a service or product for its own use if such product or
service can be procured from private enterprise through ordinary business
channels."[5] This order became the point of departure for Office of Management and Budget (OMB) Circular Number A-76, whose basic aim was
to put activities currently performed by government out for public-private
competition. Functions identified as "inherently governmental" were not
to be candidates for outsourcing.

Eisenhower's concerns were a rational response to a dramatically new
postwar institutional environment. The National Security Act of 1947 had
created a brand new national security architecture that included the new
Department of Defense and made wartime-sized federal budgets a peacetime norm, increasing both the size of government and the scope for outsourcing. Despite the dramatic demobilization of American forces, after
World War II the federal budget would never return to prewar levels. The
government's projected total outlays for 1947 were roughly four times what
they had been in 1940, and they escalated exponentially from there. Even
with the reductions in military spending after the Cold War's end, America's 1995 military budget approximately equaled the 1980 budget in real
terms.[6]

The drive to harness private sector power to the public good cannot be
properly understood without an awareness of the enormous impact of the
new Pentagon on the size of government. Big government's shortcomings,
the Eisenhower administration reasoned, could be circumvented by harnessing private sector energy, efficiency, and initiative to government ends.
Outsourcing followed directly from core American values: faith in free
markets and free trade, distrust of big and distant government, and the belief that individuals deserve to reap the benefits of their own striving.

Eisenhower's exhortation also cannot be separated from his anxieties
about the consequences of creating a peacetime defense establishment. As
he memorably noted in his 1961 farewell address, "We have been compelled
to create a permanent armaments industry of vast proportions. . . . We annually spend on military security more than the net income of all United
States corporations." This massive concentration of federal power, while
"imperative," also had potential for great abuse. The United States had to
"guard against the acquisition of unwarranted influence, whether sought
or unsought, by the military-industrial complex."[7] Viewed in this light,
Eisenhower's support of privatization may have been intended as a check
on expanded federal power, consistent with the founders' desire to let "ambition counter ambition."

Outsourcing took a back seat during the Vietnam years, but the Reagan administration enthusiastically revived the privatization theme. Its 1983 revision of the OMB A-76 process amounted to a free-market call to arms: "In the process of governing, the government should not compete with its citizens. The competitive enterprise system, characterized by individual freedom and initiative, is the primary source of national economic strength. In recognition of this principle, it has been and continues to be the general policy of the government to rely on commercial sources to supply the products and services government needs."[8]

For the Reagan team, the privatization impulse also extended to foreign policy. When Congress cut off funding to the Contras rebel group in Nicaragua, Oliver North and the rest of Reagan's National Security Council outsourced the job to private actors, with wholly disastrous consequences. But Iran-Contra was a scandal that exposed a covert operation; Reagan's Contras had no government contracts. The security contractors hired by our government today work for firms whose shares are traded on the New York Stock Exchange.

Surprisingly, it was the Democrats who expanded outsourcing to include armed security contractors. During the Clinton years, the U.S. government sanctioned the use of third-party military personnel in Colombia and the former Yugoslavia. Back at home, the Clinton team sought to "reinvent government," which in turn brought them, like their Republican predecessors, to revising the A-76 process. The Clinton administration restated the outsourcing principle in less idealistic terms, releasing guidelines that explained, "Americans want to 'get their money's worth' and want a government that is more businesslike and better managed. . . . Circular A-76 is not designed to simply contract out. Rather, it is designed to . . . empower federal managers to make sound and justifiable business decisions."[9]

The Clinton administration also promulgated the Federal Activities Inventory Reform (FAIR) Act of 1998, which requires federal agencies to submit annual inventories of their commercial activities—an exercise that is meant to encourage smart outsourcing. As part of this process, agencies are required to identify work that can be outsourced.[10] By definition, then, anything identified as suitable for public-private competition is not inherently governmental. Agency officials were thus indirectly left to determine, on an ad hoc basis, the purposes of government.

In theory, the revised A-76 process is supposed to compel government agencies to divide what they do into core and peripheral functions. Core functions are those activities that are "inherently governmental," and peripheral functions are candidates for outsourcing to the private sector. The reigning definition of "inherently governmental" can be found in the Federal Acquisition Regulation (FAR), Office of Federal Procurement Policy Letter 92–1.[11] An inherently governmental job, it says, is a "function that is so intimately related to the public interest as to require performance by federal government employees."[12] In practice, agencies over time have found such functions to be fewer and fewer.[13] Government has gradually been hollowed out.

The question of how the U.S. Constitution assigns sovereignty sheds interesting light on the accountability predicament that follows from hollowed-out government. In his thoughtful book *Outsourcing Sovereignty*, Cardozo law professor Paul Verkuil draws upon Gordon Wood's important work on the debates leading up the Constitution's ratification to show how the Federalists and Anti-Federalists resolved a thorny dispute over sovereignty. Put simply, for Anti-Federalists, sovereignty resided with the states, and they saw the new federal constitution as raising the prospect of divided sovereignty between the Congress and the states. Wood tells us that James Wilson forged the key compromise by arguing that sovereignty actually resided with the people, who delegated powers in such proportions as they saw fit among the states and the three branches of government. As a result, the Constitution begins with "We the People" rather than "We the States."[14]

That sovereignty ultimately resides with the people opens up new ways of thinking about both privatization and accountability in the information age. Privatization can be more than what Princeton professor Paul Starr has called "an effort on the part of conservatives to enhance their own power position."[15] If the people are sovereign, they can in theory give tacit consent to government's delegation to the private sector—once they are fully informed that the government has indeed been doing this for quite some time. That the people are ultimately sovereign also creates possibilities for improved accountability above and beyond better congressional oversight. But those solutions will not spontaneously arise. Government and the people must make them happen.

As this book was being written, Congress was heading down another road. In May 2008, a House bill, the Fiscal 2009 National Defense Authorization Act, passed out of committee but did not become law before the close of that session. If the bill is reintroduced and becomes law in the next session, it would freeze competitive sourcing for three years and impose stricter standards for contractor ethics.[16] In so doing, the dynamic fueling outsourcing since the Eisenhower years would be temporarily suspended. Would this amount to turning the clock back and reasserting top-down government authority? If government itself had been wholly untouched by privatization, then perhaps. But that is hardly the case.

The Hollowing-out of Government

Despite the natural human inclination to defend turf, over time government power has gradually been diffused. The story does not reside in one definitive statistic but in a series of numbers that make the overarching trend eminently clear. One fact, however, speaks louder than most others: the size of the executive branch federal workforce in 2008 was the same as it was in 1963. The federal government had 1.9 million civilian employees (including temporary workers but not the Post Office) in 1963, and the same number in 2006. But the federal budget in 1963 was roughly $111.3 billion, versus $2.7 *trillion* in 2006.[17] Adjusting for inflation, the differential is still staggering: $733.3 billion in 1963 versus $2.7 trillion in 2006.[18] That enormous gap is filled by contractors.

Using these inflation-adjusted figures, each government employee has gone from being responsible for overseeing $385,947 in 1963 to $1,421,053 in 2006. This might be less worrisome if the acquisition workforce (those involved in buying goods and services on behalf of the government) had expanded dramatically in the same period. But it hasn't. As the scope and character of contracting has changed, the number of acquisition professionals within government has not kept pace with the demand for their skills.

Using effectively the same number of people to oversee almost four times the number of dollars has had several unintended consequences. The first is a human capital crisis of staggering proportions, which in turn, has two key facets to it. For starters, there simply are not enough warm bodies in government service to man the oversight positions. Testifying before Congress in January 2008, retired army general David M. Maddox reported that the Pentagon's acquisition workforce shrank by 25 percent from 1990 to the end of fiscal year 2000. During the same period, the volume of contracting increased sevenfold. In 1990, the army had five general officer slots for career contracting positions; today it has none. In addition, only about half of the military personnel in the contracting field today "are certified for their current positions."[19]

The second key facet of government's human capital crisis follows from the diminished attractiveness of low-paying government positions when comparable work in the private sector is available at higher pay. As the Partnership for Public Service's landmark 2006 study diplomatically put it, "These increasingly difficult work conditions have made the retention of experienced staff a pressing challenge for the acquisition community."[20] Few people can resist the temptation to serve in government only long enough to land a lucrative position at the other end of the contract relationship.

The long-delayed reckoning with this human capital crisis may well be upon us, as policymakers struggle to deal with the future of the Iraq intervention, an enterprise wholly reliant on contractor support. But even if that crisis can be successfully finessed, another is sure to follow. Brookings Institution scholar Paul Light has identified what he calls a "thickening" of the federal government over time, a rise in the ratio of middle managers to subordinates as the shadow government of contractors has grown. In 1997, for the first time federal employees of the middle ranks of government outnumbered those occupying the lowest rungs of the organizational chart.[21]

It is easy to understand how this thickening came into being. As basic functions were outsourced, there was no longer a need to keep line-level talent in-house. The majority of government employees became managers. But with a big wave of middle management retirements on the horizon, the federal government will soon face an existential crisis. Does it need to replace the retirees, or should it simply let their positions wither away as a precondition for redefining itself? No one should want a federal government that outsources freely but has in place neither appropriate mechanisms for oversight nor the full-time employees in-house to ensure responsible management.

Another unintended consequence of the hollowing-out of government is a potentially huge accountability crisis. Since our government ventures abroad depend on contractors, and since most contracts prompt a chain of subcontracting (remember, the government only recently started tracking subcontracts), much of our foreign policy has consequently been rendered opaque. The oversight gap creates the perfect conditions for all variants of corruption and abuse of power. As a result, our government is disbursing enormous sums abroad without having the capacity to assess properly whether this money has actually reached its destination or accomplished what it was dispatched to do.

In part, this uncertainty follows from the necessary tradeoff between efficiency and responsibility. Stephen Goldsmith and William Eggers have argued that the "accountability dilemma" presents "networked government" with its greatest challenge. The central problem is that traditional accountability mechanisms "clash with the very purpose of the network: to provide a decentralized, flexible, individualized and creative response to a public problem."[22] Acknowledging that "ensuring accountability in a government of networks," which is precisely what the web of relationships forged through privatization constitutes, "is more of an art than a science," Goldsmith and Eggers see the accountability problem as a human capital issue. Without the right sorts of managers in government, the right sorts of partnerships will not be forged, and the potential for networked government to go badly awry will be ever present.[23] But it is not easy to put in place the right sorts of managers during a human capital emergency.

The seriousness of the accountability challenge is reflected in disturbing war stories from Iraq. There were over three hundred reported cases of contracting mistakes or abuses in Iraq from 2003 through 2007. In January 2008, Stuart W. Bowen Jr., special inspector general for Iraq reconstruction, and William M. Solis, director of defense capabilities and management for the Government Accountability Office, testified before Congress that they knew of not a single instance of anyone being fired or denied promotion in connection with those cases.[24] In a stunning confession, the Pentagon itself acknowledged that $8.2 billion of taxpayer money flowed through contracts into Iraq, some in stacks or pallets of cash, without appropriate record-keeping or oversight. Huge sums of money were also funneled to our allies without any accompanying explanation. For example, $68.2 million went to the United Kingdom, $45.3 million to Poland, and $21.3 million to Korea, yet Pentagon auditors were unable to determine why the payments were made.[25] Government knows that something has gone wrong, but it is so shorthanded that it cannot do anything about it.

How did we arrive at this alarming state of affairs? Some have argued that the hollowing-out of government is the result of legislation limiting the size of government; the resulting reduction of government capacity then necessitates further contraction, producing a host of negative unintended consequences. For example, "the reduction of USAID staff over the past 30 years has been so severe," said former USAID administrator Andrew Natsios, that "it can't adequately manage the programs it has contracted out."[26] Others focus on the pay differentials that siphon the best and the brightest from government service to more lucrative positions in the private sector. Still others are not sure that head count limits for civil servants are a cause or a consequence; they argue that the real driving force is the sea change in socioeconomic relations brought about by technology.[27] One does not have to solve this chicken-and-egg problem to see that the problem is unlikely to abate without direct and forceful intervention.

The trends already in motion are only further reinforced by a longstanding American suspicion of concentrated government power. Faith in the transformative power of private property and free markets has been a feature of American political life since the founding. When compared to citizens of other countries, Americans are off the charts with their unwavering faith in the superiority of market solutions to social problems. It is not a stretch to depict the American revolution itself as a struggle for the right to the fruits of one's labors, to keep surplus value in the hands of the local population rather than surrendering it to imperial governors. The collapse of communism as a viable alternative to market forms of economic organization only strengthened the existing American inclination to rely on the private sector, broadly defined, whenever possible.

This distinctive attitude facilitates an equally distinctive understanding of privatization. In the former communist bloc and parts of the developing world, privatization means restructuring the state to facilitate markets and civil society. In the developed capitalist countries, privatization changes the public-private balance. But the United States, with little nationalized industry, has uniquely understood privatization as private sector involvement in public policy.[28] Treasury secretary Henry Paulson's $350 billion bailout in fall 2008 was emblematic. His plan sought to rescue the financial system with a cash infusion to banks and one very large insurance company so that the private sector could rescue itself.

Even within that carefully defined frame, privatization can mean different things to different people. There are three principal forms that privatization can take. First, it can refer to delivery of goods and services (contracting and government grants to private entities) as well as societal infrastructure (public-private partnerships to build things that people need). Second, it can refer to privatization of financing (getting money from the private sector rather than government) or the utilization of private sector personnel to accomplish government ends. Finally, privatization is sometimes used to refer to the application of private sector best practices to the public sector's work. For example, government employees can simply realize they have customers and services and act accordingly, rather than hand their work to the private sector.[29]

If government deems the private sector better suited to pursue its agenda in some situations, it has a complementary responsibility, as custodian of the public good, to delineate clearly what only government can and should do well. Absent that declaration of purpose, government behaves irresponsibly, and its choices unwittingly undermine the public's faith in its legitimacy and accountability. The most ominous consequence of hollowing-out is a government that has lost its sense of purpose. Responding to that disaster, however, will require the direct involvement of the American people. Since every contract represents jobs in some congressman's district, Congress has little incentive to devise or facilitate desperately needed postindustrial strategies for oversight and accountability unless ordinary citizens demand that it do so.

Transparency and Accountability

In writing this book, I struggled to come to terms with the magnitude of change in how our government functions. A few stories cannot, on their own, pin down this transformation, but they can illuminate the challenges ahead.

Until recently, data on the broadening scope of government-wide procurement was unavailable to the general public. That changed in 2003 with the launch of the General Services Administration's Federal Procurement Data Service (FPDS), which made data on contract spending (both for-profit and not-for-profit) available to registered users.[30] Since FPDS issued annual reports and made them publicly available on its Web site, its launch marked the start of a new era of relative transparency. In 2006, the Federal Funding Accountability and Transparency Act (FFATA) took things a step further when it instructed the White House Office of Management and Budget to create and maintain a user-friendly searchable database that covers all federal spending. To public acclaim, USAspending.gov came online one month ahead of schedule, in December 2007. For the first time, the public could see in detail how the federal government spends taxpayer money. The Web site crossed all sorts of divides. Not only did Barack Obama, then just the junior senator from Illinois, and Sen. Tom Coburn (R-Oklahoma) co-sponsor the legislation, but the Office of Management and Budget partnered with OMB Watch, a nonprofit organization founded to keep OMB honest, to devise the new Web site's software.

The Web site is dramatically expanding the scope and quality of information available to the public on contracting and subcontracting. The legislation stipulated that the database be updated within thirty days of a contract or grant being formalized. While the deadline was not met, it also mandated that OMB's database be expanded by January 2009 to include information on subcontracts and subgrants.[31] USAspending.gov relies on FPDS contracting numbers but corrects for inaccuracies it detects in its by-agency figures before presenting them to the public.[32] Its welcome screen boasts: "Where Americans Can See Where Their Money Goes." The site provides greater detail and is much more user-friendly than its predecessor, FPDS. Think plug-and-play rather than having to register as a user before being able to make full use of the data.

FFATA was long overdue. Despite the tremendous amounts of money involved, government needed a push to launch a concerted effort to track those flows accurately. In a 2005 letter to OMB director Joshua Bolten, Katherine Schinasi of Congress's Government Accountability Office (GAO) flagged the many problems that persisted with FPDS data, despite the progress that had been made on gathering the data and making it more readily accessible. Thanks in part to this prodding, the first bird's-eye view of federal procurement data was presented to the public in early 2006. All available evidence suggests that the numbers were hastily cobbled together to address GAO concerns. In other words, it is not as though government always had an internal tracking system that it has only recently disclosed to the public. Putting together a government-wide system for tracking contracts and subcontracts was spurred by FFATA and remains a work in progress.

Unbelievably, while the Department of Defense has always represented at least 60 percent of total contracting in the federal government, its numbers seem not to have been fully integrated within the FPDS system and database until early 2007. I tried to determine when the governmentwide General Services Administration (GSA) reports that track contracting over time had been updated to include Defense Department numbers. The evidence at hand suggests that OMB was at first forced to estimate these numbers after the Pentagon could not supply the requested figures. When I inquired at the Pentagon in January, March, and June 2007, Pentagon officials did not say they refused to deliver the figures in order to protect classified information; they simply had never collected the data that would have allowed them to respond properly to the OMB request. As Stanley Trice, the Pentagon's director of finance, audits, and internal management controls, put it in June 2007, "We tried to figure it out retroactively, but it would have taken too long since there were no databases in place."[33]

As of early 2008, FPDS had yet to release 2006 numbers, so I tried to use USAspending.gov to see how the 2007 troop surge in Iraq had affected the Pentagon's contract spending. FPDS summary reports showed exponential growth in Department of Defense and Department of Homeland Security (DHS) spending on contracts from 2000 to 2005 (DOD spent $268.4 billion and DHS $10.3 billion in 2005). When I logged on to USAspending.gov for the first time in early March 2008, I expected to see a continued upward trend. Yet my first visit yielded something less than transparent. As promised, the site features data on Defense and Homeland Security contract spending. But it was already displaying total figures for 2006 and 2007, citing FPDS as the source of the numbers. That would have been about two months ahead of schedule, as the official numbers for

2006 were released to the public only on May 18, 2008. There was no indication, however, that the agency numbers weren't final and definitive.

I poked around a little bit more and pulled up DOD total contracting figures for 2007. They revealed a downward trend from 2006. The same was true of DHS. How could it be, I wondered, that we actually spent less on DOD contracts in the year of the surge than we did in 2006? Perhaps all the results were not yet in? The summary graph suggested otherwise; the asterisk next to 2008, signifying incomplete data, implied that prior years were complete.

I checked back a month later, in April 2008, and discovered that the numbers had shifted profoundly. Now DOD contracting was on an upward trajectory from 2006 to 2007. That made more sense, yet the summary chart still suggested that the fiscal year had already been closed out. So why were the numbers a moving target? I made some calls and turned up two surprising bits of information. First, all appearances to the contrary, the summary numbers for both 2006 and 2007 were still a live data stream that changed as more reports flowed in; nothing tells visitors to the site when a year has been officially closed out. Second, and more disturbing, the numbers on OMB's site disagreed with other established sources, because OMB is "cleansing" the agency data. But nothing on the site says how or through what process the data is being cleansed.

There is nothing wrong with data cleansing in principle. When numbers are less than accurate for whatever reason, cleaning up data can give us a clearer picture. Yet if USAspending.gov aims for transparency and accountability, visitors to the site obviously need to be told why and how data is being cleansed. When this happens without full disclosure of the methods deployed, Americans cannot possibly see where their money goes.[34]

To their credit, after I had expressed my concerns in the *Washington Post*, both OMB Watch and OMB publicly acknowledged the problems with FPDS data and pledged to improve both data quality and transparency.[35] Figure 1, which compares FPDS with USAspending.gov figures for fiscal year 2005, illustrates the magnitude of the challenge.

Clearly, the governmentwide FPDS numbers have been cobbled together in a rickety way. This will surely improve as the system is further developed and OMB's consolidation and elaboration plans are enacted. Nevertheless, since even the uncleansed FPDS data tracks basic trends over time, which is our main interest, we can draw some conclusions from the patterns that emerge. For example, it is clear that the Bush administration has overseen, according to New York University professor Paul Light, "the most significant increase in recent history" in the number of contractors

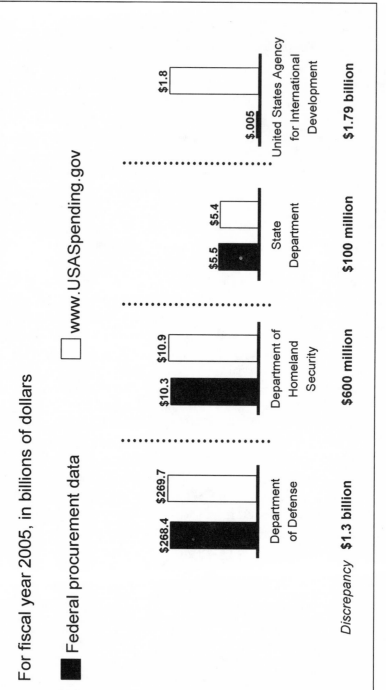

Figure 1. Spending amounts reported for specific agencies for fiscal year 2005, in billions of dollars. Two Web sites offering information on government spending get their contract data from the same source—one is just easier to access and provides more detail. But the USASpending.gov final tallies for 2005 don't match the official numbers. (Sources: www.USASpending.gov [accessed May 15, 2008], Federal Procurement Data System. Graphic: Carolann Davis)

and grantees employed by the federal government, with the Department of Defense accounting for the biggest slice of the total procurement pie.[36] According to the Partnership for Public Service, federal procurement expenditures grew by some 60 percent from FY2000 to FY2005; the increase from FY2004 to FY2005 alone was 18 percent, with the federal government issuing $388 billion in contracts in FY2005.[37] The most recent FPDS trending analysis shows that the total dollar amount spent on contracting nearly doubled from FY2000 to FY2006, from $219 billion to $415 billion.[38] Figures from the parallel OMB Web site, Federalspending.org, track an increase in total contracting dollars from $208.8 billion in FY2000 to $384.2 billion in FY2005, and an increase in total grant dollars from $294.5 billion to $440.9 billion in the same period.[39] If you notice a similarity between the government and the watchdog Web sites, it is no accident. OMB purchased its software from OMB Watch for $600,000 in November 2007.[40]

The available numbers also show that outsourcing is no partisan issue. FPDS has produced some basic summary charts that track patterns of spending from 1995 through 2005. The trend line, in total procurement dollars per year, rises steadily over this period. While some numbers differ, OMB's and OMB Watch's parallel federal spending sites map an identical trajectory.[41] Both the total dollars spent on federal procurement and the number of actions per year—the former a rough measure of the scope of contracting and the latter of its velocity—have exploded since the end of the Cold War.[42]

Again, these numbers are a work in progress and will no doubt become more accurate as government continues to render contracting processes more transparent. What is most important is not the absolute accuracy of governmentwide contracting data but the trends the available numbers manage to capture. They clearly reveal a dramatic change in the way government conducts its business—and that transformation has taken place with no public discussion of its significance or consequences.

What Shouldn't Be Outsourced?

In the Pentagon, the State Department, and the Department of Homeland Security, outsourcing takes place for the same simple reason: it is a means of getting jobs done that needed doing yesterday. Government increasingly relies on the private sector to deliver what government flying solo cannot deliver. But if the private sector can routinely trump government in delivering what the country needs, what is government for? Privatization pursued without proper reflection on its implications for the ends of government raises the possibility of undermining the authority of government itself.

There have to be boundaries: the march of privatization demands that government and the general public come to some basic agreement on the limits of private sector efficiency. Functions that are somehow integral to the very purpose of government—so-called inherently governmental functions—should never be tasked to the private sector. Defining what those functions are, however, is more difficult than it appears.

The matter cannot be resolved by returning to first principles. The Constitution is largely mute on what the founders thought about the proper balance between private and public interests. In Articles 1 and 2 it assigns powers to the executive and legislative branches, but does so in an artfully ambiguous way that is the backbone of an ingenious system of checks and balances. If in reviewing Articles 1 and 2 we asked which of those executive and legislative powers can be legitimately privatized, the answer would be virtually everything. For example, the Constitution assigns Congress all decisions on spending money; Congress has the appropriation power—in theory. But in practice, contractors routinely decide who will be paid and what they will actually do. The only reference in the Constitution of potential relevance to contracting is the Marque and Reprisal Clause, which allows licensed "privateers" to act on the government's behalf in certain carefully circumscribed situations when the country is at war.[43] But as Paul Verkuil points out, this clause has important limitations, since the Constitution requires congressional approval for its authorization (Art. I, Section 8) and forbids states from deploying privateers (Art. I, Section 10).[44] The bottom line, according to prominent Washington attorney Herb Fenster, is that there are no explicit constitutional limits on privatization.[45]

Others have offered guidance where the Constitution provides none. The economist Milton Friedman wrote, "The basic functions of government are to defend the nation against foreign enemies, to prevent coercion of some individuals by others within the country, to provide a means of deciding on our rules, and to adjudicate disputes."[46] Secretary of Defense Donald Rumsfeld would later misquote Friedman as saying: "Government has three primary functions: it should provide for the military defense of the nation. It should enforce contracts between individuals. And it should protect citizens against crimes against themselves or their property."[47] Under either rendition, even this leanest of all definitions is violated by government's current practices. Running a prison or policing the streets seems like an inherently governmental function—an essential part of "preventing coercion" or "protecting citizens"—yet both prisons and policing have been privatized. Collecting taxes seems to be an inherently governmental function, since government needs revenue to do anything at all, yet large portions of tax collection have been privatized. Friedman explicitly named fighting wars as an inherently governmental function, but much of war has been privatized.

As these examples suggest, the federal government has no firm position on what is inherently governmental. Individual agencies and state and local governments do, but their definitions are not consistent. Even within a given government department, there is no means of assessing whether various in-house definitions are consistent. The Pentagon, for example, has official guidelines as to what constitutes an inherently governmental function, but they leave much latitude to individual offices. "Inherently governmental" is not defined globally at the Pentagon.[48] This latitude is highly conducive to continued privatization by departments that see advantages in contracting out what had previously been routine government business.

Even if an activity has been identified as inherently governmental, it can be broken down into core and peripheral functions. Former comptroller general of the United States David Walker cites national defense and law enforcement as examples of inherently governmental activities. We will not hire mercenaries, he argued, but the work of supporting the troops—by servicing weapons systems or serving meals—can rightfully be outsourced. Walker has maintained that you need to distinguish among the functions that constitute an inherently governmental activity. "Government doesn't necessarily have to provide all support services tied to an inherently governmental activity."[49]

But the distinction between core and peripheral can blur when there are not enough people in-house to get the job done. Under those circumstances, government may have no choice but to outsource a function it might otherwise have viewed as beyond the rightful bounds of outsourcing. Exhibit A is our use of private security contractors in Iraq and Afghanistan. Armed contractors have been deployed there because however much government might like to keep their function in-house, it is simply unable to recruit the requisite number of employees—in this case soldiers—to fill its needs. As Walker has put it, "Even if you'd like to be able to do it inside government, you have to ask, can government attract and motivate an adequate number of workers to get the job done? . . . If the answer is no, you may not have a choice but to contract out the function."[50]

Outsourcing has slowly nibbled away at government authority in all three of the realms—national security, adjudication, and law enforcement—that Friedman's bare-bones definition acknowledges as critical roles of government. This is not wholly a bad thing. Privatization typically puts problem solving closer to the problem, unleashing the innovation that only free markets can catalyze. But privatization without proper management is also a recipe for delegitimizing government and the slow erosion of the general public's trust in government over time. When armed contractors are no longer a temporary fix but a permanent crutch, government is outsourcing things that it shouldn't.

One way of defining the limits of privatization would be for Congress to insist that oversight functions remain within government. Such a restriction would prohibit government from delegating the role of Lead Systems Integrator (LSI) to the private sector, a choice the Coast Guard made with its Deepwater program to recapitalize its equipment (including aircraft, ships, logistics, and command and control systems) and an alternative whose appeal grows with the technical expertise needed for supervising such projects. When a contractor or team of contractors is LSI on a new weapons system, for example, they have responsibility for everything from technology development to final testing. In May 2007, the House Armed Services Committee considered legislation that would bar contractors from serving as LSI in U.S. defense programs.[51] This could be the wave of the future: Congress might easily present itself to the electorate as taking necessary action on the privatization issue by simply legislating restrictions of this sort.

But federalizing programs without also attending to government's shocking human capital crisis will only make matters worse. The Defense Department, for example, cut its acquisition workforce by more than 50 percent between 1994 and 2005. Banning contractors from certain activities would necessitate hiring to bring the function back in house at a time when Congress is unlikely to allocate funds for additional government employees at the expense of programs. The business of government would grind to a halt if contractors were banned without expanding the federal workforce to replace them.

Deciding what shouldn't be outsourced ultimately requires government to take a hard look at what it has become and think about what it might instead be. The ad hoc outsourcing of the past two decades, according to Walker, has "expand[ed] the use of contractors in some ways that are wholly inappropriate and in others that are high risk."[52] It should be obvious that the private sector cannot on its own defend the nation, uphold the rule of law, or render justice at home. Justice and security are still public goods that demand direct government involvement. While contractors can clearly provide support for government, neither security nor justice is a function democracy should entrust to private hands. Oversight is also, of necessity, a core governmental function. Only government is properly equipped to manage costs, schedule, and performance in a manner that serves the public interest rather than private interests.[53]

General Anthony Zinni, former commander-in-chief of the U.S. Central Command, said, "If I had to revamp how we do things, I would start with what should be contracted and what should not."[54] He's right. America needs a public debate on the proper limits of privatization, and this debate must take place not simply within government but across the public-private divide. Both the public and the private sectors have a shared interest in collaborating to enhance transparency and address government's very real human capital concerns.

Foreign Policy, Privatized

Globalization and the information revolution have expanded the field of contracting possibilities. The full extension of the privatization paradigm to defense and diplomacy is a post–Cold War development. This is not to say that earlier private contractors played no significant role in American power projection. Government may have bankrolled the effort, but contractors rebuilt Europe through the Marshall Plan. All but five thousand of the sixty thousand people employed by the Atomic Energy Commission in 1951 were contractors.[55] But the range of functions that have been privatized and the volume of contracts have increased dramatically since the end of the Cold War—and have become genuinely global.

Not surprisingly, overseas contracting has been the real growth area. The U.S. contract presence abroad is stunning (Figure 2); in 2005, the federal government had contractors operating in every UN-recognized country of the world except Bhutan, Nauru, and San Marino.[56] DOD procurement spending has increased by 89 percent from 2000 to 2005. State Department contracting has gone up by an astonishing 258 percent in the same period. From its birth in 2003 through fiscal year 2006, the new Department of Homeland Security nearly quadrupled its procurement outlays.

The trends captured in the chart do not begin with the Bush administration. The definitive case must wait for the chapters that follow, but a snapshot of State Department budgetary trends clearly situates the origins of the outsourcing turn in the Clinton years, especially when one factors in the effect of the peace dividend, which reduced outlays to the State Department in that same period. State Department procurements have risen steadily since 1988 and exploded in the last five years. American foreign policy has been privatized by Democrats and Republicans alike.

Growth in Federal Contracts
2000-2005

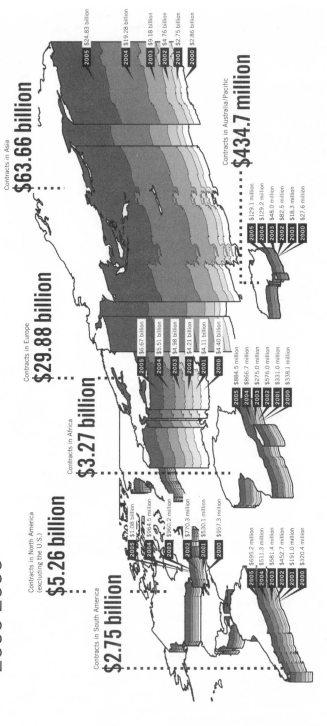

Contracts in North America
(excluding the U.S.)
$5.26 billion

2005	$1.08 billion
2004	$964.5 million
2003	$960.2 million
2002	$770.3 million
2001	$530.1 million
2000	$957.3 million

Contracts in South America
$2.75 billion

2005	$695.2 million
2004	$511.3 million
2003	$581.4 million
2002	$452.7 million
2001	$191.0 million
2000	$320.4 million

Contracts in Africa
$3.27 billion

Contracts in Europe
$29.88 billion

2005	$6.67 billion
2004	$5.51 billion
2003	$4.98 billion
2002	$4.21 billion
2001	$4.11 billion
2000	$4.40 billion

2005	$884.5 million
2004	$866.7 million
2003	$275.0 million
2002	$576.0 million
2001	$331.0 million
2000	$338.1 million

Contracts in Asia
$63.66 billion

2005	$24.83 billion
2004	$19.28 billion
2003	$9.18 billion
2002	$4.76 billion
2001	$2.75 billion
2000	$2.86 billion

Contracts in Australia/Pacific
$434.7 million

2005	$129.1 million
2004	$129.2 million
2003	$48.0 million
2002	$82.5 million
2001	$18.3 million
2000	$27.6 million

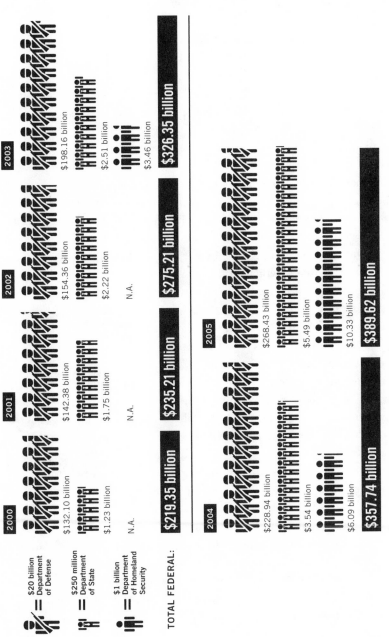

Figure 2. Growth in federal contracts, 2000–2005 (Graphic: Omnivore)

What is new, therefore, is not the use of contractors but the broadening scope of their deployment across the various institutions of American government, particularly in foreign policy. One key indicator of the shift's effect is the private sector's relative influence on policy outcomes. Lawrence Jacobs and Benjamin Page found business to be the number one shaper of contemporary American foreign policy, outranking expert opinion, labor, and public opinion in degree of influence.[57]

The delegation of the execution of America's international agenda to private actors is part of what Berkeley professor Jacob Hacker has called the "great risk shift." This phrase refers to the precarious status of America's middle class after "the massive transfer of economic risk from broad structures of insurance, whether sponsored by the corporate sector or by government, onto the fragile balance sheets of American families."[58] The same dynamic applies to the impact of privatization on the international policies of the United States. Hidden behind any risk shift, Hacker argues, is a transfer of responsibility.[59] When government delegates functions to the private sector, it has a ready alibi when things do not go as planned and other countries or individuals pay the price. Rather than shouldering the full responsibility for policy failure, government can point a finger at others outside of itself.

The great risk shift has been on full display in the U.S. intervention in Iraq. Jacquelyn Williams-Bridgers, managing director of the Government Accountability Office's International Affairs and Trade team, said the two big themes emerging from the GAO's early work on Iraq were lack of government oversight over government-led functions and activities, and the outsourcing of oversight. It had been difficult to get the numbers the GAO needed, and the layers of subcontractors created a considerable degree of mystery.[60] Since the federal government has only just recently started tracking its contracting systematically, and the FFATA-mandated effort to render subcontracting transparent is still in its infancy, a good portion of the business of the U.S. government remains shrouded in secrecy.[61] Yet our overseas military interventions plunge ahead.

If private sector experience with similar issues is any guide, the current state of misinformation and opacity is cause for great concern. In the private sector, firms that shift work outside their enterprise typically eliminate the managers who tracked these operations when they were internal. The idea is that these tasks will be picked up by the contracting firm, but often the result is an evaporation of clear lines of responsibility. Risk itself winds up being outsourced in a less than wholly conscious way. In any networked system of production, no one is ultimately responsible for ensuring that the system itself endures.[62] The current wars are no different. The United

States has "ad hoc-ed" its way into a set of arrangements where it seems to bear no responsibility for either the consequences of its contracts or the sustainability of the circumstances it has inadvertently endorsed.

On balance, does the explosion of overseas outsourcing in "emerging markets" advance the cause of free markets and liberal capitalism? Probably not. For market benefits to accrue, free and fair competition must prevail. But the present competition for federal contracts is anything but free and fair. Multinational corporations usually trump local business, especially abroad. The large corporations do not typically compete in free and fair fashion, in part because there are not that many of them; the startup costs for setting up a high tech weapons business are formidable. The majority of federal contract awards are less than fully competitive. In 2006, for example, according to a report prepared for Henry Waxman (D-California), chair of the House Committee on Oversight and Government Reform, "50.2 percent of federal procurement spending—$206.9 out of $412.1 billion—was awarded without full and open competition."[63] The picture for privatized foreign policy is even worse. In 2007, according to USAspending.gov, 69 percent of DOD contracts and 73 percent of DHS contracts were awarded without full and open competition. The ratios were scarcely better for the State Department and USAID, with 62 percent and 66 percent, respectively, being awarded without full and open competition.[64] Business is making money, but it is the largest corporations that currently benefit the most, and the free market is hard to locate.

Overseas contracting to date exemplifies the unintended consequences of willy-nilly privatization. On the one hand, outsourcing promises greater efficiency, surge capacity, and government responsiveness to rapidly changing events. Contractors have allowed the Bush administration to fight two simultaneous wars without a draft. The last extended conflict in which the United States participated without resorting to a draft was the American revolution.[65] But these advantages have come at the expense of accountability, a fact that has not escaped the Government Accountability Office. Managing federal contracting more effectively was on the GAO's 2007 High-Risk List as an item demanding immediate attention. DOD was the department whose contracting processes the GAO considered most out of control.[66]

Since privatization is intimately connected to globalization, we cannot turn the clock back on privatization without unwittingly undermining some of globalization's gains. Strategic outsourcing done well can advance U.S. interests; uncontrolled outsourcing of the sort on display in Iraq creates more problems than it solves. We need to be able to tell the difference.

3

State Power in a Privatized World

Everything is undergoing an invisible but ceaseless transformation, the
unsettled holds more of the future than the settled, and the present is
nothing more than a hypothesis that has not yet been surmounted.
—Robert Musil, *The Man Without Qualities*

"There are many who are errant," said Sancho. "Many," responded Don
Quixote, "but few who deserve to be called knights."
—Miguel de Cervantes, *Don Quixote*

URING THE Cold War, the White House met the threat of nuclear weapons with deterrence and arms control summits with
the Soviet Union. Weapons of mass destruction cast a shadow
over the prospects for world peace, and, while they may not have done all
they could, the U.S. and Soviet governments led the effort to avert nuclear
catastrophe. In 2006, however, Washington did not set the agenda but took
a back seat to private initiative by the megarich investor Warren Buffett.

Buffett offered $50 million, provided the U.S. government matched
it, to establish an international nuclear fuel bank under the auspices of the
International Atomic Energy Agency (IAEA), an autonomous international
organization committed to the use of nuclear power for energy and other
peaceful purposes. In pledging his $50 million, Buffett had the support of
the Nuclear Threat Initiative (NTI), a charitable organization founded by
former Georgia Democratic senator Sam Nunn with the financial backing
of cable television mogul Ted Turner. NTI strives to keep weapons of mass
destruction from falling into the wrong hands. In late December 2007, the
Bush administration announced that it would match Buffett's pledge and
included the requisite funds in the FY2008 Omnibus Appropriations bill.
For the fuel bank to become reality, the IAEA must officially approve the
initiative, and other IAEA member states must contribute another $100
million. The idea that an individual could set Washington's foreign policy
agenda in this fashion would have been unthinkable during the Cold War.

But this tale reminds us that American foreign policy was not privatized in a vacuum. Globalization and the information revolution have both facilitated and accelerated the hollowing-out of government and the creation of the shadow government. At the same time, the new international context has unleashed the ingenuity and initiative of people like Nunn, Turner, and Buffett. That independent activity, too, has foreign policy implications.

Privatization needs to be understood as a more pervasive phenomenon than has often been acknowledged. At the broadest possible level, it is not only government outsourcing (contracts plus grants) but also independent private sector initiatives with foreign policy impact. It is to these bottom-up ventures that we now turn.

The Emergent Fourth Sector

During the Cold War, organizations could be neatly classified into three sectors: business (for-profit private sector), NGO (not-for-profit private sector), or government (public sector). Today the number of hybrid entities that do not fall neatly into one of these categories is growing exponentially. These entities do not operate in conventional ways. For example, social entrepreneurs have an NGO mission that they pursue using a business tool set. "Philanthropreneurs" simultaneously pursue not-for-profit philanthropy and for-profit entrepreneurship. Al Qaeda does not exist to make money, improve socioeconomic conditions, or govern; it, too, is a fourth sector organization. The privatization of power is an equal opportunity employer that provides opportunities for individuals bent on destruction as well as for those interested in making the world less violent.

From the vantage point of other countries, many initiatives might seem like official American foreign policy, yet they are often without direct government involvement. Nunn's NTI illustrates this new reality. Its principal funders to date have been Turner and Buffett. NTI has successfully intervened directly abroad to fill a vacuum that would once have been entirely covered by the U.S. government. At the Vinca nuclear reactor in Belgrade, for example, NTI paid to have more than one hundred pounds of potent nuclear materials flown from Belgrade to Russia for blending down. In exchange for giving up their highly enriched uranium, the Serbs wanted money for cleaning up Vinca's spent reactor fuel, but there were a range of bureaucratic obstacles to using U.S. federal funds for that purpose. So NTI covered the $5 million cleanup fee. It has taken similar independent action in Kazakhstan. The Energy Department's Global Threat Reduction Initiative, a program designed to remove nuclear materials from civilian reactors around the world, was in part inspired by the NTI example.[1] When the Bush administration matched Buffett's donation to finance an international nuclear fuel bank, NTI became part charity, part agenda-setter for the U.S. government.

Creative capitalism was already changing the world long before Bill Gates articulated its message at Davos. Muhammed Yunus, founder of the legendary Grameen Bank, has been pursuing a similar vision for decades. Yunus began the Grameen Bank in Bangladesh in 1983 with the conviction that small loans (microfinance) could make a big difference in helping people lift themselves out of poverty. The bank lends money without collateral to the poorest of the poor in Bangladesh. Yunus believed that "these millions of small people with their millions of small pursuits can add up to create the biggest development wonder." The bank's success—as of December 2007 it had 7.41 million borrowers, 97 percent of them women—has made it a prototype for microcredit programs around the world. In 2006 Yunus and the bank were jointly awarded the Nobel Peace Prize, and in 2007 *Business Week* named Yunus, along with Benjamin Franklin, Andrew Carnegie, John D. Rockefeller, and Bill Gates, one of the thirty greatest entrepreneurs of all time.[2]

Other social entrepreneurs are also working from the creative capitalism playbook, pursuing independent action that expands American influence abroad without government involvement. Ashoka: Innovators for the Public is a venture capital organization for social entrepreneurship. Its Web site defines a social entrepreneur as neither business nor government: "While a business entrepreneur might create entirely new industries, a social entrepreneur comes up with new solutions to social problems and then implements them on a large scale."[3] It cites Jean Monnet, architect of the European Community, as an example of the best sort of social entrepreneurship. Along parallel lines, the Schwab Foundation for Social Entrepreneurship defines its goal as applying "practical, innovative and sustainable approaches to benefit society in general, with an emphasis on those who are marginalized and poor."[4] Its founder is the Swiss economist and businessman Klaus Schwab, perhaps better known for creating the World Economic Forum that convenes every January in Davos, Switzerland.

There are many other such ventures. The Acumen Fund is "a nonprofit social venture fund that uses entrepreneurial approaches to solve the problems of global poverty."[5] Endeavor Global "transforms the economies of emerging markets by identifying and supporting high impact entrepreneurs." The Omidyar Network, founded in 2004 with eBay wealth, funds both for-profits and nonprofits as tools for social change. As its Web site states, "Omidyar Network believes that all individuals have the innate potential to make life better for themselves and their communities." One of its investment choices is the nonprofit DonorsChoose, an online marketplace to connect individual donors with school projects in need of funding.[6] Another organization, Kiva, also facilitates charity with a venture capital twist. Kiva allows individuals to lend money directly via PayPal to "a specific entrepreneur in the developing world, empowering them to lift themselves out of poverty."[7] With a slightly different twist, GlobalGiving connects individual donors to prescreened grassroots charity projects around the world.[8]

Steve Case, CEO of AOL, offers an example of how more-traditional organizations are increasingly crossing the profit/nonprofit divide and thus becoming, in effect, part of the fourth sector. The National Geographic Society, sustained by sales of everything from magazines to toys, is now a billion-dollar business set up as a nonprofit. Case explained to the *New York Times* that "it doesn't have to focus on collecting money or holding black-tie balls to raise money, because its sales are sustaining its mission of educating the world about the world." Pierre Omidyar, founder of eBay and the Omidyar Network, cites the huge positive social impact that eBay has had simply by running its core business, yet obviously eBay is not a charity. Omidyar points as well to the accomplishments of the Grameen Bank. In the sense that its revenues exceed its costs, it is a business, yet Grameen has made an enormous contribution to the cause of pulling people out of poverty. To Omidyar, this provides "proof that you can have it both ways."[9] Nicholas Kristof of the *New York Times* has labeled social entrepreneurs "do-gooders with spreadsheets."[10]

Fourth sector organizations also blur the line between business investment and charitable giving. While social entrepreneurs often advance government agendas, they call the shots, not government. In some instances, government aid offered in support of private ventures has been rejected as a potential impediment to sustainable development. Endeavor Global's founder, Linda Rottenberg, for example, turned down an offer of $450,000 from the Chilean government for efforts to support entrepreneurship in that country because of the stipulations the government attached to the funding. Chilean president Ricardo Lagos called her "crazy" for rejecting the money, but, once word got out, $3 million came in from private sources.[11]

Google's new for-profit philanthropic venture capital firm, Google.org, is another prominent example of the new "philanthropreneurship." Google founders Larry Page and Sergey Brin set it up in 2006, giving it $1 billion of seed money and a mandate to change the world. As a hybrid philanthropy, Google.org can pursue traditional charitable pathways or fund for-profit ventures and partner with venture capitalists. When it turns a profit, the for-profit arm must pay taxes; in contrast, the activities of the Google Foundation, also part of Google.org, are tax-exempt.[12]

The explosion of hybrid ventures over the past decade suggests that the fourth sector will continue to be a growth industry. The Slate 60 list of the world's most generous philanthropists, started in 1996, provides one measure of the spike in social action. Ted Turner seems to have gotten it right when he predicted that were someone to publicize the identity of the world's top donors, the wealthy would compete among themselves to be the most generous, with positive results for the world. Economists look to market mechanisms to correct the failures of government. Government seeks to correct the failures of markets. In channeling funds directly to civil society, hybrid charitable organizations may be able to address government and market failures simultaneously.[13]

The potential to do some good while simultaneously positioning one-self for the next big moneymaking idea will no doubt inspire many others to climb aboard the hybrid philanthropy train, making it a formidable new force in the international system. But does it matter if social causes are thinly disguised marketing efforts, and ostensible donations are actually high-risk investments? If one believes that positive outcomes require purity of motives, then perhaps it does matter. But it isn't clear why motives always need be pure for outcomes to be positive. Over 225 years ago, Adam Smith reasoned that optimal large-scale outcomes often result from leaving individuals free to pursue their parochial interests. According to Smith, empires make no economic sense, since the costs of maintaining them always exceed the benefits.[14] While he has sometimes been caricatured as seeing no positive role for government in public lives, in fact Smith believed government had an important role to play in enforcing contracts, encouraging entrepreneurship, and providing public works.

The emergence of this lively fourth sector means that it is no longer possible to draw a clear line between for-profit and not-for-profit activity. Rather than quibble over distinctions between for-profit business and not-for-profit social entrepreneurship, it is more useful simply to refer to both as private sector activity. If they are successful, social entrepreneurs open up new markets. And the opening of new markets for the parochial purpose of making money can have a variety of positive social effects. Since entrepreneurship in any form typically allows people to employ their neighbors, even wholly self-interested action can produce beneficial outcomes. That is the radical idea at the core of these extragovernmental hybrid ventures; they refuse to accept the antiquated distinction that it is government that does good and business that makes money. They challenge the equally obsolete assumptions that one best helps the poor by aiding their governments and that one cannot do good and make money.

Tapping into the positive energy of social entrepreneurs and channeling it productively should be an important agenda item for U.S. policymakers.[15] To do that, however, government must come to terms with just how dramatically the landscape of America's interaction with the world has changed. The privatization of U.S. power is the result of both the intentional devolution of authority by government and the concurrent explosion of independent private sector action. A good place to start understanding this changed landscape is with the reigning paradigms for interpreting the behavior of states. These frameworks create the strategic horizon by which American international behavior orients itself.

Realism and Liberal Internationalism After Westphalia

Grand strategy, the preserve of states and statesmen, traditionally focuses on deterring enemies through the right configuration of military power. In the modern world there are two dominant frameworks for thinking about war and peace. The one known as realism focuses on the world as it is, not as it might be. It defines a world where the strong do as they can and the weak as they must. The ultimate end of states in the international system is self-preservation. As such, they seek to balance power so that one state does not become too powerful, thereby threatening the sovereignty of all the others. The other lens is known as idealism to philosophers and liberal internationalism to political scientists. From its first articulation by Immanuel Kant to its first implementation under Woodrow Wilson, liberal internationalism has sought to transcend the traditional realist logic of war and peace and instead focus on building international institutions that would tame humanity's violent inclinations, rendering war obsolete or at least less likely.

While realism focuses on the worst in human nature and liberal internationalism on the best, both frameworks presuppose sovereign states as the building blocks of international order. Both were built on the logic of the 1648 Treaty of Westphalia, which laid out the terms of peace for Europe after the Thirty Years' War. Westphalia endorsed the principle *cuius regio, eius religio*—whoever rules determines the religion of his subjects. There followed a long tradition in which the international system endorsed respect for sovereignty and noninterference in other states' internal affairs as its supreme values. That tradition was the foundation for the Congress of Vienna, the League of Nations, and, later, the United Nations.

Writing prior to 9/11, Henry Kissinger described the 1990s as the decade of the overturning of Westphalia.[16] America intervened in the internal affairs of Somalia, Haiti, Kosovo, and Bosnia, trampling on the sovereignty of states in the name of human rights. The final nail in Westphalia's coffin was the American invasion of Iraq, which openly sought to remove Saddam Hussein from power. The United States acknowledged that this intervention took place without United Nations Security Council authorization, but nonetheless declared it "legitimate." This revolutionary dethroning of both sovereignty and the principle of noninterference undermined the very foundation of the Westphalian worldview. Of course, European colonialism had never respected the prior claims of indigenous peoples; the Westphalian system acknowledged the rights of states only, not colonies.

State sovereignty is obviously challenged by the proliferation of relationships between individuals and organizations that transcend state affiliations. Their increasing importance does not mean that the state is disappearing. To the contrary, as Anne-Marie Slaughter has argued, the state is "disaggregating" to confront and exploit the changed international environment it inhabits.[17] Slaughter used the term "disaggregated state" to capture the explosion of global networks that link individuals and organizations in common cause regardless of state boundaries or government hierarchies, but there is no reason it might not also be extended to encompass the impact of overseas outsourcing as well. The reality of the disaggregated state, however defined, makes building global order using either the realist or the liberal internationalist frames a precarious business indeed.

In contrast to liberal internationalism, the balance of power at the heart of the realist doctrine is premised on zero-sum thinking. One nation's gain is always another nation's loss; the system of costs and benefits is airtight. Yet economic transactions, by definition quid pro quo exchanges, are not built on zero-sum thinking. Trade, for example, presupposes mutual gain; without it, there would be no point in making deals. Realists have squared this circle by arguing for a hierarchy of interests, with national security (defined as the defense of state sovereignty) trumping economic concerns; this perspective sees economic matters as important until they conflict with national security concerns. The sovereign state may labor under the constraints of economic interdependence, realists argue, but like the other states that inhabit the international system, it does so as a coherent actor in a bleak world where force is ultimately decisive.[18] In contrast, liberal internationalists beginning with Woodrow Wilson have focused on the interdependent nature of interests. They seek to expand the scope of international cooperation, primarily through multilateral institutions and international law. I don't have space here to do justice to the rich traditions that these two ideal types generated as the Westphalian system developed. What is important to the argument at hand is their common focus on states as the principal building blocks of international order.

Today, the disaggregated state and the privatization of power call both visions into question. Realism mandates the unfettered pursuit of U.S. interests, but its Westphalian-inspired emphasis on the state as the only important actor on the international stage blinds it to the considerable devolution of power to private actors. Liberal internationalism urges states to abandon the shortsighted pursuit of parochial interests and submit to the mandates of international law and institutions, but it does not explain why doing so is prudent if private actors have no incentive to do the same. As frameworks that assume state predominance in a world in which states no longer have a monopoly on significant action, realism and liberal internationalism can offer less and less guidance. Stating this point slightly differently, Tony Blair said, "Globalisation begets interdependence. Interdependence begets the necessity of a common value system to make it work. In other words, the idealism becomes the realpolitik."[19]

Well ahead of its time, Robert Keohane and Joseph Nye's 1977 book *Power and Interdependence* first identified this gap between the international system as it actually is and the frameworks deployed to analyze it. They argued that the realist paradigm was still relevant if one was fully aware of its limits. Writing in *Foreign Policy* in 2000, however, Keohane and Nye argued that interdependence, as they conceived it in 1977, and globalization are not interchangeable. Globalization refers to something new. What distinguishes it from interdependence as they first understood it is the genuinely global scope of interdependence, the increased velocity of interdependent interaction, and the complexity of the network of transnational ties.[20]

Many valiant and praiseworthy books have since acknowledged the gap between theory and practice and have endeavored to transcend it by combining the best insights from both realism and liberal institutionalism. Their proliferation beyond the ivory tower is a barometer of rising intellectual frustration.

The titles of these new calls to action, which often borrow from both traditions directly, capture the concerted effort to bolster aging paradigms to fit a transformed world. Francis Fukuyama argues for the adoption of a "realistic Wilsonianism" that can better match means to ends. "What the US now needs," he writes, "is new ideas, neither neoconservative nor realist, for how America is to relate to the rest of the world—ideas that retain the neoconservative belief in the universality of human rights, but without its illusions about the efficacy of American power and hegemony to bring those ends about."[21] Anatol Lieven and John Hulsman call for "Ethical Realism," a vision inspired by the humility and restraint of Reinhold Niebuhr, George Kennan, and Hans Morgenthau, all prominent realists whose views shaped the policy of the Truman administration.[22] Others seek to remind liberals that the United States has in the past fought for truth and justice without making a mess of things—and Democrats have led the cause. Peter Beinart would have us adopt the fighting faith of Truman Democrats.[23] The final report of the Princeton Project on National Security urged Americans to uphold "Liberty under Law," which seeks to build a "worldwide web of cooperation" and "networked order."[24]

These are all well-intentioned efforts build on dysfunctional foundations. Beinart usefully reminds us that Democrats do not have to be cowardly proponents of moral equivalence, but taking a strategy designed to contain the expansionism of another state and reconfiguring it for a world dominated by nonstate threats is an idea that cannot help but come up short. The Princeton Project's Liberty under Law concept rightfully emphasizes the importance of cooperation and the rule of law, but it does not explain how international law is to function in a world where power has been privatized. Similarly, rejecting neoconservative excess makes good sense given the destruction it has wrought, but for all its attention to the importance of soft power, Fukuyama's realistic Wilsonianism does not tell us how this doctrine is to function when other values trump state sovereignty. Realistic Wilsonianism provides norms of restraint and cooperation for states but not for nonstate actors. Lieven and Hulsman's Ethical Realism does not accommodate the impact of the disaggregated state and how it is to balance threats from nonstate actors. In short, all of these ideas suffer from the same flaw: They implicitly assume that the only sort of power that really matters in international relations is state power.

The end of Westphalia has rendered both liberal internationalism and realism, inherently state-centric frameworks, impotent far too often. They explain aspects of the global system but no longer explain its entirety. It is understandable that we deploy these frameworks, as they are all we have. But we must build from the ground up as well if we are to avoid having a foreign policy that has, in Donald Kettl's memorable phrase, "outrun the existing theories."[25]

One reason both realism and liberal internationalism come up short is that globalization has unleashed a host of problems that are simply beyond the resources of individual nation-states to solve. This forces the debate about America's future away from a focus on realism vs. liberal internationalism or some hybrid that tries to capture their best attributes, and requires us to think in wholly new ways. Each of our state-centric principal foreign policy frameworks sheds light on different aspects of the misuse of American power, but they do not account for the ways in which power itself has changed. We don't need a new prescription for our glasses. We need a new eye chart.

Globalization and the Changing Nature of Power

Government's privatization turn and the explosion of fourth sector entrepreneurial activity are both enabled by significant changes in the international economic system and the global information environment. The ingredients of Westphalia's demise include government choice as well as private sector innovation. But globalization is the catalyst for the complex post-Westphalian world that policymakers must now navigate. Globalization is not the same as privatization, but the scope of government outsourcing and the extent of private sector innovation in pursuing social change would be unthinkable without it.

In his best-selling book *The Lexus and the Olive Tree*, the *New York Times*'s Thomas Friedman characterized globalization as the democratization of three things previously controlled by American elites. First is the democratization of information. Ordinary citizens now have access to a vast range of resources that have transformed the way individuals think about the world and their place in it. Second is the democratization of finance. The common man now plays the market right alongside the Wall Street tycoon, linking the destinies of the ultrarich and the middle class in unprecedented ways. Third is the democratization of technology. The Internet and e-mail have radically lowered communication barriers between elites and the general public, dramatically expanding the range of options for expressing an opinion. These three forces combined to eradicate the old Cold War categories of First, Second, and Third Worlds and replace them with a Fast World and a Slow World. The great divide is now between the countries and individuals who have climbed aboard the globalization train and those who refuse to do so, clinging to a past that cannot produce prosperity. The hyperconnected and hypercompetitive economy has, in turn, leveled the global playing field; in Friedman's more recent incisive turn of phrase, the world is flat.[26]

Globalization thus encourages an empowerment of the private sector that has profound yet often unacknowledged consequences for diplomacy, development, and national security strategy. All of the standard models for framing the national interest, forged for the most part in nineteenth century continental Europe, make three assumptions that are increasingly inapplicable to the contemporary international system: (1) The state has a monopoly on important information, (2) The state has financial leverage that other competing entities do not, and (3) The state has an unchallenged monopoly on the legitimate use of force. Let us take these one at a time.

1. *The monopoly on information.* Information is power, and since information is now available to all (with the technology and the energy to access it) in a dizzying array of new ways, power cannot help but flow to new actors. The simple fact of a radically changed information environment has wide-ranging implications. Long gone are the days when an ambassador was the principal source of vital intelligence about the country to which he was posted. Even fifty years ago, professors had an unchallenged monopoly on expert information. Today, any student with a PDA can relax in a lecture hall and pull down information from the Internet with which to stump the pontificating sage in front of the class. International leaders can now learn as much from CNN and the Internet as they do from their own bureaucracies.

Not only has access to information been democratized, but the velocity with which that information can be exchanged has risen exponentially. Elites no longer have access to information that ordinary folks do not, and they often lack valuable information that entities closer to the decision point have. Since large and hierarchical business organizations developed to minimize transaction costs,[27] it follows that the Internet, in lowering the transaction costs associated with gathering and storing information to practically zero, makes hierarchical organization less valuable and in many instances renders it an impediment to efficiency. This transformation of the cost of information gives unprecedented power to individuals within the international system—both the enemies of globalization and its principal emissaries.

2. *The monopoly on financial leverage.* If money is power, then the quiet shift in power from the public to the private sector is easy enough to see. Bill Gates has amassed a personal fortune that surpasses the GDP of many states. Turbo-philanthropy has recast the calculus of development. With a commitment of $1 billion, Ted Turner can single-handedly set up a whole new apparatus for UN partnerships. Former presidents Bill Clinton and George H. W. Bush can raise private contributions for tsunami relief ($1.8 billion) that more than double the direct contribution of the U.S. government ($841 million).[28] To cite one further illuminating example, the government of the world's sole remaining superpower shut down in 1996, and the world's business simply went on. Such a scenario would have been impossible to imagine in the Cold War era.

Since power, in the sense of the ability to advance one's interests, is not a zero-sum game, none of these developments strips the state of relative power. As Jessica Matthews put it, "National governments are not simply losing autonomy in a globalizing economy. They are sharing powers—including political, social, and security roles at the core of sovereignty—with businesses, with international organizations, and with a multitude of citizens groups, known as nongovernmental organizations."[29] But as the number of actors that can affect U.S. foreign policy has increased, this in turn has required the state's policymakers to think differently about American interests. The point is that globalization is not something that happens to states but something that state and nonstate actors construct as they make choices about how to deal with its implications.

3. *The monopoly on the legitimate use of force.* In the Westphalian world of state supremacy, states were the only entities authorized to exercise force. In Max Weber's classic definition, the state is "a human community that (successfully) claims the *monopoly of the legitimate use of physical force* within a given territory."[30] But it is precisely this monopoly that has broken down. The West's embrace of universal human rights undercuts the primacy of state sovereignty. So does Western support for the dismemberment of existing states such as the former Yugoslavia, the former Czechoslovakia, and the former Soviet Union. Challenges to the state's monopoly on the legitimate use of force within its borders come from such disparate entities as human rights activists, who urge intervention in the internal affairs of other countries to prevent abuses, and suicide bombers, who seek destruction.

That the world's military power has never before in human history been distributed so disproportionately compels those forces committed to remaking the status quo. Today the U.S. military budget is larger than the next twenty powers' budgets combined. The second- and third-strongest economic powers, Japan and Germany, have militaries for self-defense only. This state of affairs would have been unthinkable prior to World War II, when military and economic power always went hand in hand. This disparity between economic and military power suggests two possibilities: either something has fundamentally changed, and military spending does not yield the return that it once did, or the present state of affairs is unsustainable, and Japan and Germany will inevitably once again become full-fledged military powers. Either way, the state's monopoly on the legitimate use of force has been undercut in at least three ways: nonstate actors now claim at least equal legitimacy; force itself has lost much of its former moral legitimacy; and military power has been decoupled from other kinds of power.

Along the way, something peculiar happened to power itself. In 2008, even after America had been in Iraq for five years, its military power was quite simply off the charts compared with that of other countries. As David Rothkopf writes, "Among the world's roughly two hundred armies, there are only between thirty and forty with weapons of mass destruction. There are fewer than twenty with any kind of missile capability, only nine with nuclear weapons capability, only six armies with roughly five hundred thousand or more troops, only three air forces with more than one thousand planes, and arguably, among these, only one that—thanks to its unequaled technology, presence in space, and financial and material resources—is truly capable today of waging modern global warfare."[31] Yet despite this unprecedented military advantage, we seem incapable of controlling world events.

Power has been redefined in commercial relations as well as in interstate relations. The vertically integrated corporation that fueled industrialization has given way to what IBM CEO Samuel Palmisano has called "the globally integrated enterprise." Rather than focusing on production within states, "the emerging globally integrated enterprise . . . fashions its strategy, its management, and its operations in pursuit of a new goal: the integration of production and value delivery worldwide. State borders define less and less the boundaries of corporate thinking or practice."[32] In the global economy, production gravitates to the place where the job can be accomplished at the lowest possible cost, and the key consideration is securing a supply of high-value skills. In such a world, innovation is about more than simply launching and creating new products. "It is also about how services are delivered, how business processes are integrated, how companies and institutions are managed, how knowledge is transferred, how public policies are formulated—and how enterprises, communities, and societies participate in and benefit from it all."[33]

At one level, then, globalization constitutes privatization, the march of the free market into realms where it previously had no place. But globalization is ultimately more than just economic change. Since the information revolution and air travel have rendered distance largely irrelevant, globalization compresses our very notions of time and space.[34] It is the high octane fuel for a shrinking world.

Does this then mean that the nature of power has been transformed? Do we dwell in a fundamentally different world, or are international relations what they have always been: states in a state of nature, struggling for survival in a war of all against all? The answer seems to be simultaneously yes and no. We dwell in a fundamentally different world, in which life for the majority of the world's citizens is nasty, brutish, and short (and now hot, flat, and crowded) but for a privileged minority is one of unprecedented comfort. We dwell in a world full of conflict, but conflict is no longer the exclusive monopoly of states. Power has been redistributed from states to business and civil society. For good or for ill, clever individuals who understand the changing nature of power can make their presence felt.

This reconfigured global system means that the principal threats to American interests and security no longer lie exclusively in the military power of other states. Threats also flow from those who despise the West's values and are willing to sacrifice their lives to stem the spread of Western bourgeois influence. As Tony Blair has stated, "This is not a clash between civilizations; it is a clash about civilization. It is the age-old battle between progress and reaction, between those who embrace the modern world and those who reject its existence—between optimism and hope, on the one hand, and pessimism and fear, on the other." In its purest form, Blair continued, it is "a struggle between democracy and violence."[35]

What blogger and author John Robb has called "global guerillas" are the dark side of the privatization of power. Unlike standard insurgency movements, which aspire to seize control of the state, Robb's global guerillas are bent on disrupting the networks that support the daily life of inhabitants of Friedman's flat world. They conduct "open source" warfare that relies on uncoordinated swarm tactics yet creates the appearance of centralized organization. For example, it is impossible to decapitate the Iraqi insurgency and declare victory, since no head organizer exists. Traditional armies can expend endless sums of money and never defeat those bent on what Robb calls "systems disruption."[36] Moreover, the model is wholly exportable to other parts of the world. It is built on a virtual community united by technology and, like a parasite, can thrive as well in the anarchy of a war zone as in the open society of advanced industrial capitalism.

Nontraditional threats to American interests and values are not confined to the terrorist challenge alone. Climate change is a first order security threat that imperils the future of the planet itself. But here we find another dark side of privatization. The profit motive has fueled some of globalization's greatest accomplishments, but on its own it provides no short-term incentive for meeting the threat of global warming. How can government muster the will to promote globalization's sustainability when through its contracting practices it has willingly ceded so much authority to the private sector?

In short, even for the uniquely powerful United States, globalization is a revolution that has shifted power from the state and its representatives to the private sector and a range of entrepreneurial forces. The U.S. government has itself played an active role in reconfiguring authority through its outsourcing, but the forces are much larger than government choice. No longer able to attain its objectives solely by armed force, the United States now relies heavily on private security companies to advance its interests.

No longer able to control information and financial flows, the United States still retains considerable power but must exercise it differently.

An Empire of the Willing

Despite the changing character of American power in what Fareed Zakaria aptly called "the post-American world," the ambitious military ventures of the United States look like old-fashioned imperialism. Surveying the voluminous and contentious literature these expeditions have spawned, one may discern an embryonic consensus: If America has an empire, it is a peculiar one compared with its European predecessors.

The American position has several unique features. For starters, the foundational geography is different. In traditional empires, the periphery interacts through the core; the resulting command and control arrangement resembles a rimless wheel with a hub and spokes. As one commentator pointed out, "the idea of all roads leading to Rome accurately describes the imperial structure."[37] The American empire, in contrast, is not a hub with spokes but an international network with multiple nodes[38] that binds individuals and communities anywhere in the world who share the values that first took full shape on American soil.[39] Some of the critical nodes in this network are neither government nor public institutions.

A different geography ensures that American influence functions differently as well. To secure economic benefits, traditional empires required political control of territory, but the United States profits without actually governing the countries it influences. Whereas past empires depended on political domination to dominate markets, market power and profit extraction no longer require imperial control. Contractors can reap enormous profits without the permission of the U.S. government simply by operating in the wake of disasters. The United States does not need to govern the territory for money to be made. Remarkably, free-market enthusiasts and leftist critics agree on this central difference.[40]

A variety of adjectives have been deployed to describe America's unique empire. The director of the Norwegian Nobel Institute, Geir Lundestad, calls it an "empire by invitation," placing the term *empire* in quotation marks.[41] The Harvard historian Charles Maier sees is as a "consensual empire."[42] For former UPI editor-in-chief Martin Walker it is a "virtual empire," with America's technological advantage playing the critical role in its dominance.[43] William E. Odom and Robert Dujarric describe America's unprecedented relative power as having created an "inadvertent empire" that ultimately follows from the strength of American liberal institutions and depends on prudent American leadership.[44] Princeton political scientist John Ikenberry also connects American power to liberal values and institutions, but he argues that talk of empire is ultimately misleading. It keeps us from absorbing the significance of the long peace between the great powers, as well as the ways in which American leaders differ from their European counterparts: "When all is said and done, Americans are less interested in ruling the world than they are in creating a world of rules."[45]

Parting with the majority, the philosopher Michael Walzer rejects the term *empire* in favor of *hegemony*. South Korea's rejection of U.S. policy toward North Korea, Turkey's refusal to offer its soil as a launch point for U.S. troops entering Iraq, and the international outcry against the Iraq war all indicate that the United States hardly dominates its allies politically as a traditional empire would do. In contrast, hegemony requires consultation, persuasion, and compromise; "hegemony, unlike empire, requires consent."[46]

Does hegemony suffice to describe America's relationship with the world? It is a word with even more historical baggage than empire. While it is common to note the cultural and scientific accomplishments of empires, no one lauds hegemony's contribution to human progress. Italian Marxist philosopher Antonio Gramsci's understanding of hegemony, which inspires Walzer's usage, focuses on the negative dimensions of consent. For Gramsci, the majority of people who "consent" to the existing power structure are not consenting at all but suffering from false consciousness. They unwittingly uphold hegemony when their interests align with resistance. Were they to understand what alternatives actually existed, they would act otherwise.[47] For Gramsci, and by extension for Walzer, capitalism is a problem, not a solution. It forces ordinary people to acquiesce in their own subjugation.

Walzer's hegemony argument presupposes the continued salience of false consciousness—the possibility of an individual's not knowing where his or her true interests lie—after communism's exit. But false consciousness is a less useful concept in a world where sustainable modern alternatives to bourgeois democracy no longer exist. The very idea of false consciousness presupposes an option that will be readily chosen when the oppressed see their predicament clearly. What is that alternative today in the already developed world? It cannot be Islamic fundamentalism, which makes no universalist appeal and longs to turn the clock back. It is unlikely to be Chinese-style market authoritarianism or Russia's gangster capitalism. It must be possible for individuals to support the existing system and seek to reform it without by definition acting against their own interests.

If the United States today has an empire, therefore, it is an empire of the willing—the first in human history. The empire of the willing advances its core interests through the universal appeal of the ideals it embodies: economic freedom and equality of opportunity. It unites human beings across borders, inviting the newly enfranchised to rise in its ranks, regardless of national origin, race, gender, or religion. In measuring value through socioeconomic achievement, it lays waste to all other prestige hierarchies, which is why traditional elites around the world find its core values so threatening to their interests.

Many have noted that with their shared celebration of free trade and liberal democracy, the empire of the willing has much in common with the former British Empire. But the differences between British imperial power and contemporary American power are actually more illuminating. The East India Company was a state within a state, a wholly British entity within a British colony. The most powerful firms in the empire of the willing are not tied to the American state in any such way. Whereas the British Empire's representatives abroad were uniformly British citizens, those of the empire of the willing can hail from any country. Indeed, with the advent of the globally integrated enterprise, the point where American power ends and that of another country begins can be an arbitrary designation. British imperialism—like all the variants that preceded it—was a thoroughly nationalist venture. The empire of the willing is a global concern, a transnational web of common economic and political interests.

Like its British predecessor, by empowering individual innovators, the empire of the willing lays the groundwork for both liberal democracy and prosperity. But its relationship to military force is more problematic. Unilateral military action in the information age, regardless of ultimate ends, is by definition at odds with the ideals that underlie American power. The United States is a central contributor to a like-minded partnership that spans countries, private sector organizations, and individuals. The empire of the willing is thus an inclusive club whose members are committed to the principles of the Declaration of Independence: "We hold these Truths to be self-evident, that all Men are created equal, that they are endowed by their Creator with certain unalienable Rights, that among these are Life, Liberty and the Pursuit of Happiness."

With these words as its founding principles, the United States is well suited to serve as a key node in the empire of the willing's network; Americans both play a vital role in, and are the beneficiaries of, a system of economic organization whose fundamental aspects many non-Americans find desirable. Yet the values that inspire participation in the global economy are not intrinsically American, and American citizens are not the only ones motivated by the American dream. Its pursuit was first celebrated in America, but its contours are not culturally bound. Otherwise, immigrants from around the world would not be attracted to it.[48]

The American empire, therefore, is neither American nor Anglo-American but is instead a transnational phenomenon. Yes, the United States and Britain are most intimately connected with the promulgation of its core values of free trade and free markets. But what Harvard political philosopher Michael Sandel has characterized as the "empty center" of liberalism—the elevation of tolerance over all other values—is precisely what makes it so readily adoptable elsewhere.[49] Liberalism's defining values are bourgeois virtues as opposed to aristocratic or traditional ones, and bourgeois norms and aspirations can be adapted to a wide variety of cultural contexts—look at the differences between capitalism as implemented in Europe, the United States, and China. The empire of the willing's principal stakeholders are thus genuinely global. They are not all liberal, but they share a belief in the power of individual initiative as an engine of economic growth and shared prosperity.

The Bush years made it clear that the empire of the willing has enemies. While this empire is a club open to all, traditional societies are not interested in membership, especially the elites governing them, who stand to lose all. The flawed assumption in the Bush administration's grand strategy was that American influence could be extended through military force; once dictators were toppled, the people of Iraq and Afghanistan would rise up after decades of oppression and enthusiastically embrace the American way of life. The Bush administration fundamentally misunderstood the sources of American power. The empire of the willing is all about choice, not coercion. It was once possible to completely dominate the information environment and mask what was in reality coercive manipulation; this was the modus operandi of the Soviet leadership. But the information revolution makes it impossible for such a strategy to succeed today; brute force is quickly exposed for what it is. The Bush White House conducted its foreign policy as though this wasn't the case. The glaring hypocrisy of celebrating liberty and free markets while occupying other countries seriously compromised American interests.

America can renew its positive role in the world if it can acknowledge the real source of its strength and resilience: an unlimited capacity to deploy the talent of the world in the solutions it devises to a particular problem. As Anne-Marie Slaughter, State Department director of policy planning, has put it, the measure of power in a networked world is connectedness.[50] And who is more committed to global connectedness than multicultural America, educator and champion of the world's best and brightest? This is what we have always done best, despite making some egregious errors now and then. The founding fathers sought to build the new republic on what Thomas Jefferson, in an 1813 letter to John Adams, called "the natural aristocracy" not of class but of "virtue and talent." Americans today still believe in a natural aristocracy, one no longer confined to white European males of British descent. The empire of the willing is a community of strivers that anyone of talent and initiative is free to join. Its members have a shared interest in sustaining a system in which it is possible for exceptional individuals to rise, regardless of race, creed, gender, or national origin.

Unlike all previous empires, the American sphere of influence is one that other countries volunteered to join. The NATO alliance has expanded from eleven members at its founding in 1949 to twenty-eight members and an additional twenty-two partner countries in 2009. A central player in the empire of the willing, the United States is also the first great power in human history to rise to prominence with its women fully enfranchised (women did not win equal voting rights in Britain until 1928). Having been forged through consent, the empire of the willing, properly understood, is the first empire without subjects. As such, it is also the first genuinely global empire that does not require nationalism to sustain itself. Its integrative potential thus greatly exceeds that of any world power to date. Because it is the first empire to harness the creativity of men and women alike, its potential to do the unprecedented should not be underestimated.

Previous studies have claimed that the United States is an empire either in denial, endangering the world by refusing to shoulder its responsibilities for world order, or in decline. Both perspectives miss what is most important. The Achilles heel of American power is our failure to appreciate the unique features of American strength: our unrivaled potential to collaborate in innovative ways and inspire the aspiring. The interwoven character of the global economy renders other countries, organizations, and individuals willing partners. Americans are not the only ones who have a vested interest in the empire's sustainability, but we are uniquely well-positioned to prosper in a networked world, where "the state with the most connections will be the central player."[51]

Of course, simply identifying the distinctive features of American strength does not preclude the adoption of strategies that are either at odds with American ideals or hopelessly unrealistic. The Bush administration's foreign policy was a case in point. Our values do not immunize us against shortsighted and misguided nationalistic policies that unwittingly undermine those values. The ideals of the French revolution—*liberté, égalité, fraternité*—were similarly at odds with traditional empire, but the French Revolution quickly arrived at precisely that destination. The challenge will be to define the empire of the willing through partnerships that serve mutual interests rather than unilateral projections of force.

The Roman historian Livy wrote that an empire remains powerful so long as its "subjects yield obedience gladly."[52] At its most basic level, the empire of the willing defines enlightened self-interest in the information age as unleashing the power of the individual to solve problems in his neighborhood. Genuine opportunity for individuals is the bedrock of the empire's appeal. Yet American decision makers in recent years made traditional imperial gambits. The main threats to the empire of the willing's legitimacy and sustainability are of our own making.

Innovate or Decline

In December 2005, the United States Agency for International Development (USAID) formally offered over $1 billion to "any type of entity" to "design and implement" a plan for stabilizing ten strategic cities in Iraq, the number of which "may expand or contract over time." During the Cold War, U.S. government funding for development exceeded that of private capital. Today, private investment dwarfs government aid by a factor of six, and charitable giving to international development is roughly three times greater than Washington's philanthropy. Warren Buffett's gift will eventually require the Bill and Melinda Gates Foundation to dispense at least $2.5 billion annually, comfortably exceeding the 2005 aid outlays of Australia and many EU member states. With the demise of the Soviet empire, America's relative power has grown, but that power is increasingly executed through private sector and philanthropic organizations. While our attention was focused elsewhere, American foreign policy has been privatized.

Across the board, the U.S. government can no longer pursue its foreign policy objectives without the private sector. Beyond Iraq—where private employees, who constitute 53 percent of the total number of boots on the ground, actually outnumber U.S. military personnel—contractors now feature prominently in everything from diplomacy to development to intelligence, and only a fraction of them carry weapons. Outsourcing is not just Blackwater and Halliburton. Humanitarian organizations such as Save the Children, CARE, and Catholic Relief Services have relied heavily on U.S. government funding. In many instances, contractors are forces for the good, especially when the United States indirectly employs the local population.

Taken at face value, the inability of the United States to bring peace and stability to Afghanistan and Iraq suggests that American power is on the wane. Our militarized foreign policy and arrogant unilateralism mobilized anti-American sentiment that our enemies prudently exploited. But to conclude that the situation is irreparable requires an exclusive focus on military power. For those who measure state power in terms of the ability to compel others to do one's bidding, the power of the United States is indeed in irreversible decline. Yet George Soros, Ted Turner, Bill Gates, Starbucks, Google, corporate social responsibility, philanthropreneurship, Halliburton, and Al Qaeda all register zero on the traditional military power scale while having an enormous impact on global politics.

In his illuminating book *The Future of Freedom*, Fareed Zakaria points out that we dwell in an era where little is demanded of our elites, in part because our commitment to democracy blinds us to their presence. Americans want to believe that our society is so meritocratic and dynamic that it no longer even has a governing elite. But a change in the structure of American elites should not be confused with their disappearance. The rich and powerful always will be with us. The difference is that we no longer expect anything of them. "We have freed our upper classes of any sense of responsibility," Zakaria writes, "and they have happily reciprocated."[53]

Changing elite perceptions of their own self-interest—bringing them to the realization that they stand to lose all if they do not step up and serve as stewards of liberal order, rather than focusing on short-term gain at the expense of long-term viability—is the central challenge that the privatization of American power poses. Those who exercise power globally have an obligation to be part of the solution to global problems, precisely because it is in their own self-interest to do so. One thing is certain: we cannot get where we need to go when government outsources in unenlightened fashion while effectively telling business to focus on what they do best: making money. The current status quo leaves too many powerful forces as spectators rather than participants. It would be both prudent and thrifty for the U.S. government to nurture those forces, harnessing them to appropriate purposes.

At least part of the private sector understands its long-term interests quite well. The corporate social responsibility movement, Bill Gates's call for creative capitalism, and the independent force of the emergent fourth sector create a reservoir of support for new forms of business-government collaboration among globalization's principal stakeholders. But it is up to government to channel these diverse forces into a genuine political force that is harnessed to the common good.

Acknowledging that American power has been misunderstood, misused, and, above all, privatized, is the key to restoring American vitality.

American strength and prosperity do not flow from military might but instead from the values that have shaped American political institutions and the economy they govern. Those core American values of liberty and equality of opportunity are shared by many non-Americans and bind a wide range of individuals and organizations—an empire of the willing—in common cause. The changing nature of power, once properly understood, opens up an enormous window of opportunity for the United States to restore its reputation, recover its values, and serve once again as a beacon to the world.

4

The End of Statesmanship

The unripe grape, the ripe bunch, the dried grape, all are changes, not
into nothing, but into something which exists not yet.
—Marcus Aurelius, *The Meditations*

Modern politics is, at bottom, a struggle not of men but of forces.
—Henry Adams, *The Education of Henry Adams*

THE Treaty of Westphalia of 1648 ended Europe's Thirty Years'
War between Protestants and Catholics by enshrining the principle
of state sovereignty and ushering in the era of modern diplomacy.
Building on that foundation in 1814–15, the Congress of Vienna brought
together Europe's great powers to forge a peace settlement based on a balance of power. The aim of great statesmen like Austria's Metternich and
Britain's Castlereagh was to inoculate the continent against the sort of dev-
astation in the name of universalism that Napoleon's forces had wrought in
their drive to dominate the European continent.[1] Today, while violence
rages in Iraq and Afghanistan, the leadership of one party to the conflict
sends no representative to a high-level peace conference but instead hides
in caves. Whereas the Congress of Vienna was the fulfillment of the Treaty
of Westphalia's promise, the attacks on the World Trade Center symbolize
its official end.

The end of Westphalia means that contemporary diplomats can never
convene to forge a comparable peace settlement, because the West's principal enemy is not another state with diplomats at the helm but a global network of stateless nihilists. The potential disruption that suicide bombers
with Internet connections can pose to globalization's interdependent processes is enormous. The twenty-first century military of the world's remaining superpower thus finds itself mortally challenged in a standoff against
an opponent with no standing army and no embassies.

This conflict cannot be won by military might and top-down information control. It is a war of the future—an information war of communica-

tions strategies. As counterinsurgency expert David Kilcullen explained to *New Yorker* writer George Packer, "If bin Laden didn't have access to global media, satellite communications, and the Internet, he'd just be a cranky guy in a cave."[2] That means while diplomacy is of fundamental importance, the traditional state-centric diplomacy of a Metternich or a Castlereagh, so successful in restoring order in nineteenth century Europe, can no longer suffice. The billions of dollars in contracts that firms like Blackwater, DynCorp, and Triple Canopy have received from the State Department since 2003 are both a reflection of and a response to this changed world.

Former British prime minister Tony Blair's June 2007 appointment as the West's Middle East envoy, representing no state in particular, should be understood as a symbol of diplomacy's newly privatized face.[3] Rather than pursuing parochial national interests, the diplomacy of the twenty-first century must instead exploit the privatization of power and globalization's connectivity to the West's advantage. How can that be done? A precondition for getting the formula right is a clear understanding of the forces that have catalyzed the privatization of diplomacy, as well as the inherent contradictions that hobbled the Bush administration's diplomatic strategy.

The Rise and Decline of the State Department

Following European nomenclature, the U.S. Department of Foreign Affairs was created in July 1787 as part of the larger project to forge a deeper union through a new federal constitution. After certain domestic duties were added to the new department's portfolio, it was renamed the U.S. Department of State on September 15, 1787. Later that month, Thomas Jefferson, then ambassador to France, was sworn in as the first U.S. secretary of state. The U.S. Department of State thus predates the ratification of the Constitution and is the oldest institution of American foreign policy. In contrast, both the National Security Council and the U.S. Department of Defense were twentieth century creations, products of the National Security Act of 1947.

At the beginning of the twentieth century, two independent and poorly coordinated federal services looked after American interests overseas: the diplomatic service, whose employees were accredited by the foreign country in which they served and based in its capital city; and the consular service, whose employees were accredited to the local authorities and often based outside the capital in areas of commercial activity. The latter far outnumbered the former, and the consular service at that time was charged with protecting the rights of U.S. citizens abroad, as well as issuing visas and the like. The Rogers Act of 1924 consolidated these two services into the Foreign Service of the United States.[4]

The diplomatic corps was founded on noblesse oblige and public-spiritedness. Over time, according to the diplomat and strategist George Kennan, it became something else entirely. It shifted from an enterprise that placed the practice of diplomacy beyond politics to one that was thoroughly politicized from start to finish. The politicization of ambassadorial posts symbolized this larger transition. "By 1950," Kennan wrote in the seventy-fifth anniversary issue of *Foreign Affairs,* "the Foreign Service bore little resemblance to the corps its authors had intended."[5]

The National Security Act of 1947 created two brand new entities, the National Security Council (NSC) and the Central Intelligence Agency (CIA). It also reorganized the military under the Department of Defense, which absorbed the old Department of War and the Navy Department. In the process it initiated another slow change in diplomacy as traditionally understood. Both State and Defense had one equally weighted vote on the new National Security Council, and the national security advisor reported directly to the president, which had the effect of redistributing responsibility for foreign policy. One of the many reasons behind the new National Security Council apparatus was to ensure that the new Department of Defense, whose secretary shared a seat at the NSC table with the secretary of state, would be able to hold its own against the powerful State Department.[6] Few worried about whether State could hold its own against Defense.

These administrative changes swiftly undercut ambassadorial power overseas. Once the State Department was just another institution of foreign policy, rather than the main institution, there was no reason other agencies should not have a presence overseas as well. USAID and the United States Information Agency claimed a seat at the diplomatic table during the Cold War. After the Cold War, the FBI and the Drug Enforcement Agency added their voices to the mix. By opening up new venues for economic interaction, globalization provided the rationale for still more diversification of American overseas representation. The Departments of Commerce and Agriculture are today major players in trade promotion.[7] As Kennan pointed out, by 1997 "regular State Department personnel account[ed] for only some 30 percent of the total official presence at these missions; the remaining 70 percent [came] from other agencies."[8]

The diversification of the official American presence overseas went hand in hand with radical changes in communications and intelligence. Until World War II, the State Department was the principal channel of communications. The National Security Act of 1947 added the CIA to the mix and created the potential for big information gaps between the CIA's and the State Department's sense of a given crisis. For example, former U.S. Ambassador to Peru Anthony Quainton recalls how his official residence in Peru was ripped apart by a car bomb in February 1992 while he was just three blocks away. At the time, the information he had from multiple sources initially persuaded him that the attack was symbolic and not directed against him personally. As part of a subsequent official review of the event, he was shown a CIA assessment, one he had not previously seen or approved, which concluded that he had in fact been personally targeted.[9]

Encryption technology improved in the 1980s to the point where communication between home and abroad no longer had to be hand-carried in secure boxes. It could be done on a desktop computer and later a laptop computer without risk of external penetration. This meant, in practice, that every agency represented abroad had the capacity to communicate directly with Washington without the tacit approval of the ambassador. The Internet revolution also undercut ambassadorial power by enabling anyone to send an e-mail directly to the secretary of state. The potential access points for influence by government employees or private actors became virtually unlimited.[10]

Two important things happened simultaneously in the 1990s to further undermine the power of the State Department. First, the Clinton administration's efforts to reduce the federal deficit meant that budgets were cut across the board, with the State Department taking a large hit. Foreign affairs fell from 2.5 percent of the federal budget in 1984 to roughly 1 percent in 1996. Both aggregate dollars and numbers of full-time employees were cut. Second, the Clinton administration embarked on a "reinventing government" campaign that reduced the number of employees on government payrolls while keeping the workload largely unchanged. Contracting filled the gap. The State Department began to rely heavily on contracted guards at U.S. embassies during the Clinton years.[11]

Another manifestation of the growing willingness to outsource responsibility beyond formal governmental structures was an increased reliance on special envoys. The demise of Soviet power, and with it the old bipolar world order, made formerly black-and-white issues more nuanced and complex. It was one thing to determine who had responsibility for an issue when the principal threat to American security was the other superpower. It was another thing entirely to do so in an environment where multiple government agencies could legitimately claim ownership of any given policy. Turf battles, adjudicated by the NSC, became the order of the day. Appointing a special envoy to deal with the issue became a way to transcend both gridlock and the tyranny of the in-box at a stroke. The fact of daily government life is that there is so much going on that it is very difficult to give extended attention to any one issue, yet negotiations need just that to succeed. Special envoys, like contractors, can expand government capacity.

For example, when Clinton's former national security advisor, Anthony Lake, served in 1998–2000 as special envoy to the Ethiopia/Eritrea border conflict, he traveled to Africa for negotiations over a dozen times. Lake reported both to Assistant Secretary of State for African Affairs Susan Rice and to the NSC. The use of this extradiplomatic tool both reflected and reinforced presidential power. In Lake's view, if a special envoy, especially a senior person, is clearly working for the State Department or, better still, for the White House, he or she can be very useful. But costs emerge as the practice proliferates, and the official position of the U.S. government becomes a moving target. Overreliance on extradiplomatic channels can amount to outsourcing diplomacy, which Lake finds imprudent and potentially dangerous.[12]

The Bush administration saw things differently. With the administration's June 2007 proposal that Tony Blair be appointed special envoy to the Middle East, representing the diplomatic "quartet" of the United States, the European Union, the United Nations, and Russia, President Bush and Secretary of State Condoleezza Rice showed that they had no qualms about outsourcing diplomacy to other countries.[13] The Bush administration also continued the practice of devolving diplomatic authority to special assistants. That same month, the president appointed General Douglas E. Lute "war czar" for Iraq and Afghanistan, reporting directly to the president. In confirmation hearings, several senators wondered why this was not the responsibility of National Security Advisor Stephen Hadley. Defense Secretary Robert Gates explained to the *New York Times* that "this is what Steve Hadley would do if Steve Hadley had the time, but he doesn't have the time to do it full time."[14] The Obama administration has expanded the use of special envoys and representatives still further. If regular government channels are inadequate to handle the biggest challenges the nation faces, it is hard to avoid concluding that something is terribly wrong with our current national security architecture.

The well-documented conflict between the State Department and the Pentagon over Iraqi reconstruction illuminates the problem.[15] Defense Secretary Donald Rumsfeld's Pentagon gained the upper hand over State after the fall of Baghdad, but as Iraq unraveled it became increasingly obvious that the Pentagon's ad hoc leadership of Iraqi reconstruction was proving unsatisfactory. In early 2004 Sens. Richard Lugar (R-Indiana) and Joseph

Biden (D-Delaware), respectively the chairman and ranking minority member of the Senate Foreign Relations Committee, took steps to highlight the lack of civilian operational capability. They introduced legislation for a new office within the State Department, effectively designed to wrest leadership of reconstruction policy from the Pentagon and place it in civilian hands. For the U.S. military, tasked with a nation-building agenda in postwar Iraq that it had never been trained to pursue, this was a welcome and timely reform. To Secretary of State Colin Powell's State Department, it looked like an attempt by the administration to drop DOD's mess in State's lap. The initiative understandably drew little enthusiasm from Foggy Bottom.[16]

Yet with Iraq descending into civil war, the National Security Council effectively endorsed the Lugar-Biden position in April 2004, agreeing that State should coordinate interagency responses for reconstruction. The State Department created an Office for Reconstruction and Stabilization (S/CRS) in August 2004. The office got to work immediately, but despite the declared urgency of the task its authorities were not formally approved for over a year.[17] In December 2005, the White House announced the creation of the new office within the State Department through National Security Presidential Directive 44.[18]

Though designed to be the lead civilian coordinator for stabilization and reconstruction efforts abroad, S/CRS instead quickly became a poster child for bureaucratic inertia. Congress provided only $7 million of the $100 million in funding the administration had requested. Ironically, the new office never took part in the two biggest reconstruction challenges, Iraq and Afghanistan. The White House did not protest loudly. And the balance of funds were never delivered. The new institution that the president himself had tasked to lead reconstruction never got off the ground. In mid-2008, the office still had fewer than ten employees.[19]

Since life and death issues in Iraq and Afghanistan could not be put on hold while government agencies jockeyed for power, the Pentagon stepped in to fill the gap as best it could. One Defense innovation was provisional reconstruction teams (PRTs), designed to bring civilian expertise and military protection together in one unit. It was unprecedented for the military to acknowledge the necessity of cooperation with the civilian side, yet that is precisely what the PRT concept called for.[20] But the State Department has been unable to staff the PRTs in Afghanistan and Iraq, in large part because its employees have little incentive to take such dangerous postings without the clear promise of career advancement for service in war zones.

Another factor also played a role in State's inability to staff the PRTs. Since resources and the opportunity to make a difference now exist elsewhere, the allure of a State Department career seems to have diminished. The Foreign Affairs Council announced in June 2007 that some two hundred State Department jobs, most of them overseas, are unfilled. To make matters worse, in the first two years of Secretary Rice's stewardship, "almost no net new resources" for the State Department were realized, despite increased expectations for its role in the world. None of the new positions requested for training and transformational diplomacy (a new State Department agenda launched in 2006; see discussion later in this chapter) were granted in fiscal years 2006 and 2007.[21] All of this further increased the Pentagon presence overseas at the expense of the State Department.

When responsibilities increase but requests for new positions are denied, outsourcing can be a way to get the job done. The Bureau of Diplomatic Security, the entity responsible for the safety of U.S. diplomatic personnel deployed overseas, is a case in point. In 2003, the State Department turned to Blackwater USA and a consortium of other companies to provide private security for its personnel. It is one thing for embassy guards in Prague to be private sector employees; it's another thing entirely for diplomatic security to be privatized in a war zone. When seventeen Iraqi civilians were gunned down by guards under contract with the U.S. State Department in September 2007, the effect was anything but diplomatic.

When the Pentagon has a much greater overseas presence than the State Department, we have traveled a long way from the early days of the republic, when the writers of the Constitution did not even anticipate the existence of a Department of Defense. We have also traveled far from the traditional definition of diplomacy. Diplomacy in Metternich's or Bismarck's era presupposed the primacy of foreign policy over all government realms *(das Primat der Aussenpolitik)*. The ambassador or foreign minister would speak on behalf of the sovereign, and the lines of accountability and power were crystal clear. *Das Primat der Aussenpolitik* became an impossible goal at precisely that indefinable moment when foreign service became more than simply residing abroad, winning friends there, and reporting one's observations back to the capital. Once that tipping point was reached, there was no turning back. The shifting balance of power between the military and the foreign service has deeper roots than Donald Rumsfeld's ambitions.

The relative decline in State Department input to the foreign policy of the United States has dangerous unintended (and often unacknowledged) consequences. During the Cold War, the top concern in U.S. embassies abroad was information security. Today it is the physical security of the building and its inhabitants—which contractors are hired to defend. This focus on physical security in turn creates enormous pressure to reduce the

American footprint overseas in order to reduce the number of targets for terrorists. As service abroad becomes more dangerous, it becomes difficult to persuade personnel to serve on the front lines. Robert Blackwill, former National Security Council deputy for Iraq, recalled how he couldn't get Treasury Department employees to set up the currency in the country; they didn't want to risk getting killed.[22]

Besides creating an image of Fortress America, a zero-risk mentality is ultimately a recipe for inaction, and since Washington wanted to do something it wound up hiring contractors to act on its behalf. The direct-hire employee figures tell the story here. During the Vietnam War, USAID had fifteen thousand total employees; to meet the development challenges in Iraq and Afghanistan, it has roughly two thousand. USAID has become a contract clearinghouse. As former USAID administrator Andrew Natsios puts it, "Unless we allow for a tolerable level of managed risk—even risk to life and limb—neither our diplomats nor our aid missions can do the work for which they exist, at a time when their contribution is more needed than ever."[23]

With jobs to be done that no one else wanted, the military became the executive branch's go-to institution. The Pentagon's willingness to step in is, in some basic sense, heroic. But it has had huge consequences for the U.S. image abroad. Unlike every other liberal democracy in the world, America today clothes its lead diplomatic team in a military uniform.

The Statesman of the Future

The statesman of the future must operate in a world where, as Ambassador Quainton put it, "diplomacy is no longer the function of diplomats."[24] This is not simply because other agencies have gotten into what used to be State's game. It is also because private sector forces often represent the face of the West abroad as much as traditional diplomats and sometimes exert more influence. Globalization gives private actors enormous and unprecedented impact. Private citizens such as rock star Bono, actress Angelina Jolie, Bill Clinton, and Al Gore undeniably advance a diplomatic agenda without official government backing; so do countless other individuals without celebrity status. So does Osama Bin Laden.

Just as presidents can call on individuals to speak over the heads of government, so too can private actors perform governmental functions without being asked. Independent Diplomat, a nonprofit venture funded by George Soros and headed by a former British diplomat, Carne Ross, provides an illuminating example. Independent Diplomat seeks to ensure that the poor and powerless get access to the decision makers and organizations that make policy, such as the EU and the United Nations. Ross's book, *Independent Diplomat: Dispatches from an Unaccountable Elite*, argues that the foreign service routinely makes bad decisions in closed rooms with little or no consultation with the people those decisions affect most. Independent Diplomat offers advice to politically marginalized regions and groups in places like Kosovo and Western Sahara. Its motto is "a diplomatic service for those who need it most."[25]

As this example suggests, the privatization of power has transformed traditional diplomacy in at least four ways. First, whereas traditional diplomacy was largely a bilateral affair, the new diplomacy is multilateral and hence strategic in a wholly different way. Bismarck catapulted Germany to unification and prominence through the skillful manipulation of bilateral relationships. The politics of friends and enemies was both a domestic and an international pursuit, but the battles at home were largely distinct from those waged abroad. Today, because of the revolution in communication flows, it is no longer possible to separate domestic from foreign concerns in this systematic way. An American ambassador's traditional function was to penetrate the society of the country to which he was assigned in order to serve as a two-way conduit of information between the foreign country and decision makers in Washington. The statesman reported on events; he did not endeavor to shape them. Today the Internet, carefully perused, can instantly relay much of the same information without intermediaries. As a result, the State Department's function as an indispensable node in the strategic information network necessary to formulate prudent policy is irretrievably undermined.

The second major point of contrast between the traditional and contemporary statesman also follows directly from the information revolution. Since information is and always has been power, the potential to preserve information partitions (that is, to keep secrets), with the elites in the know and the masses in the dark, both facilitates and reinforces hierarchical chains of command. If ordinary people do not have access to the information the elites do, they are by definition less capable of contributing to the dialogue regarding alternative courses of action. In such circumstances the statesman serves as gatekeeper, helping to decide whose information merits inclusion in decision-making and who deserves to be admitted to the circle of those in the know, with the sovereign's complete access to all secrets placing him in the supreme position. The presence of airtight information silos and power relationships that preclude taking seriously any conflicting intelligence that might emerge from outside the silo and lower in the chain of command is commonly called stovepiping. Stovepiping may focus the organization's attention on a set of common goals, but it also produces a tunnel vision that can both reinforce misconceptions that develop within the silo (such as the misconception that Iraq possessed weapons of mass destruction) and introduce inefficiencies that undermine overarching national interests. Stovepiping is rational when relevant information is the exclusive domain of elites and strict hierarchy prevails for access to it.

For the new diplomacy, however, stovepiping is itself the problem. Rather than hoard information, the new global statesman must strive to forge a network of fruitful relationships with international organizations, NGOs, business, and other governments to advance American interests. A strict division of labor determined from on high does not exist, relevant information is ideally shared among the parties to which it is useful, and multiple overlapping lines of responsibility prevail. The leader of the new diplomacy is not a gatekeeper but a boundary-buster and traffic conductor: According to Brian Hocking, a professor of international relations, "The claims of the gatekeeper role are being redefined in terms of that of facilitator in the management of multifaceted policy networks."[26] Still, since it serves a basic human need to feel powerful, stovepiping is not instantaneously eradicated by the information revolution. Moving beyond it will require a different understanding of power.

The third significant difference between traditional diplomacy and global diplomacy is who determines which employees populate American embassies. By 1996, the State Department accounted for just over a third of the staffing at most U.S. embassies; a full 63 percent of those under the authority of U.S. ambassadors and other chiefs of mission were not State Department employees. The percentage of employees who hail from government agencies without direct ties to the State Department ("Chief of Mission" jurisdiction) grew significantly from 1986 to 1996, as the embassies responded to the challenges of globalization (Table 1). In Mexico in the mid-1990s, for example, U.S. interests were promoted by representatives of thirty-two different agencies, including the Departments of Justice, Agriculture, Treasury, Commerce, and Defense; the Immigration and Naturalization Service; the FBI; and the Drug Enforcement Agency. As the 1996 report of the U.S. Advisory Commission on Public Diplomacy concluded, "Relations between the United States and Mexico are far more complex than what happens between the State Department and the Mexican foreign ministry."[27] The point is clear: if any one of thirty-two agencies might be represented by that person at the embassy desk, the State Department is no longer the first voice of the U.S. government abroad.

The fourth crucial distinction between diplomacy as Metternich knew it and as it is practiced today is the critical importance of public diplomacy in advancing state interests. For the European realist, the idea that random

Table 1   U.S. government positions overseas under chief of mission
authority, 1986 vs. 1996

Agency	Change (%)
Health and Human Services	+250.0
Justice	+76.3
Transportation	+11.6
Defense	+7.7
Treasury	+5.8
Commerce	−2.3
Agriculture	−10.5
U.S. Information Agency	−14.1
U.S. Agency for International Development	−23.9

Source: U.S. Department of State; published in Strobe Talbott, "Globalization and Diplomacy: A Practitioner's Perspective," *Foreign Policy,* no. 108 (1997).

subjects who were not directly employed by the government could advance state interests in a predictably favorable way seemed ludicrous, a most dangerous gamble. Since the nineteenth century international system did not have NGOs and international business concerns that were not under direct state control, the building blocks of public diplomacy were not discernible.

Circumstances today are radically different. The number of significant players with an influence on foreign policy has grown exponentially.[28] For example, to implement the Dayton Peace Accords in Bosnia, nine agencies and departments of the U.S. government cooperated with more than a dozen other governments, seven international organizations, and thirteen major NGOs.[29] As Kiva's microlending activities in Iraq illustrate, private citizens can now make their own diplomacy. Here, too, the rise of privatized power has redefined the situation.

The numbers for State Department procurement between 2000 and 2005 display yet another dimension of the privatization of diplomatic power (Figure 3). In that period, State had the largest percentage increase in procurement spending of any major federal agency, including the DOD. In 2000, the State Department spent $1.2 billion on federal contracts. By 2005, this spending had grown to $5.3 billion, an increase of 332 percent.[30] At the same time, the State Department's budget has declined in real terms by nearly 50 percent since 1984.[31] As a result, the proportion of its budget that State spends on contracts has grown dramatically in the twenty-first century. Since contractors can be deployed strategically as needed, and the market for services is now genuinely global, it is small wonder that State's procurement figures have shot through the roof.

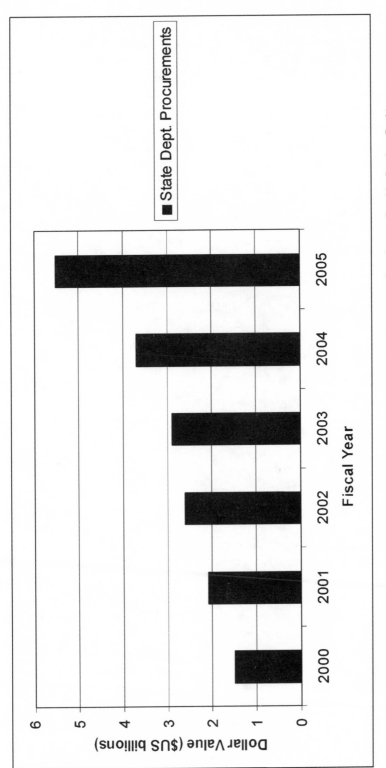

Figure 3. State Department procurements, 2000–2005 (Source: Federal Procurement Data System. Graphic: Carolann Davis)

Today's emissaries also rely on private security contractors rather than soldiers or government employees to pursue their mission abroad. State Department costs for private security have gone from $1 billion in 2003 to nearly $4 billion in 2007.[32] Even in Washington, the Iraq Desk at State is administered by the management and technology consultant BearingPoint, which is paid more than $2 million a year to schedule, set agendas for, and take notes at all Iraq policy meetings.[33]

For the statesman of the twenty-first century, leveraging nongovernmental forces through strategic partnerships is the key to accomplishment and even survival. Writing prior to September 11, Marc Grossman, then director general of the Foreign Service, described the State Department as "changing from an organization whose main job is to observe and report into an organization that tells America's story, promotes America's interests, and confronts new dangers to our democracy."[34] Diplomacy still matters, but diplomats are managers of multifaceted networks that extend into quasi-governmental and nongovernmental space. And the people occupying the various nodes in these networks have power comparable to and sometimes greater than the ambassador's. As former ambassador Robert Oakley remarked, "A lot of people would rather see the CEO of Citibank than the American ambassador."[35] In his April 2006 visit to the United States, President Hu Jintao of China met with officials of Starbucks, Microsoft, and Boeing before connecting with his counterpart in the White House. If Bismarck and Metternich were in their prime today, they'd be heading Internet startups.

Transformational Diplomacy

In January 2006, with the deepening quagmire in Iraq as a backdrop, Secretary of State Rice unveiled a new mission for the State Department, saying it "must rise to answer a new historic calling." In challenging times, ordinary diplomacy was no longer enough. The moment called for something far more radical: "transformational diplomacy." "The resources we commit must empower developing countries to strengthen security, to consolidate democracy, to increase trade and investment, and to improve the lives of their people," Rice announced. "America's foreign assistance must promote responsible sovereignty, not permanent dependency." Working hand in hand with the imperatives of transformational development, transformational diplomacy would be "rooted in partnership, not paternalism—in doing things with other people, not for them. We seek to use America's diplomatic power to help foreign citizens to better their own lives, and to build their own nations, and to transform their own futures." Rice concluded,

"Transforming the State Department is the work of a generation. But it is urgent work that cannot be deferred."[36]

The embrace of transformational diplomacy brought immediate, dramatic shifts in foreign service staffing. Fifteen new positions were created at the U.S. Embassy in China, and twelve in India. Five new slots were added in Jakarta. In total, transformational diplomacy created seventy-four new foreign service positions, the vast majority in the developing world. To pay for the new postings, other positions were eliminated: ten in Russia, seven in Germany, and two or three each in Belgium, Poland, Italy, Spain, Japan, and Brazil. With these changes, the face of the State Department turned squarely to the developing world.

Transformational diplomacy prescribed one-year, unaccompanied tours of duty in the world's hotspots. The idea was to move people quickly in and out of the more demanding embassies, keeping their families at home for safety. In practice, this means that the entire staff in a place like Kabul turns over every summer, with damaging implications for effective engagement.[37] It is impossible to determine how much of this dramatic reorientation was driven by budgetary constraints and to what extent these reforms were the authentic expression of an emergent alternative vision for America's role in the world.

Changes on the other side of the Atlantic suggest that there is something more at work here than mere budgetary realities. Great Britain has made comparable staffing changes in the Foreign Office, closing embassies and high commissions in Africa to reopen embassies in Baghdad, Kabul, and North Korea. The cuts also helped pay for the recruitment of counter-terrorism and drug trafficking specialists for deployment in the Middle East. Since 9/11, Germany has created two hundred new positions for posts in North Africa, the Middle East, Indonesia, Pakistan, and Afghanistan.[38] That Britain and Germany have made parallel redeployment decisions suggests a redefinition of diplomatic strategy for the era of globalization that transcends particular national interests. Speaking at Georgetown University in May 2006, British prime minister Tony Blair explained, "Interdependence—the fact of a crisis somewhere becoming a crisis everywhere— makes a mockery of traditional views of national interest. You can't have a coherent view of national interest today without a coherent view of the international community."[39]

That a crisis in a far-off place can become a crisis everywhere reflects a radically changed communication environment. The Bush administration called its effort to adapt to that new media world transformational diplomacy. Transformational diplomacy of necessity relies on public diplomacy, but not as it is traditionally understood. During the Cold War, the

United States employed print and radio as well as high culture to present a positive American face to the world. It was standard operating procedure to send the Boston Symphony Orchestra and the New York Philharmonic on international tours. Today, the United States utilizes little print and radio, and no longer sees high culture as an emissary.[40] For the Rice State Department, public diplomacy largely meant engaging the private sector in innovative ways, often while neglecting more traditional public initiatives.[41]

The State Department established its Office of Private Sector Outreach in 2006, but a shrinking budget limited its effectiveness. In 2006, the State Department was allocated just $1.5 billion—roughly what the Pentagon spends in a day—for public diplomacy efforts.[42]

Joint efforts with the private sector fared better. In December 2005, Keith Reinhard, the president and founder of Business for Diplomatic Action (BDA), discussed with Karen Hughes, under secretary of state for public diplomacy and public affairs, the establishment of a public-private foundation for public diplomacy. He proposed BDA as the embryo for such a venture, with State Department financial support. Reinhard reported that the Government Accountability Office found his proposal promising.[43] BDA built its vision on Peter G. Peterson's earlier argument for the establishment of an independent, not-for-profit Corporation for Public Diplomacy, to be modeled on the Corporation for Public Broadcasting.[44] The Corporation for Public Diplomacy would be a "focal point for private sector involvement in public diplomacy," and, like the Corporation for Public Broadcasting, it would have tax-exempt status.[45] This ability to tap into private resources would ensure that quality initiatives could continue even when government resources were stretched to the limit. In underwriting public diplomacy efforts without increasing the federal budget deficit, public-private partnerships can be a particularly useful instrument in an era of deficit spending.[46]

The Discover America Partnership provides a fine example of wholly self-interested private sector behavior that advances transformational diplomacy. This partnership was founded in 2006 by leaders in the travel and tourism industry, who made the shrewd connection between the dip in America's popularity abroad and the smaller number of foreigners vacationing in the United States. Even with a weakening dollar, America's market share in international tourism has declined 36 percent since 1992. Since the country's declining image affects its ability to lead successfully, these changes are pertinent to national security. The Discover America Partnership commits itself to advancing public diplomacy through foreigners having fun in the United States. Its central premise is that tourism shapes foreigners' attitudes toward the United States. What's good for tourism is good for public diplomacy.[47]

Transformational diplomacy's public-private partnerships provide a window on its innovative potential. After the 2005 Kashmir earthquake, President Bush announced the formation of the South Asia Earthquake Relief Fund, appointing five private sector executives—Jeff Immelt of General Electric, Jim Kelly of UPS, Hank McKinnell Jr. of Pfizer, Anne Mulcahy of Xerox, and Sanford Weill of Citigroup—to lead a national effort to mobilize private resources for earthquake relief, so that the U.S. government's contribution to the cause might be effectively leveraged. These business leaders, in conjunction with the U.S. government, raised more than $100 million, surpassing the goal they had set. For its timely assistance, the team was presented with the Sitara-i-Eissar (Star of Sacrifice) award by Pakistan president Pervez Musharraf in a 2006 ceremony at the Pakistan Embassy in Washington.[48] Concurrently, USAID announced a $600,000 partnership with Proctor and Gamble to provide clean drinking water to earthquake survivors.[49]

The U.S.-Lebanon Partnership was created in September 2006 through a business delegation to Lebanon led by Under Secretary of State Dina Habib Powell.[50] Traveling with Powell were the CEOs of Cisco Systems, Intel, Ghafari Inc., and Occidental Petroleum. Upon returning from their long weekend in Lebanon, they met immediately with President Bush and announced a collaborative effort to raise funds for Lebanon's reconstruction. The president blessed this public-private partnership's efforts with a pledge of $230 million in government financing.[51]

The State Department's Web site describes the Middle East Partnership Initiative (MEPI) as "transformational diplomacy in action."[52] MEPI works to promote four main objectives: spreading democracy, expanding women's freedom, improving education, and creating economic opportunity. MEPI educates people in the region on political party building, campaigning, and election monitoring. It has created the Arab Women's Legal Network, uniting women lawyers and judges across national boundaries. MEPI trains teachers and provides civic education opportunities. It has also funded initiatives such as the Middle East Entrepreneur Training (MEET US), which provides business training and networking opportunities to increase entrepreneurship in the region. In sum, MEPI "has set in motion more than 350 programs in 15 countries of the Middle East and in the Palestinian territories."[53]

In an effort to connect with educators and promote international exchange arrangements, Bush took a step in the right direction when he held the first university presidents' summit on international education on January 5–6, 2006. With the secretary of state and the president present, it clearly signaled the administration's newfound commitment to public diplomacy and the pivotal role that international education of necessity plays in undergirding it. The administration used the occasion to unfurl its National Security Language Initiative, which was designed to increase dramatically the number of Americans with facility in critical foreign languages.[54]

The Bush administration also sought to reward independent private sector initiative that advances transformational diplomacy's goals. The Award for Corporate Excellence (ACE) was launched by the Clinton administration and was first awarded in two categories: small to medium-sized businesses and multinational corporations. In 2006, the State Department added an award for large companies, with Goldman Sachs of New York receiving the first ACE for its outstanding corporate stewardship in Chile.[55] In the multinational category, General Motors got the 2006 honors for its efforts in Colombia. In the small to medium-sized business category, Sambazon took the prize for its work with organic agriculture in Brazil. Secretary Rice stressed the direct connection between private sector initiatives like these and the administration's agenda for democracy promotion.

Finally, transformational diplomacy endorsed the Clinton administration's American "presence posts" (APPs). American presence posts involve deploying a single American officer outside of the capital, to staff a regional hub for diplomacy. The brainchild of Felix Rohatyn, they were first implemented in France during his tenure as ambassador there and are a means of extending America's reach at minimal cost.[56]

The implementation of Rohatyn's concept met with resistance at first, especially from Sen. Jesse Helms (R-North Carolina), then chair of the Senate Foreign Relations Committee. Helms had been a staunch proponent of slashing the State Department's budget, which had forced the State Department to close the consulate in Lyon. Felix Rohatyn explained, "I devised the idea of the American presence post as a way of having a viable presence in Lyon without a full blown consulate. We simply could not do our business without a presence in the provinces. I proposed reallocating some funds from the embassy in Paris to foot the bill. Some people in the State Department did not like the idea of devolving power in this fashion. But I thought we had to do it. So I went to Jesse Helms and told him that globalization involves the decentralization of power, and I needed the American presence posts to do business. I told him, 'We are like a multinational global business, and we need access to our customers.' He listened carefully, and replied, 'So, these presence posts are like your regional teller's windows?' And I said, 'Exactly.' He supported the concept from there on out."[57]

In her January 2006 speech that unveiled the details of transformational diplomacy, Secretary Rice embraced the economical idea of the American presence post, describing it as having "one of our best diplomats move outside the embassy to live and work and represent America in an emerging community of change." In the same speech she also endorsed the more radically cost-effective concept of a virtual presence post, where an Internet site would replace the face-to-face connection of a real-time presence post.[58] "As of June 2007, there were eight APPs operating worldwide: five in France (Bordeaux, Lille, Lyon, Rennes, and Toulouse) and one each in Egypt (Alexandria), Indonesia (Medan), and Canada (Winnipeg). New APPs are scheduled to open in China (Wuhan) and Korea (Busan). The State Department plans to triple the number of APPs in operation."[59]

The State Department's January 2007 Private Sector Summit on Public Diplomacy, a cooperative initiative between the State Department and the PR Coalition (a coalition of public relations associations), broke new ground in engaging the private sector and putting an official governmental seal of approval on their freelance efforts to date. With the department's top-ranking officials all present, the conference brought together representatives from the business and NGO communities to discuss new forms of collaboration and showcase best practices in private sector innovation to date. In her introduction to the conference report, Rice proclaimed the necessity of the gathering in direct language: "The solutions to the challenges of the twenty-first century are not going to be met by government alone. The solutions must come from all sectors of American society working together, enhanced by a close and vital partnership between government and the private sector." In her remarks Rice also referred to the public-private partnership represented by the gathering itself as representative of "the true aim of transformational diplomacy: to devote America's energy to help foreign citizens better their own lives, build their own nations, and transform their own futures."[60]

In short, the State Department under Bush devoted a lot of effort to reinventing its standard operating procedures. Marc Grossman, who served as Colin Powell's under secretary of state for political affairs (the number three job at State), put the challenge this way in an interview with David Rothkopf: "One of the things we had tried to do is tell everybody here that if we don't change the way we do business, then we're going to go out of business. There will still be a building here and people will come to work, but it will be like any other irrelevant bureaucracy. And we don't want to do that. . . . Our whole struggle here for the past four years has been to try to change that culture, and say to people, this isn't about observing, reporting, and sending it back for other people to act and decide on."[61] In other words, the State Department felt its options were either transformational diplomacy or obsolescence.

When crisis strikes, of course, there is no substitute for traditional diplomacy. "Crisis diplomacy," shrewdly noted Robert Blackwill, former U.S. national security deputy for Iraq, "is not an endeavor for rookies."[62] But transformational diplomacy inevitably entailed the elevation of market and private authority, since all private actors associated with the United States have the potential to influence how foreigners view the world. If public diplomacy seeks to combat America's poor image overseas, every American interacting with foreigners abroad is a potential force for good. Transformational diplomacy thus blurred the line between government and business agendas as well as between philanthropy and business.[63]

The Millennium Challenge Corporation and Transformational Development

Transformational diplomacy was a calibrated adjustment to a world where the locus of national security threats had shifted to developing countries. Globalization allows ideas, goods, and people to move across borders at unprecedented velocity. Word travels fast about what behavior the U.S. government rewards. At the same time, the emerging consensus in the aid community that building capacity at the local level is the key to sustainable development has designated the standard top-down solution—government-to-government aid—as part of the problem rather than the solution. Designed with those insights in mind, transformational development expressly used foreign assistance as a tool for rewarding "good performers—governments that govern justly, invest in people, and create opportunities for economic growth."[64]

Though it does not often receive proper credit, the Bush administration made foreign assistance a Republican issue. With the United States occupying last place among developed countries in overseas direct assistance as a percentage of GDP, the Bush administration was not well positioned to shine at the March 2002 UN-sponsored conference on development in Monterrey, Mexico. Just before his departure for the meeting that would produce the Monterrey Consensus (the agreement of fifty heads of state that they share an interest in eliminating extreme poverty), Bush pledged an additional $5 billion in U.S. foreign aid and announced the creation of a new U.S. aid institution, the Millennium Challenge Account

(MCA). "The goal," he said, "is to provide people in developing nations the tools they need to seize the opportunities of the global economy. . . . Countries that live by these three broad standards—ruling justly, investing in their people, and encouraging economic freedom—will receive more aid from America."[65]

The story of the MCA is one of then Secretary of State Colin Powell's greatest achievements. But the State Department had plenty of help from both the National Security Council and prominent activists. In summer 2001, the rock stars Bob Geldof and Bono, along with their principal strategist Jamie Drummond, had coffee with then National Security Advisor Condoleezza Rice at the G-8 summit in Genoa. Rice told them that she was impressed with their work on debt relief in the developing world and wanted to build on it. Soon thereafter, in spring 2002, Rice's deputy Gary Edson, an intellectual force behind the new approach to development, invited Drummond to Washington to work on what would become the Millennium Challenge Corporation. While he would later build a hundreds-strong global advocacy organization, Drummond had no Washington office at the time, so he worked out of a Kinko's copy shop.[66]

The improbable collaboration produced something unprecedented. The Millennium Challenge Corporation (MCC) oversees the MCA and is the institutional embodiment of the new approach to foreign assistance. The corporation's board features key members of the president's cabinet— the secretaries of State and Treasury, the United States trade representative, and the administrator of USAID—along with a bipartisan group of four citizens appointed by the president on the advice of Congress. The public-private governance structure is distinctive; writing in the *New York Times* in December 2008, the four private sector appointees described their role as ensuring that the program "remains faithful to the principles that Congress laid down for it."[67] Creating the MCC was an explicit end run of USAID, an agency whose career employees are almost uniformly Democrats inclined to be hostile to a Republican president.[68] But the core ideas transcend partisan divides and are worthy of sustained exploration.

There are four principles that, when packaged together, are innovative in the MCC approach. First, the MCC has a narrow focus of reducing poverty through sustainable growth. The MCC does not do disaster relief, need-based humanitarian assistance, or political favors. Second, it is designed to work with a select group of countries that are doing things right and therefore most likely to benefit from significant MCA funding. The MCC selects this group of countries on the basis of seventeen indicators, which assess nonpolitically whether a country is ruling justly, investing in its people, and adopting sound economic policies.[69] Based on this methodology, as of January 2009 MCC had selected forty-one countries as eligible to receive MCA funding. That number includes what the MCC calls "threshold countries"—those that currently fall short of its compact-eligibility standards but might benefit from a push in the right direction.[70]

Third, the MCC requires local input and country ownership in all aspects of program selection, design, and implementation. MCC-eligible countries themselves must determine what they want funded and provide MCC with funding proposals that reflect the results of a broad and public consultative process with civil society and the private sector. Once a compact is signed, the MCC typically has four or five MCC employees on the ground in any given country to oversee program implementation, an extremely small footprint when compared with traditional approaches to aid. The implementing institution in Honduras, for example, is called MCA-Honduras and is established and run by the country. The country, therefore, is expected to carry out all procurements and all aspects of implementation, not the MCC. To continue with the example, MCA-Honduras is run by a board of directors that includes government, civil society, and private sector representatives, all with one vote and all with access to the same information. Board meetings are public, not private, which is the case in any country in which the MCC operates. In addition, there is no "buy American" or "buy local" requirement, with the goal being to obtain the best value for money for the country and to create a level playing field for local suppliers. Tenders for works and services are international, and the competition is global. Through its investments, MCC hopes to create opportunities for the private sector, thereby resulting in a multiplier effect on its original investment.[71]

The fourth critical difference between MCC practices and those of the past is that the MCC insists on measurable results, on outcomes rather than on how much money is spent or other inputs. This transfers the responsibility for success to the countries themselves, which are held accountable for their performance. Unlike USAID, the MCC is not designed to carry out the implementation of a project; the country is responsible for handling this as well. Also unlike USAID, the MCC funding is not subject to any congressional earmarks (set-aside money for particular programs). Backsliding on the key performance indicators is not tolerated; when things go wrong the MCC tells countries, "Don't lobby us, lobby the ratings agencies." In essence, in a way unlike any previous development program, the MCC seeks to incentivize countries to govern well, invest in health and education, and adopt sound economic policies. The MCC effect seems to have worked like EU membership. Countries compete to become eligible for MCC funding and in so doing improve their own performance.[72]

To create the Millennium Challenge Corporation as an engine for re-inforcing good performance, the Bush administration effectively side-stepped all existing aid programs. It was perceived by many people to be a vote of no confidence in USAID. A primary aim was to differentiate the new "performance-based" aid from the traditional USAID "need-based" aid. The MCC was designed to give a fresh face to U.S. foreign aid, be more cost-efficient, and have greater capacity to exploit partnerships.[73] Identifying and providing funding to those most likely to be successful—an investment or venture capital approach to aid—required someone with business as well as development savvy at the helm. Its first CEO, Paul Ap-plegarth, was previously a managing director of Emerging Markets Part-nership, an asset management firm specializing in international private equity and debt investments in emerging markets. Applegarth was also the founding managing director of the Emerging Africa Infrastructure Fund, an innovative public-private partnership created by the United Kingdom and three other European governments to promote development in sub-Saharan Africa.

After Bush announced the venture in his 2002 speech in Monterrey, eleven months of extensive consultations within government were neces-sary to create its basic design and legislation. Congress then took eleven more months to pass the Millennium Challenge Act in January 2004, al-most two years after the initiative was first announced. Applegarth was sworn in as CEO in May 2004, and the first compact was signed eleven months later: $110 million worth of aid for Madagascar. By July 2005, grants for Honduras, Cape Verde, and Nicaragua were in the works, bring-ing MCC's total commitments to $610 million.

It wasn't long before the MCC's unorthodox approach met with con-troversy. In June 2005 five African presidents complained in a White House meeting that the MCC had been too slow in providing them assistance. A subsequent editorial in the *New York Times* blamed the corporation's found-ing leadership for failing to spend the funds the corporation had at its dis-posal. However, of the five countries that complained, two did not qualify because their incomes were too high according to the legislation governing the MCC, which focused operations in its first two years on the very poor-est countries. A third did not qualify because it was too corrupt. Ghana, which did qualify, simply protested the rate of disbursement and later in-sisted it had not complained at the meeting. The disgruntlement grew in part from a genuine misunderstanding about how one qualified for MCC aid, not a failure by MCC to deliver.[74]

It is certainly clear that the question of blame is more complicated than the *Times* editorial made it initially appear. The Millennium Challenge Corporation was supposed to be funded with entirely new money, but the promised funding never materialized. President Bush's original proposition was to fund $5 billion annually. In 2005, he asked for just $3 billion, and by mid-2006 the MCC had only disbursed some $400 million.[75] Further, congressional concern that the MCA would take away desperately needed funds for need-based aid slowed the initiative still further. After the president asked for less than he had promised, the House proceeded to cut his reduced $3 billion dollar request to $1.75 billion.[76] The uncertain financing created understandable bottlenecks. From the MCC's perspective, the uncertainty about its funding put it in the awkward position of asking countries to make hard decisions to qualify for uncertain benefits.[77]

From the perspective of developing countries and Congress, however, things looked differently. After approving a smaller amount, the money Congress did appropriate flowed into MCC coffers and was not immediately dispatched to the recipient countries. The delay followed from the MCC's innovative approach to development itself, which for the first time required the countries themselves, rather than American technocrats, to write the proposals. There were obviously significant startup costs in asking developing nations to participate directly in the actual crafting of programs, so the expectations of seeing an immediate impact were misplaced. The MCC approach was premised on using money well rather than simply spending it. But it was difficult for Congress to understand why taxpayer money that was supposed to have been desperately needed was not quickly put to use. The unavoidable time lag was also frustrating for the countries in need. The MCC leadership can perhaps be faulted for not better managing these expectations. At the same time, the enormous gap between Bush's promises and what actually materialized made some countries question whether the effort was even worth it.[78]

All of these factors combined to make MCC's waters increasingly difficult to navigate. As a result, Applegarth's tenure as CEO was relatively brief. In August 2005 he tendered his resignation after only a year on the job.[79] At the time of his resignation, the MCC had given final approval to only two countries, Madagascar and Honduras, and had disbursed very little money. His replacement, Ambassador John Danilovich, took the helm in November 2005, with explicit instructions from Bush "to complete and sign several more compacts in the coming months."[80] As of February 2006, the MCC had identified twenty-three eligible countries and approved aid for eight.[81] In January 2009, the MCC had signed eighteen compacts for $6.7 billion.[82]

The MCC's history underscores the serious political obstacles that can arise in any effort to engage local forces directly in sustainable development. For example, the first signed compact, with Madagascar for $110 million to assist land titling, bank reform, and agribusiness centers, was meant to put the essential elements in place for an increase in agricultural yields and food production. Following MCC's formula, it required local populations to write the grant proposals themselves, which takes time. When extreme poverty exists, however, a preoccupation with abstract things like sustainability over feeding the famished can appear misplaced. Hungry people are unlikely to be looking for the bank, pointed out a *New York Times* editorial after Applegarth's resignation.[83] It is hard to dispute this assertion, but it also skirts the main point. To focus exclusively on aid to address short-term needs, as the *Times* implicitly urged, would take the United States back to an approach to development that had not delivered in the past.

There is a striking degree of bipartisan consensus that the MCC model provides a promising blueprint for the future of foreign aid. Lael Brainard, the former deputy national economic advisor for the Clinton administration, "would take the MCC model and have it cover a lot more countries. Everything we have learned about development tells us that telling developing countries what they should do is crazy."[84] According to Steve Radelet, former deputy assistant secretary of the treasury, "There is a growing recognition that we are working with a spectrum of countries with different needs and abilities. That recognition is reflected in the MCC mission, but it extends beyond the MCC's walls. We need a spectrum of approaches."[85] Even the MCC's most severe critics like the MCA idea and its insistence on transparency and country ownership. As former MCC official Jim Vermillion put it, "The MCC was a horrible implementation of a really good idea."[86]

Yet despite enthusiastic support among foreign aid experts at the level of ideas, the MCC's future is by no means clear, for at least three big reasons. First, the MCC came about partly as a response to Bono, who essentially told the president, "I'm in if you up the ante." The interagency process that ensued had NGO input and limited Capitol Hill involvement. Part of the reason was the MCC's "no earmarks" approach, which at a stroke eliminates pork and makes lobbying a futile effort. As a result, the MCC has no real champion in Congress.[87] Second, the MCC has run out of money, and the financial meltdown makes foreign aid a tough sell. The MCC dispenses monies unlike any previous assistance institution: all funds are obligated up front. As of January 2009, all of the money in the till has been committed, and, if no additional funding comes through, there will be no way of signing the compacts currently pending.[88] Finally, there is the political fallout that may come when companies from problematic countries start bidding in earnest for MCC-financed projects. The MCC presently has no legal requirement that assistance monies be channeled through U.S. firms. This could change in a hurry as soon as a U.S. firm loses a contract.[89] John Hewko, vice president for compact development, predicts that "when the Chinese start bidding, we will have an issue."[90]

As the institutional embodiment of transformational diplomacy, the MCC is equipped, at least in theory, to produce unprecedented results by encouraging local initiative and entrepreneurship. In insisting that the "how" of foreign aid matters more than the "what," and by empowering countries to shape their own futures, the MCC reinvented foreign assistance in dramatic and important ways. That it presently seems poised to be swallowed up by politics as usual is a measure of the serious predicament we are in.

The Limits of Transformational Diplomacy

The U.S. failure to bring democracy to the Middle East looms large in all discussions of the future of information age diplomacy. The transformational vision embodied in the MCC approach strives to encourage "democratic" and "well-governed" states. How do we know a democratic and well-governed state when we see one? One necessary condition is that it allows free enterprise and entrepreneurship to thrive. The core premise of transformational diplomacy, therefore, is the quite radical notion that aid from without can't solve problems on the ground without an engaged and like-minded local leadership within.[91] Respecting the importance of context and individual initiative, the new diplomacy in theory rejects top-down, command and control approaches in favor of democratization. Without empowering indigenous populations to take charge of their own destinies, development efforts—no matter how much money is pumped into the country—will not yield fruit.

Juxtapose the MCC vision of diplomacy's mission in the developing world with the image of the brand new U.S. Embassy in Baghdad, open for business in January 2009. As Iraq descended into civil war, the State Department spent $600 million to erect a walled fortress the size of Vatican City inside the heavily guarded Green Zone. The compound is expected to cost $1.2 billion per year to run. While the people of Iraq struggle to stay alive outside its walls, America's emissaries can feign relaxation in a heavily fortified, blast-proof compound with all the amenities of life back home: movie theaters, a food court with free food, a telephone center (Virginia area code), a cell phone center (New York area code), and tennis courts. Whatever the American fortress's inhabitants may think they are doing, they won't be engaging and empowering the local population. For the State Department, the "new embassy compound," or NEC, is a blueprint for the future of diplomacy.[92]

"The Mega-Bunker in Baghdad" reveals the limits of transformational diplomacy as well as the obsolescence of the nineteenth century statesman. There is a glaring disconnect between the transformational vision that created the MCC and the Bush administration's overseas military ventures. Even setting aside mistakes like disbanding the Iraqi military and shock therapy privatization, the aftermath of devastating defeat in war and years of dictatorship was not exactly an optimal time to encourage Iraqis to be entrepreneurial. As the journalist George Packer writes, "Confused, frightened Iraqis, who had never before been allowed to take any initiative, turned to the Americans, who seemed to have all the power and money; the Americans, who didn't see themselves as occupiers, tried to force the Iraqis to work within their own institutions, but the institutions had been largely dismantled."[93] Whatever the good intentions were, in the information age local ownership and self-empowerment are unlikely to emerge from the barrel of a gun, especially with such grotesque inequality between the occupiers and the local population.

What's more, the heavy reliance on Western rather than Iraqi companies for Iraqi reconstruction did little to lay the groundwork for domestic stability. The problem wasn't excessive coziness between the Bush administration and firms like Bechtel and Halliburton, but the scope of the projects they contracted to undertake and who they chose to undertake them. These projects were so sweeping, and the official American procurement protocols so cumbersome, that money made its way into Iraqi society at a snail's pace. "By August 2004," Packer writes, "ten months after the appropriation, only $400 million of the $18.4 billion—barely two percent—had been spent. By the time Iraqi subcontractors saw any of the money, all but a small fraction had been lopped off in overhead, security (as much as forty percent of contracts), corruption, and profits. The Coalition Provisional Authority . . . kept promising Iraqis that the spigot was about to be turned on and the country was going to be flooded with lifesaving cash that would put tens of thousands of people back to work. It never happened."[94] The result was lots of jobs and profits for everyone but the Iraqi people, who were forced to watch foreigners grow rich from their suffering. As for the transparency and accountability on which private sector cost-effectiveness relies, these were impossible to secure in the midst of a war zone.

So what can we learn from past mistakes? While transformational diplomacy looks great on paper, the implementation of its central ideas—the *how* of transformational diplomacy—is problematic for at least three major reasons. First, the paltry resources allocated to diplomacy, and the necessary reliance on contracting that resulted, caused oversight to be outsourced along with diplomatic security. An October 2007 audit of DynCorp's work for the State Department exposed the seriousness of the issue. The audit, prepared by the Special Inspector General for Iraq, showed that documentation of DynCorp's work was in such disarray that it was impossible to determine what specifically State had received for the $1.2 billion it had paid the company since 2004. The same audit also reported that, prior to 2007, the State Department had only two employees in Iraq supervising the work of nearly seven hundred DynCorp employees.[95]

The State Department's reluctance to take full responsibility for Blackwater's misdeeds in Iraq shows the same abdication of responsibility. Anyone who has outsourced work knows that the key to getting results is to know just what needs to be done and who is in charge. If something goes wrong, the person or entity that oversaw the contract is ultimately responsible. If the contractor has not delivered, it is the job of the overseer to terminate the relationship. Instead of punishing Blackwater for its transgressions, the State Department renewed its contract in May 2008.

Getting transformational diplomacy right will require the State Department to acknowledge the shortcomings of privatized diplomacy as presently practiced. As Philip Zelikow, a former special assistant to Condoleezza Rice and executive director of the 9/11 Commission, told me, "While the Department cannot and should not do all of this work itself, it must become more than just a general contractor, with little in-house expertise or field capability of its own. Managing this work is challenging, and we need expertise in-house to guarantee its professionalism, and to internalize and apply best practices."[96]

Second, transformational diplomacy was hamstrung by the enormous gap between theory and practice that until now has characterized its implementation. The main problem with the well-intentioned Middle East Partnership Initiative was straightforward: it was addressed to a region with a significant American military presence, which meant that anyone who participated in its programs risked being tarnished as a collaborator, thereby undermining the very forces capable of transforming state and society. Our blueprint for "reconstruction" in both Iraq and Afghanistan, meanwhile, was straight out of the traditional imperial playbook and had little relation to the message of self-empowerment and entrepreneurship that transformational diplomacy promoted. The United States is extremely hypocritical to stress the importance of empowering individuals to take charge of their own destiny in other parts of the developing world when it denies and suppresses these values in the countries to which we have devoted the lion's share of our blood and treasure. Transformational diplomacy in support of colonial occupation is a contradiction in terms.

At the level of ideas, there was a powerful connection between the transformational vision and what the Bush administration claimed to be doing in Iraq. But the manner in which those ideas were pursued badly undermined the goal of building democratic capacity. Transformational diplomacy was an agenda for peacetime, not wartime. Initiative and bottom-up problem-solving skills cannot be summoned through imperial coercion and military force. The irony is that the administration failed in Iraq and Afghanistan by the very MCC metric that it itself devised. The MCC would never sign a compact with a country divided by civil strife. Sri Lanka's descent into civil war, for example, put negotiations on hold. Small wonder, then, that the rest of the world looked upon the actions of the United States in the Bush era with considerable suspicion. The pieces of the Bush administration's approach to the external world did not add up to a coherent policy.

The perception of American hypocrisy, in turn, compromised initiatives to restore the nation's standing in the world through public diplomacy. The State Department's public diplomacy efforts can be only as effective as the underlying policy, and if the underlying policy is incoherent or hypocritical, the public relations challenges may become insurmountable. As former ambassador Edmund Hull put it, "You can't solve public diplomacy problems without addressing the policy issues that underlie them. The administration has no credibility in selling a line when the policy itself contradicts it."[97]

Finally, and perhaps most importantly, transformational diplomacy underperformed because of the central role coercion played in the face that the United States presented to the world. To have the Pentagon lead reconstruction efforts put brute force at the heart of American efforts to rebuild countries whose infrastructure our military intervention had helped destroy. With the Pentagon effectively the leading diplomat in many of the world's hotspots, the DOD footprint cannot avoid shaping perceptions of U.S. aspirations in ways that directly contradict cherished American values. The gross imbalance between State Department and DOD power and budgets must be remedied before the empire of the willing is rendered wholly illegitimate by a rival empire of the billing.

5

The Privatization of Defense

I have no desire to attack the Pentagon. I want to liberate it.
We need to save it from itself.
—Secretary of Defense Donald Rumsfeld, September 10, 2001

And by experience one sees that only princes and armed republics make
very great progress; nothing but harm ever comes from mercenary arms.
—Niccolo Machiavelli, *The Prince*

THE USE OF CONTRACTORS on the battlefield is as old as organized warfare. American revolutionaries fought Hessian troops-for-hire in the Revolutionary War. In the Civil War, the Union army hired British and Canadian volunteers as well as a range of immigrants aspiring to citizenship.[1] Eighty thousand contractors supported U.S. operations in Vietnam.[2] Hiring help to bolster American power is an American tradition. It is also wholly consistent with standard corporate practice. When an American business faces a new challenge, it typically brings in an expert team of consultants to help chart its future course. Yet the current scale of privatization in its application to war is unprecedented.

Over the past fifteen years, the deployment of contracted military support has changed in both scope and kind. In Iraq in 2007, more than 180,000 government contractors were on the ground, compared to 160,000 U.S. soldiers. And this figure does not include the large array of subcontractors who also were given a piece of the action.[3] Even the Pentagon itself was until recently unaware of the explosion in nonuniformed personnel deployed on its behalf; its prior estimate of 25,000 was off by a factor of at least seven. The 180,000 figure dwarfs its equivalent for the Persian Gulf War, in which only about 10,000 nonuniformed personnel were deployed to support U.S. operations.[4] Most would think of war-fighting as something reserved to governments, but when contractor personnel now outnumber U.S. forces in Iraq, the character of war itself would appear to have changed significantly.

Subcontracting in war and the deployment of mercenaries are nothing new. The British developed a citizens' army only in the latter half of the nineteenth century. But there are two major structural differences between the nineteenth century British and twenty-first century U.S. empires. First, publicly traded companies now conduct private military operations. Incorporation connotes legitimacy. Second, the market for this force is now genuinely global, which raises new concerns should other countries do as the United States does.

The Pentagon's Privatization Turn

The lessons of World War II and the challenges of the early Cold War were the catalyst for the creation of the Department of Defense. Established by the National Security Act of 1947, DOD consolidated the old War Department and the Navy Department under a single secretary. Part of the intent was to reduce the interservice rivalry that had undermined America's war-fighting effectiveness during the war. Following the U.S. withdrawal from Vietnam, the same concerns about counterproductive turf wars fueled the 1986 Goldwater-Nichols Defense Reorganization Act. In an effort to produce more effective collaboration ("jointness"), Goldwater-Nichols restructured the command of the U.S. military, centralizing military advice in the Joint Chiefs of Staff, whose chair was to serve as the principal military advisor to the president, National Security Council, and the Secretary of Defense.[5]

The preconditions for the privatization of national security were in place before the Cold War ended. Four factors intrinsic to the Department of Defense would conspire with the imperatives of globalization to transform the American approach to war in the 1990s. The first was the 1922 decision by the Navy and War Departments to discontinue building ships and planes themselves, which launched the military's romance with the private sector. Second, the shift from a conscripted to an all-volunteer military force after Vietnam meant that the Pentagon had to provide a range of new services (such as four flavors of ice cream for our troops stationed in Iraq) to fill its ranks; many of these services required expanded contracting. Third, during the Cold War, America's strategic imperative had been to match the quantity of Soviet weaponry with the quality of the American arsenal, an effort that was thought to be enhanced by privatization's efficiency. Finally, because government pay scales meant that the Pentagon could not match the salaries available in the private sector to the best men and women, it resorted to contracting to draw on top talent.[6]

Victory in the Cold War and the subsequent budget cuts forced the

DOD to economize. Privatization emerged as the remedy of choice. The Defense Department issued a report in March 1996 extolling the virtues of outsourcing: "Like the best companies and organizations in the United States, DOD has embarked on a systematic and vigorous effort to reduce the cost and improve the performance of its support activities" through "outsourcing, privatization and competition."[7] A subsequent report, "Outsourcing and Privatization," released by the Defense Science Board Task Force, put the argument in more forceful terms, recommending that "all DOD support functions should be contracted out to private vendors except those functions which are inherently governmental, are directly involved in war fighting, or for which no adequate private sector capability exists or can be expected to be established."[8]

In 1997 the Defense Science Board's calls for sweeping change were incorporated directly into the Pentagon's *Quadrennial Defense Review* and *Defense Reform Initiative Report*. The latter report, in particular, challenged DOD to replicate private sector practices (including outsourcing) that had enabled American business to flourish: "The Department of Defense must adopt and adapt the lessons of the private sector if America's Armed Forces are to maintain their competitive edge in the rapidly changing global security arena."[9] Consistent with Vice President Al Gore's "Reinventing Government" initiative, Secretary of Defense William Cohen vowed to adopt a "corporate vision for the Department of Defense" based on a "revolution in the department's business affairs."[10]

Having gathered force under Clinton, this trend accelerated dramatically during the Bush administration. In a landmark speech to twenty-three thousand Pentagon employees on September 10, 2001, Secretary of Defense Donald Rumsfeld labeled the Pentagon's wasteful bureaucracy a threat to national security and promised to transform the organization. Rumsfeld bravely told the gathered, "Some might ask, 'How in the world could the Secretary of Defense attack the Pentagon in front of its people?' To them I reply, I have no desire to attack the Pentagon. I want to liberate it. We need to save it from itself." Calling for the outsourcing of all noncore functions and for harnessing private sector power on multiple fronts, the secretary memorably asked, "Why is DOD one of the few organizations around that still cuts its own checks?"[11] The next day, the attacks on the World Trade Center instantly changed perceptions of the principal threats to American national security and created a sense of urgency about making the right sort of change. In January 2002, Rumsfeld urged military leaders "to behave somewhat less like bureaucrats and more like venture capitalists."[12]

DOD contracting has been rising since 1998. Total procurement levels held steady in the early and mid-1990s despite reductions in overall defense spending due to the "peace dividend" following the Cold War's end. But outsourcing exploded under George W. Bush, as contractors were dispatched in unprecedented numbers to both Afghanistan and Iraq. After September 11, the Rumsfeld vision quickly sank deep roots, producing a huge across-the-board transformation in Pentagon attitudes toward contracting (Figure 4).[13]

The effects are immediately obvious to any visitor to the Pentagon. Most administrative functions have been contracted out, so on multiple visits related to this book I was greeted in the lobby and escorted to my interviewee's office by a contractor rather than a federal employee. The reduction in the armed forces after the Soviet collapse explains the reliance on contractors to escort visitors and provide administrative support; the Pentagon now has money but not personnel. As Theresa Whelan, deputy assistant secretary of state for African affairs, put it, "We crossed the Rubicon in 2002, when we allowed Northrop Grumman to do training for peacekeeping in Africa. Before then, we had used contractors for training in the classroom and for computer simulation exercises, but never before had they been deployed in the field."[14] Things have only accelerated from there; in 2008 the Pentagon was hiring contractors to train the Iraqi army.[15] Between 2002 and 2005, the number of DOD contract employees swelled from 3.4 million to 5.2 million.[16] The number of contracts exploded accordingly. According to Susan Yarwood, deputy director of enterprise services (Office of the Secretary of Defense), speaking in June 2007, "We don't even know how many contracts we have now."[17]

A range of sources document the unprecedented outsourcing the Pentagon has pursued to get its work done. In its landmark 2002 investigative journalism series "The Business of War," the Center for Public Integrity extensively documented the rapid growth of the private military industry, especially the explosion of contracting brought by the Iraq war. From 1994 to 2001, the DOD entered into 3,061 contracts at a total value of more than $300 billion. Nearly 90 percent of those contracts were held by just two companies: Kellogg Brown & Root (KBR was a subsidiary of Halliburton until 2006, when Halliburton severed ties) and Booz Allen Hamilton. Information obtained from the Pentagon via the Freedom of Information Act indicates that it is impossible to determine how these contracts break down in terms of allocations for training, security, or logistical support; only aggregate data are available.[18]

The more recent numbers are even more dramatic. Adjusted for inflation, DOD service contracting grew by a whopping 72 percent from fiscal year 1996 to 2005.[19] A full 57 percent of the Pentagon's procurement dol-

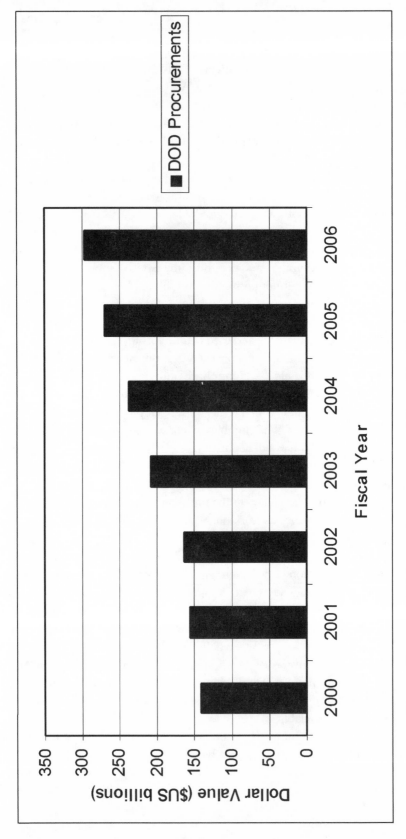

Figure 4. Department of Defense procurements, 2000–2006 (Source: Federal Procurement Data System. Graphic: Carolann Davis)

lars are today spent on services rather than equipment.[20] The Brookings Institution's Peter Singer estimates that a third of the U.S. Army's operating budget is spent on private military contractors, deployed in over fifty different countries; estimates vary, but the ratio of private contractors to U.S. soldiers on the ground has grown by at least a factor of ten since the Persian Gulf War.[21] According to DOD officials, the dollar value of service contracts in the period from 1996 to 2005 exceeded what the department spent on major weapon systems.[22] Rep. Henry Waxman's (D-California) 2007 report on contracting trends under the Bush administration captures the upward trend. From 2000 to 2006, the Defense Department increased its contract spending by 123 percent. In 2005–6 alone, procurement spending increased by $27.6 billion, an increase of 10 percent. As a result of this reorientation, the Defense Department consumed over 72 percent of the total federal procurement budget in 2006.[23]

While the amount, nature, and complexity of DOD contract activity have increased, its acquisition workforce has not adjusted accordingly, remaining relatively unchanged in size.[24] Consequently, the incredible flurry of contracting means that the Pentagon's capacity to monitor the activities it outsources has never been lower. As contracting expert Steve Schooner has aptly remarked, "It's been an unmitigated disaster . . . there are not enough trained professionals in the government to manage the contractors that the government needs every day."[25] Add it all up and it becomes quickly obvious that a rapid increase in Pentagon contracting, coupled with a decrease in resources devoted to oversight, have been a recipe for mismanagement and corruption.

Understanding what private military companies (PMCs) do is critical to understanding the market in which they operate. While there is some overlap between categories, private military firms break down into three basic types: (1) military provider firms, (2) military consulting firms, and (3) military support firms.[26]

Military provider firms offer services on a battlefield's front line; they engage in combat, and in command and control operations in the military theater. Often they operate alongside a client's regular armed forces, enhancing its military capacity. AirScan of Rockledge, Florida, for instance, specializes in sophisticated aerial military surveillance and is among the few U.S. corporations that operate in the foreground of military theaters. Other examples are Blackwater Worldwide (now Xe) and DynCorp, which guard State Department personnel in Afghanistan and Iraq.

Military consulting firms do not engage in frontline combat but instead offer strategic, training, and operational services. These firms are the functional equivalent of business consultancies in that they improve the man-

agement and readiness of a client's armed forces. Because such firms employ experienced former military personnel and officers, they offer advice
from seasoned professionals, which constitutes their comparative advantage. For example, Military Professional Resources Incorporated (MPRI),
based in Alexandria, Virginia, typifies this type of PMC. MPRI not only
employs thousands of ex-military personnel but maintains a database of
340 retired generals and several thousand retired senior officers available
for contracting assignments.

Finally, military support firms provide a variety of logistical services at
the tail of a military operation, including building base camps, feeding the
troops, and other services. Kellogg, Brown & Root has been the Bush administration's military support firm of choice.[27]

The Costs and Benefits of Privatizing Security

The practice of contracting has a host of unintended consequences. On
the battlefield itself, contractors operate in a murky legal zone outside the
regular chain of command. Employees of private military firms answer
neither to the U.S. military nor to the indigenous population they are involved in defending. They answer to the company that employs them. One
can easily imagine scenarios where a contract employee, unlike his uniformed counterpart, has the right to walk away. He or she cannot be ordered to fulfill a dangerous mission, yet attainment of shared objectives
depends on the contractor's support. When American life and liberty are
on the line, financial incentives alone cannot inspire selfless and courageous
action. Contractors thus introduce into any military operation a degree of
uncertainty that is not present when soldiers perform the same task.

The controversial Tim Spicer—former employee of private military
company (PMC) Sandline International and now at the helm of Aegis, the
London-based private company coordinating contractor activity in Iraq—
has argued that PMC employees are every bit as accountable to securing
mission aims as uniformed personnel. In his sensationalist memoir, Spicer
responds to the charge that PMCs are not accountable by asking, "Not accountable to whom? World opinion? Outside politicians? I can only speak
for Sandline, but we are always accountable, to our own policies and ethos
and to our client government, with whom we always have a binding contract."[28] While obviously self-serving, Spicer has a point: in most conflict
situations, those loyalties will carry the day. But then again, today's PMCs
operate in a geostrategic world dominated by the United States. In a multi-
polar environment, things might well be different.

Beyond the battlefield, no one would dispute that contracting generates troubling accountability issues. A Congress poorly informed about PMC activities cannot exert the oversight over the executive branch needed to sustain effective checks and balances. As Steven Aftergood, a secrecy specialist with the American Federation of Scientists, notes, "the kind of routine oversight that official military activities would be subjected to are evaded by contractors as a matter of course."[29] Add subcontracting to the mix, and the opacity only grows.

When commerce expands globally, the potential realms of extraconstitutional operation grow accordingly. The private military sector is distinctive in that it can easily expand quite rapidly without that growth being properly scrutinized. PMC contracts typically prohibit firms from publicly disclosing their provisions, and the State Department is disinclined to discuss PMC contracts for "commercial proprietary" reasons. Meanwhile, the president and the State Department have no legal obligation to inform Congress of contracts smaller than $50 million.[30] The Pentagon can circumvent the State Department's licensing procedures by selling services abroad through its Foreign Military Sales program; here, DOD pays the contractor for services offered to a foreign government, which then turns around and reimburses the Pentagon. The only information available to the public about such contracts is the type of services a PMC has exported and in which country they were performed—and then only through the Freedom of Information Act.[31] Finally, contracts awarded by the Central Intelligence Agency fall outside the normal contract licensing protocols. What all this means is that while Congress is supposed to have oversight over all spending, many contracts—including any contract under $50 million—are off its radar screen.

Sometimes five or six layers deep, the intricate web of subcontracting that emerges from a substantial prime contract renders oversight even more complex. For government contracting expert Steven Schooner, the proliferation of subcontracts is itself a product of the shortage of procurement personnel. If there were enough people doing procurement, contracts would tend to be smaller and more easily managed. But when there aren't enough hands, the easiest way to move things forward is to award an enormous contract to one company, which then subcontracts and bears responsibility for the results of its choices. In effect, oversight is outsourced to the primary contractor. The consequence is that monitoring that should be done by the government is instead done by private companies with a vested interest in making it appear that things are going well, since the next contract always rides on successful fulfillment of the last.[32]

In the absence of any governmentwide agency to monitor contractor performance, the minimal oversight the departments of State and Defense—plus Congress—devote to PMC operations constitutes a basic problem.[33] The Pentagon only recently began counting how many contractors it employs; it also lacked the information systems to provide reliable data necessary for effective PMC management.[34] The State Department's Office of Defense Trade Controls does not record how much the government spends or saves on the PMC contracts it approves. Congress remains largely in the dark on these issues.[35]

The dearth of proper oversight, in turn, raises the probability that one rogue contract or bad employee can tarnish the international reputation of not only his company but the United States. While the majority of PMCs strive to maintain a professional commercial profile, since it is good for business, the employees of some firms have behaved deplorably on the job. Perhaps the most egregious example is the Abu Ghraib torture scandal, where the majority of the interrogators (twenty-seven of thirty-seven total) were contractors. The United States's reputation suffered badly after Abu Ghraib attracted international attention, yet none of the civilians implicated in the abuses were prosecuted or punished.

Abu Ghraib is hardly the only instance in which contractors have engaged in disturbing activities. In May 2001, an American missionary and her daughter were killed when the Peruvian air force shot down their airplane after a PMC had mistakenly identified it as a narcotics courier. That same year a contractor in Colombia sent a package that contained a liquid substance laced with heroin to Patrick Air Force Base; U.S. customs intercepted it.[36] In the former Yugoslavia, DynCorp employees were found operating a sex slavery ring in Bosnia, selling girls as young as twelve on an hourly, daily, or permanent basis. While a few DynCorp employees were fired, the crimes themselves were never prosecuted.[37]

The United States may provide the paycheck and be responsible for contractor presence in a conflict zone, but when things go awry, as they often do in high-stress environments, Washington has no effective means of registering strong disapproval, since contractors are not covered by the same rules that govern their peers in uniform. Contractors in enemy hands, in turn, have no legal protection; three contractors working for California Microwave Systems, a subsidiary of Northrop Grumman, were abducted in 2003 by guerrillas after their aircraft crashed in Colombia. Though on a U.S. Navy contract, the three did not have prisoner-of-war status and did not benefit from the rights accorded by the Geneva Convention.[38] This may be changing with the quiet congressional move in the FY2007 Pentagon budget to make all contractors operating in conflict zones subject to the Uniform Code of Military Justice, better known as the court-martial system, for prosecution in the event of abuses. Previously, contractors could be court-martialed only if Congress had officially declared war, something it hasn't done in over sixty-five years.[39]

Though the costs of privatizing security are considerable, the short-term benefits are substantial. Beyond the enduring reality that contractors are always there when you need them, any serious cost-benefit analysis must take into account four factors. First, the increased role of high-technology weaponry in warfare, which has transformed warfare itself, is a major element of privatization; when systems rely completely on civilian specialists for their maintenance and operation, the back room inevitably becomes the front line. The DOD traces this development to the Vietnam War, when technological complexity of weaponry began to change the typical role of a contractor from support staff to specialist working side by side with uniformed personnel.[40] No contractors, no Shock-and-Awe.

Second, the Pentagon's extensive use of contractors is a means of addressing a serious manpower shortage in the era of an all-volunteer force. The collapse of the Cold War international order and the related phenomenon of failed states both generate increased demand for the services of PMCs. Short of instituting a draft, America's ventures abroad could not be supported by the military alone. As Secretary of Defense Rumsfeld said, contractors were "freeing up additional tens of thousands of military personnel for military responsibilities—[resulting in] an increased usable military end strength without an increase in overall numbers."[41] When the army can hardly recruit enough soldiers to keep its ranks full, hiring contractors to fill the gap seems like a win-win proposition.[42] Employing the private sector in support of military operations gives the administration valuable "surge capacity" to confront threats.

Third, a range of short-term political benefits can accrue to a government that routinely outsources. Consider the extraordinary flexibility of U.S. policy in the former Yugoslavia, where permitting the government of Croatia to hire MPRI to retrain and modernize its armed forces enabled Washington to influence the balance of power on the ground while upholding the 1991 UN embargo on weapons sales to any of the warring groups—all while retaining the official position of honest broker. Providing military assistance via a PMC allowed Washington to strengthen Croatia militarily without publicly taking sides in the conflict. By April 1995, the first Croatian army officer had graduated from MPRI's Democracy Transition Training program. Four months later, Croatia launched a stunningly successful attack on Serb-held Krajina. Employing typical American tactics, the four-day assault completely displaced the Serbian forces as well as some 150,000 Serbian civilians. Croatia's military ultimately brought the Serbs to the negotiating table, and, in November 1995, Washington brokered the Dayton Peace Accords—an outcome made possible in large part by MPRI's services.[43] In this case, U.S.-sponsored military training for Croatia tipped the balance of power in Croatia's favor and set the stage for the peace negotiations. Moreover, Washington achieved this goal without significant public or congressional support and without committing its own ground forces.

Another dimension of this benefit can be seen in Latin America, where the United States turned to at least five private military corporations to execute its counternarcotics policy. Outsourcing permitted the United States to allocate military resources more efficiently, thereby enhancing the military's overall agility. To cite just one example, Washington could have implemented its Andean antinarcotics policy without DynCorp or MPRI simply by deploying U.S. special forces, pilots, and uniformed aircraft mechanics to train Bolivians, Colombians, and Peruvians in counternarcotics tactics and aircraft maintenance. But this would have left vacant key posts in the U.S. Southern Command, military training institutions, and combat divisions—a pattern of resource allocation that would have hindered military preparedness.[44] Governments are not set up to be agile, whereas private enterprises cannot survive without agility. Outsourcing key functions enables Washington to deploy force quickly and effectively where it is needed while maintaining plausible deniability. When the American people's tolerance for casualties is low and administrative will to reshape the security environment is high, outsourcing is a path of least political resistance.

Further examples of off-the-radar-screen foreign policy facilitated by privatization abound. Colombia is the third-largest recipient of U.S. military aid. Since the launch of Plan Colombia, Washington has provided more than ninety helicopters and other military hardware, all maintained and flown by private contractors. The United States has contracted logistical support for indigenous African forces in Somalia, Liberia, Ivory Coast, and Sierra Leone, and for our own presence (typically as trainers of African forces) in Senegal, Nigeria, and Ghana.[45] All of these ventures went forward quickly, with little, if any, public debate or congressional oversight, until the Iraq intervention put the Pentagon's use of contractors under the spotlight.

Does Privatizing Security Save Money?

While comparative costs are hard to pin down, the unique structure of the market for force makes corruption—or at least the appearance of it—an ever-present problem. For instance, a September 2000 GAO report demonstrated that Brown and Root Services collected more than $2.1 billion above contracted expenditures for its work in the Balkans, nearly doubling the amount stipulated in the original contract.[46] Halliburton and its subsidiary KBR came under fire for a variety of billing irregularities related to their work in Iraq, including $108 million in overcharges for gasoline shipped from neighboring Kuwait and $27 million in overcharges for meals served to American troops at five bases in Iraq and Kuwait in 2003.[47] In 2004 the Pentagon's own auditors determined that Halliburton had failed to account adequately for over $1.8 billion of contracted work in Iraq and Kuwait.[48] In testimony before Congress, the U.S. Army Corps of Engineers' top procurement official told lawmakers "unequivocally" that "the abuse related to contracts awarded to KBR represents the most blatant and improper contract abuse I have witnessed during the course of my professional career."[49]

Pentagon officials, including former Secretary of Defense Rumsfeld, insisted that privatization brings significant cost savings. In a lecture at the School of Advanced International Studies in December 2005, Rumsfeld maintained, "It is clearly cost-effective to have contractors for a variety of things that military people need not do and that for whatever reason other civilian government people cannot be deployed to do. . . . Any idea that we shouldn't have them I think would be unwise."[50] To be fair, part of the disagreement may simply be a product of conflating support and security firms. It may well be true that deploying KBR to handle logistics saves the American taxpayer money, while using contractors for action closer to combat operations does not.[51] Acknowledging the different roles that contractors play in theater is a precondition for any evaluation of which tasks should be outsourced and which should not.

Does the claim that privatization always renders operations more efficient hold up under scrutiny?[52] The ad hoc character of Pentagon outsourcing means that hard data are scarce, making estimation of costs tricky. But a simple thought experiment can raise significant doubts about the likelihood that current practices are saving money. Let's consider what it would take to assert the financial efficiency of outsourcing security functions previously performed by uniformed personnel.

We can begin by asking: What would we have to demonstrate to show that we are saving money with privatization? It's wise to start by restricting the analytical lens to combat support contracts; things quickly get murky when logistical support operations (such as KBR contracts) are in the mix. Although the bidding for contracts is often less than competitive, for the sake of the analysis below we assume that competitive bidding exists. Thus we have built in a bias toward finding that the practice does indeed save the government money. If cost savings are questionable with the assumption of competitive bidding, they are clearly all the more dubious when contracts are awarded through cronyism.

We begin by probing the assertion that the U.S. government is saving money on pensions by hiring private contractors. Some have argued that since the PMCs do not pay pensions but hire on a per-job basis, they generate significant costs savings. But on closer inspection, we find that American PMC employees have all served in the military prior to joining the private sector. The U.S. government prefers to employ U.S.-based firms, and most U.S.-based firms prefer to hire American citizens. Since the government will eventually pay a pension to the employees who are American citizens regardless of their employment status upon retirement, the savings on pension payments are not great. To reap any savings, Washington would have to encourage the private military sector to hire foreign nationals—but the conflicts of interests that emerge when non-U.S. citizens are asked to support the American army in a combat zone render this less than prudent. The idea that we save money on pensions by relying on contracted security forces is thus difficult to sustain.

Another way for the federal government to save money through privatization is by exploiting the lower labor costs of outsourcing. But is Washington actually paying less money in labor costs for military services? While it is true that contractors do not receive a set annual salary but are hired on an as-needed basis, they also make double or triple what their uniformed counterparts make doing the same job. It is difficult to argue, even with contract personnel hired and let go as needed, that the U.S. government saves money by hiring labor at a significantly higher daily rate.

At the same time, additional cost savings accrue to the private military company when it subcontracts out. For example, KBR paid carpenters, electricians, and plumbers (largely third-party nationals) working in the Balkans just $15.80 per hour on average; the government rate was $24.38. The wage gap for basic laborers was starker still. KBR paid $1.12 per hour where the government rate for the same labor was $15.99.[53]

A host of externalities can arise from resentment over the pay differentials between public and private sector employment. Many PMC employees are former members of elite U.S. special forces: former Rangers, Green Berets, Delta Forces, and Seals.[54] That can only make those soldiers who continue to serve feel less than special; it is demoralizing to work a job that employees routinely leave. To address this issue, John O. Brennan, a long-time CIA official and founder of the National Counterterrorism Center, introduced a company rule that a person cannot resign and return to do the same job as a contractor until a certain amount of time had elapsed.[55]

A third potential saving comes from the hiring of already trained employees. If the government does not have to pay to train private sector employees, it saves money. But again, when we look at the employment patterns for U.S.-based firms, this bargain too fails to materialize. If most PMC personnel come from the U.S. military, then the government bore the cost of their training. A security clearance is a marketable asset, yet the American taxpayer has paid the screening bill.

Adding it all up, a rough assessment of the market for force's underlying structure reveals that the federal government is effectively paying for the training and retirement of the contractors it hires, all appearances to the contrary, as well as paying double or triple the daily rate for their services. In addition, the government must cover the firm's profits. It is difficult to see where cost savings exist.

And remember, this analysis assumed that all contracts are competitively sourced. In fact, they are not. DOD has reported that only 41 percent of its outsourcing obligations in FY2005 were made on contracts awarded through full and open competition.[56] If the cost savings from privatization were already questionable, they become even more dubious when we acknowledge that the majority of contracts have not been tested by market forces.

The final red flag of inefficiency for economists is the government's discrimination in the labor market based on where a firm's headquarters are located. Americans are interested in contracting mostly with American firms and, in some instances, with British ones. One might even say that the United States doesn't want the competition on which cost-effectiveness relies, since that would inevitably mean more non-U.S. firms in the mix, and this would create problems for basic security. Discrimination in any labor market based on factors other than price and quality usually creates unnecessary costs. Even if we allow the argument that quality standards demand that the government contract with American firms only, the absence of genuine competition should still give us pause.

In short, while one can never prove that outsourcing security is more expensive than relying on government alone, plenty of evidence suggests that the practice does not save money. An August 2008 report from the Congressional Budget Office concluded that the cost to taxpayers was actually greater for the State Department to hire Blackwater for security in Iraq rather than relying on U.S. Army units.[57]

What the practice *does* save is time, and time is always of the essence in addressing threats to national security. Skill-based teams for particular problems can be rapidly assembled and deployed. Turning to the private sector is an easy way to create surge capacity in an era when it is hard to maintain the force at desired levels, and when government wishes to avoid incurring the huge political, social, and economic costs of a draft. Outsourcing also enables government to end-run its own bureaucracy, delivering what an urgent situation may demand without official bureaucratic approval. In particular, there are considerable benefits to using contractors for military training overseas. Getting approval for deployment of U.S. forces is a time-consuming process, but when the Pentagon hires contractors to do the job, the trainers can get right to work.[58]

Members of the military are quick to point out, however, that there are hidden costs to using contractors to train foreign forces. Contractors may be able to teach technical skills, but they cannot teach how to be a soldier. For that, said retired Marine Col. Thomas Hammes, you need the example of a man in uniform whose life has been committed to military virtues.[59] One might respond that the trainers are all former uniformed personnel— but then why has the trainer left military life for a job in the private sector, if military service is the superior occupation? As Theresa Whelan, deputy assistant secretary of defense for African affairs, memorably put it, "Sometimes certain things are easier to accept when coming from someone wearing the same boots. In the end, it is hard for a contractor in a polo shirt to be somebody's hero."[60] Whelan believes there is also a prestige factor, especially in Africa, associated with being trained by U.S. Special Forces rather than by a corporation; an important morale booster for soldiers-in-the-making is irretrievably lost when contractors are doing the training.

Privatizing military activities, in short, certainly saves time and can be politically savvy, but it does not clearly save the American taxpayer money. Perhaps more importantly, the short-term gains may come with long-term unintended costs. In hiring armed contractors, defending the national interest is transformed into a set of tasks rather than the exercise of one's patriotic duty. The desire to serve one's country is not the same as the desire to make money. The twin concerns are that extensive privatization will ultimately undermine trust in government itself if government's proper role is not properly delineated, and that market failure at an inopportune moment could fatally compromise American security. To put these fears more bluntly: What is government *for* if we assume the private sector will always outperform it? And what if America committed its treasure to fighting a future Hitler, but large segments of its (privatized) force chose to refuse the mission? American faith in private initiative and free enterprise has been extended virtually without limits to war itself, but we have yet to properly reflect on whether that faith is well placed.

The First Contractors' War

Nobody knows for certain how many American military contractors have operated in Iraq, but the number is certainly large. As Rajiv Chandrasekaran writes in his outstanding chronicle of reconstruction in Iraq, *Imperial Life in the Emerald City*, "Whatever could be outsourced was."[61] At the request of Congress, the Coalition Provisional Authority (CPA) compiled a tally listing sixty firms with 20,000 personnel. But that list clearly did not capture all firms with contracts in Iraq, as it did not include the companies CACI and Titan, which without doubt had contracts in Iraq because their employees were implicated in the Abu Ghraib scandal.[62] The CPA's report, it turns out, was off by a factor of at least six. Following the January 2007 surge, the Pentagon revised the original CPA estimate and announced instead that around 126,000 contractors were serving in Iraq alongside 150,000 American troops. After filing a Freedom of Information request with the Labor Department, which processes contractor death and injury claims, the *New York Times* reported in May 2007 that at least 146 contractors had been killed in the first quarter of 2007, the highest quarterly total to date. There were 244 military deaths in the same period.[63]

Claiming that the information is proprietary, both the firms and the government have been reluctant to reveal more than required by law, making it impossible to provide a complete listing of all contracts in Iraq, although the drumbeat for transparency grows louder as I write. In addition, the numbers that become public are typically appropriation figures, not the actual amount of money expended, so it is difficult to get a handle on expenditures. Those caveats aside, some representative contracts can suggest the range of missions Washington has assigned to private companies.

Blackwater, a U.S.-based firm, received a $21 million contract to protect the head of the CPA, Paul Bremer. The sum of $50 million went to DynCorp in 2003 to train the Iraqi police force. The Vinnell Corporation received $9 million in 2003 to train nine Iraqi battalions; the company's previous assignment had been training the Saudi National Guard. CACI Systems was awarded a $19.9 million contract in 2003 to provide interrogation services. Erinys International, a U.K. firm with South African management, got a $39.2 million contract to guard the Iraqi oil pipeline.[64]

Clearly, outsourcing the training of the post-Saddam Iraqi army shows that the Pentagon either has an unusual degree of faith in private contractor abilities or is shorthanded. Entrusting this task to the Vinnell Corporation meant that Iraqi soldiers at the end of training were assigned to U.S. Army units headed by American officers they had never met. The morale and sense of loyalty that is usually fostered through training was never built.

Chandrasekaran's book quotes Maj. Raed Khadim, the senior Iraqi officer at the Rafidain station, as saying, "The Americans misunderstood us. We will fight for Iraq. We will not fight for them."[65] Can we really blame the new Iraqi army for being less than fully loyal to U.S. forces, which were too busy to train them? As Rex Wempen, a Baghdad-based security consultant and former Special Forces operative, explained to a *Pittsburgh Post-Gazette* reporter, "It shows how embedded the PMCs are in the thinking of the Department of Defense that they would use them to train that army."[66]

The hanging of four Blackwater contractors on a bridge in Fallujah in April 2004 demonstrated the extent to which our enemies see no real difference between the U.S. military and its contract employees. After Fallujah, a consensus at long last emerged that private security contractors had to be better coordinated to ensure that they were deployed in ways consistent with U.S. interests. The solution that was devised was Kafkaesque. Just prior to the handover of sovereignty to the Iraqi people, Washington decided that the best way to remedy the confusion generated by the presence of contractors working side by side with military personnel was to hire a contractor to work the seams. Yes, even coordination of contractors was outsourced. U.K.-based Aegis Defense Services was awarded a $293 million, three-year contract in 2004 (renewed for two years in 2007) to serve as a coordination hub for over fifty other private security firms operating in Iraq, as well as to protect the U.S. Project Management Office itself. In essence, the Pentagon arbitrarily elevated one firm above its competitors to supervise business; this created a moral hazard, as its new position would make Aegis the first to know when a firm was leaving Iraq, clearly an unfair business advantage. Perhaps worst of all, Aegis was a brand new firm with no track record and was headed by a highly controversial mercenary, Tim Spicer. Aegis received its enormous cost-plus contract without having even been on the State Department's list of recommended companies in Iraq.[67]

As the torture scandal at Abu Ghraib revealed, the Pentagon also outsourced interrogation, one of the most sensitive jobs imaginable. The demand for interrogators with the right foreign language skills was so high that applicants received minimal vetting; if you spoke the language, you were likely to be given a job.[68] The security interrogators were originally hired through a computer services contract overseen by a Department of the Interior office in Arizona.[69] The Pentagon's haste to deploy people with the right skills is understandable, but the dangers of outsourcing interrogation were much larger than they initially appeared. And if the U.S. armed forces have global reach, shouldn't we find a way to have the requisite language skills in-house?

A closer look at the web of contractors and subcontractors in Iraq reveals interesting and disturbing patterns. U.S. firms won the vast majority of contracts in Iraq, with U.K. firms a distant second. Things begin to get really interesting when one tries to figure out just whom these U.S. and U.K. firms have employed in turn. The first surprise is that neither U.S. nor U.K. firms were inclined to hire Iraqis. Most of the Iraqis who won jobs with non-Iraqi contractors were hired by Erinys to guard the Iraqi oil pipeline. Many of these guards came directly from the Iraqi Free Forces, a militia once loyal to Ahmed Chalabi, the controversial leader of the Iraqi National Congress. Iraqis were paid a fraction of the compensation that their South African supervisors earned, a maximum of $4 a day, enough to buy a kilogram of meat.[70] Since Iraqis constitute a vast pool of cheap labor and are the very people the war was intended to help, it is worth asking why they have not figured prominently in U.S.-supervised Iraqi reconstruction.

Reports of the number of Iraqis that Erinys has employed vary greatly. Several sources say that they had planned to hire fourteen thousand Iraqis, but, in an interview with *Frontline* in 2005, Erinys's head of Iraq operations, Andy Melville, placed the number at closer to three hundred: "On the particular contract that I'm running for the company, I've got probably about 120 South Africans; I've got around 85 British; I've got around 38 Americans. And then the last portion, they're all different groupings of nationalities from all over the world. I've got some Polish, a couple of French, Canadian, and so on. We also employ a large group of Iraqis. On the particular contract that I run, there aren't any, but Erinys does have more than 300 Iraqi people employed on a variety of contracts. And we're very pleased and proud that we're able to interact with the Iraqi people to contribute to the economy in that way, and also provide them with high-value training." Either Erinys started with fourteen thousand Iraqis and let go all but three hundred, or Iraqis were never that well represented on the Erinys payroll. In the same interview, Melville also remarked that the American firms don't like to hire Iraqis.[71]

Apart from the pipeline security project, whose actual numbers are hard to pin down, Iraqis do not seem to have significant representation in the contractor ranks. The civilians hired by KBR to work as cooks, carpenters, mechanics, and the like are primarily third-country nationals from developing countries, mostly Filipinos. The security contractors include a large number of American and British citizens, especially in training positions, as well as South Africans, Russians, and other Europeans, and twelve thousand workers from developing countries such as Fiji, Columbia, Sri Lanka, and India. Even the vast majority of reconstruction jobs have gone to non-Iraqi nationals.[72] Only 15,000 Iraqis were hired to work on reconstruction projects funded with Congress's first emergency Supplemental (extrabudgetary outlay), rather than the 250,000 that had been promised.[73]

There were certainly more Iraqis on the U.S. indirect payroll, working for subcontractors, but the precise numbers are elusive. No single agency keeps track of the number or location of contractors, and subcontracting data is even more difficult to obtain. In response to a demand from Congress, the U.S. Central Command began conducting a census in 2006 of the numbers of contractors working on U.S. and Iraqi bases. Released to the *LA Times* in response to a Freedom of Information Act request, that census counted 130,000 contractors and subcontractors of different nationalities, a nice, round number not typically produced by a real census. U.S. military officials acknowledged that the number did not include those working on USAID or State Department contracts.

How many of the 130,000 DOD contractors were Iraqis? Here the Pentagon released conflicting information. In May 2007, the Pentagon told Congress that 22,000 Iraqis were among the contractor ranks. The next month, it reported that the number was actually 65,000, or half of the purported total.[74] The huge discrepancy demonstrates either a desire to show "Iraqization" accompanying the surge or (more likely) that the Pentagon didn't really know who was on its payroll and was providing very crude guesstimates.

Even if the United States really did indirectly employ sixty-five thousand Iraqis, this number still made up only half the contractor workforce in their own country. What explains such discrimination against hiring Iraqis? Deteriorating security conditions are the main reason Iraqi nationals were increasingly unattractive employment material. Observers report that in the initial days after the toppling of the Saddam Hussein dictatorship, many NGOs and Western companies entering town on the heels of the U.S. military hired Iraqis. By August 2003, however, the majority of Iraqis had been purged from these organizations, many of which had to move their base of operations into the safety of the U.S.-protected Green Zone.[75] Thus, even when NGOs and contractors wanted to hire the local population, the requirements of a security clearance for Green Zone entry created a major impediment. The vetting requirements for Iraqi staff were so high that few could be hired.[76] As a result, companies like KBR, which needed people who could get security clearances "yesterday," hired third-party nationals and Americans.[77] As Col. Larry Wilkerson, former chief of staff for Secretary of State Colin Powell, told me in 2007, "We essentially have a foreign legion on the ground in Iraq."[78]

The central point in these numbers is that the Pentagon and State Department have largely outsourced a big chunk of the mission in Iraq to non-U.S. citizens—to virtually everyone but the very people for whom we are allegedly fighting. A full 25 percent of reconstruction costs in Iraq to date can be assigned to private security alone, a realm strictly off-limits to Iraqi nationals.[79] As a result, and most ironically, the billions of contracting dollars that the government has exported to Iraq have not translated into significant money in Iraqi pockets.

In many respects, outsourcing in Iraq seemed like the way to get a difficult job done quickly and well, but any good cost-benefit analysis must consider long-term costs and weigh them against short-term gains. The underrepresentation of Iraqis in the contractor ranks is perhaps the biggest of these costs. Securing Iraq's stability and prosperity demands employment for Iraq's young men and women. Yet security concerns meant that most of the huge infusion of capital failed to find its way to the indigenous population. Soaring unemployment was instead the story of reconstruction, and Iraqis had to watch foreigners make good money while they sat on the sidelines. It is hard for Iraqis to believe the United States is acting in their country's best interests when foreigners profit so directly from Iraqi misery. Iraqis did not need foreigners deployed on their soil; they needed jobs. As Colin Powell acknowledged to Roger Cohen of the *New York Times*, it was a mistake not to "move more rapidly to put an Iraqi face on it."[80]

Responding to a need that had always existed, in 2005 Iraq's Ministry of Interior installed a new regime for licensing foreign security companies that encouraged the employment of Iraqis. As Aegis CEO Tim Spicer explained, the country was going through the "process of Iraqization, wanting Iraqis to have part of the action."[81] The Iraq Study Group's December 2006 report argued that we need to break the "culture of dependency": by threatening complete withdrawal unless there is progress on Iraqization. As *New York Times* reporter David Sanger wrote, reduced to a bumper sticker, the report said it was time to "train and walk backward."[82] The Iraq Study Group's recommendations were on target, but we surely should not blame Iraqis for creating that culture of dependency. Further, what does Iraqization mean when security there has been privatized to such an extent? Does it mean that private companies should hire more Iraqis? How can this be done in a way that does not amount to taking sides in a civil war?

From the start, not enough Iraqis were engaged in rebuilding or defending their own country. "The Bush administration," writes Naomi Klein in *The Shock Doctrine*, "could easily have stipulated that any company receiving U.S. tax dollars had to staff its project with Iraqis. It could also have contracted for more jobs directly with Iraqi firms. Such simple, common-sense measures did not happen for years because they conflicted with the underlying strategy of turning Iraq into an emerging market economic bubble—and everyone knows that bubbles are not inflated with rules and regulations but by their absence. So, in the name of speed and efficiency, contractors could hire whomever they wished, import from wherever they liked and subcontract to whatever company they wanted."[83] If it's all about getting the job done fast, not getting the job done so it stays done, sustainable development is unlikely to result. As economist Joseph Stiglitz has written, "It might appear to be cost-saving to hire Nepalese or other non-Iraqi workers but in terms of winning the hearts and minds of the Iraqis, or simply to improve the well-being of the Iraqi people, it makes far more sense to hire Iraqis. This is just one example of the myriad ways contractors' cost minimisation may not be in the interests of America, or the world."[84]

Democratization required Iraqization, yet contractors steered clear of hiring Iraqi nationals for the most important jobs. Sustainable development demands local involvement from the start, if counterproductive antagonisms are not to arise. With hindsight, this looks like simple common sense. Why should Iraqis entrust their future to Americans if Americans do not trust Iraqis to help rebuild their own country? The Bush administration's free-market enthusiasts overlooked the main sources of liberal capitalism's dynamism; freedom and prosperity cannot be built, let alone made self-sustaining, without the engagement of the local population. This was the very mantra of the Bush administration's transformational diplomacy, yet its maxims were never taken to heart on Iraqi soil.

Learning from Iraq

The extensive use of contractors in Iraq highlights the enormous challenge the practice presents to basic government accountability. The GAO has repeatedly warned that the DOD is courting disaster by failing to address long-standing problems in the oversight and management of contractors.[85] The Iraq operation only places those shortcomings in stark relief. To date, the Pentagon has not fully confronted the strategic dimensions of its privatization turn. Iraq may force it to do so.

Since the contracts involved are so large, they typically get executed through five or six layers of subcontracting, which only further clouds transparency. Government contracts worth more than $50 million must by law be reported to Congress. But of the sixty known firms with contracts in Iraq, only eight work directly for the Defense Department; the rest are subcontractors. That makes the majority of firms working in Iraq today accountable only to the contractor that employs them. Companies that contract with the Pentagon are obligated to abide by the Defense Acquisition Regulation Supplement, or DFARS. DFARS includes a section on "Contractor Standards of Conduct" describing appropriate behavior and providing a hotline for reporting improper conduct. It was amended on June 6, 2005, to hold contractors working in support of U.S. forces overseas accountable under U.S. and international laws as well as those of the host country. The law also explicitly allows contractors to carry weapons.[86]

The ingredients for large-scale corruption are thus firmly in place. The U.S. government transferred billions of dollars of taxpayers' money to Iraq, yet the Pentagon does not seem to have attempted to track the number or identities of companies or contractors on the ground. The demand for private security greatly exceeded supply, with the result that quality control in hiring was the first thing to go; anyone who wanted to offer his or her services was likely to receive a job. Large volumes of money changed hands under less than transparent conditions. Add a violent insurgency and the confusion of civil war, and restraint fades still further.

None of this is to assert that the story of Iraq is principally one of selfish profiteering. Many private actors there are committed and patriotic. But with the privatization of security, we have entered an era where transparency in the interactions between business and government has become imperative.

A good place to begin is the threshold between the worlds of government and business. While the revolving door between the public and private sectors has always existed, it has never spun quite so rapidly as today, and the sums of money involved have never been so enormous. To cite two prominent examples, Sir Malcolm Rifkind, former Tory foreign and defense secretary, is the CEO of ArmorGroup, a British company with millions of pounds sterling in Iraq contracts. On the other side of the Atlantic, Diligence LLC is a prominent example of former American government figures and their British friends seeking to cash in on political consulting. Diligence first set up shop in Iraq in July 2003 to provide security for reconstruction efforts there. It was founded by former CIA and FBI director William Webster; Mike Baker, the CEO, spent fourteen years in covert operations with the CIA. The co-chair of its new subsidiary, Diligence Middle East, is Joe Allbaugh, President Bush's former campaign manager. Washington insider Richard Burt, the former U.S. ambassador to Germany and President George H. W. Bush's boss at the Carlyle Group, is the chairman of the board. The vice chairman is Ed Rogers, one of the senior Bush's top advisers during his presidency. Former British prime minister John Major is now chair of Carlyle Europe; Ed Mathias, Carlyle's managing director, and Lord Charles Powell, a former aide to Margaret Thatcher, all serve on

Diligence's advisory board.[87] To map this web of relationships is not to allege wrongdoing; one could say that putting this large volume of experience to work serves the public interest. It is instead to argue that government needs to forge some norms of conduct for those moving back and forth across the business-government "divide."

That the legal status of contractors working abroad is still completely murky is another cause for concern. Armed contractors, such as the four Blackwater employees whom insurgents hanged from a bridge in Fallujah, operate in a legal gray zone. Unlike their unarmed counterparts, they aren't noncombatants under the Fourth Geneva Convention, because they carry weapons and act on behalf of the U.S. government. But according to the Third Geneva Convention, they aren't lawful combatants either; they don't wear uniforms or answer to the U.S. military. Armed contractors aren't even mercenaries under international law: mercenaries fight for a foreign government when their own country is not a party to the conflict. According to Phillip Carter, a former U.S. Army officer now teaching at UCLA Law School, "They actually have the same legally ambiguous status as the unlawful combatants detained at Guantanamo Bay."[88]

To resolve these ambiguities, in June 2003 the Coalition Provisional Authority promulgated Memorandum 17, which granted foreign contractors immunity from Iraqi law while working on contracted tasks. The workers' home country would have legal authority in the case of perceived abuses. In June 2004, just before the transfer of sovereignty from the CPA to the interim government, Paul Bremer signed a revised version of Memorandum 17 that stipulated that the rules would remain in effect until multinational forces leave Iraq or the ruling is amended by Iraqi lawmakers.[89] Memorandum 17 thus conflicts with the amended DFARS, which holds that contractors were subject to both international and U.S. law. To complicate things further, American private contractors are also subject to the October 2000 Military Extraterritorial Jurisdiction Act, signed by President Clinton, which empowers the Justice Department to prosecute crimes committed by civilians employed by or accompanying the military while overseas. As of January 2007, all contractors are also theoretically subject to the Uniform Code of Military Justice. It is unclear whether this additional legislation will help clarify the legal status of armed contractors or simply generate competing claims.

The first armed contractors' war thus raises a host of pressing questions regarding international security. As the world's preeminent military power, the United States shapes the norms that will govern this area. Are the rules of conduct the United States is shaping in Iraq the ones we want other states to adopt? Do we want to adopt them ourselves?[90]

Answering this question requires an understanding of the current market for force. Political scientist Deborah Avant has provided the best inventory to date of existing private military providers on a global scale.[91] Of the United Nations' 191 member states, just 12 are currently home to private companies that provide military advice, training, and logistical and advising support. Only 21 states are home to companies that offer site and personnel security as well as crime prevention and intelligence services. Some big states are noticeably absent. China and India, for example, do not appear on either list, while Russia is barely represented. The United States dominates both lists, followed by the United Kingdom.

America is not only the world's largest provider of private military services but also its largest consumer. At the global level, the current market for force reflects the overwhelming power of the United States in the post–Cold War international system. Should the United States lose its monopoly status, however, the advantages it derives from outsourcing could decrease accordingly, especially if other states adopt American practices, automatically increasing the number of interested parties to any conflict and complicating negotiations for peace.

The assumption is that insurmountable barriers will prevent new buyers and sellers from entering the market for force; but this is probably more rooted in wishful thinking than in the reality of globalization. Although many states lack robust financial resources, this has not deterred governments of developing countries such as Angola, Congo, Liberia, Oman, Papua New Guinea, Senegal, Sierra Leone, and Sudan from employing PMCs. And while the U.S. State Department may refuse to license contracts between American PMCs and U.S. adversaries, such states can always employ non-U.S. firms. The United States and Great Britain have led the world in commercializing realms previously untouched by market forces, with other countries following suit, and it is hard to see why the copycat dynamic would not apply to the privatization of security. It would be difficult indeed for the United States to mount a credible protest against other states for choosing the same tactics Washington itself has pursued.

The core issue is not whether the United States should discontinue the practice or bar private military firms from operating, but whether Washington can see beyond the short-term benefits of outsourcing to embrace sustainable policies. Outsourcing the implementation of policy to PMCs can be a useful solution to a range of immediate problems, but the true costs come due only in the long term. An underregulated market for force will likely have significant negative consequences in the future, and these effects will become even more dramatic if other states follow the American lead.

To address this concern, the United States should work with other na-tions to construct self-enforcing norms that serve the interests of peace and stability with adequate but circumscribed space for the private military in-dustry to function. The industry has matured to the point that established firms have a vested interest in market regulation.[92] At home, Washington should establish a robust and clearly specified oversight framework to mon-itor U.S.-based and U.S.-employed PMCs, create strict public reporting re-quirements, and substantially lower the monetary threshold that triggers congressional notification of a PMC contract. It should also ban the use of armed security contractors in conflict zones where the United States is an occupying force. The calamity that is contemporary Iraq must serve as a catalyst for the delineation of clear boundaries between the legitimate and illegitimate use of force. Our current practices blur that line, to the advan-tage of our enemies.

6

The Slow Death of USAID

A large part of what we believe to be true (and this applies even to our
final conclusions) with an obstinacy equaled only by our good faith,
springs from an original mistake in our premises.
—Marcel Proust, *In Search of Lost Time*, vol. V

We have had the morality of submission, and the morality of chivalry
and generosity; the time is now come for the morality of justice.
—John Stuart Mill, *The Subjection of Women*

THE MARSHALL PLAN of 1948–51 is one of the few undeniable success stories of American foreign policy. The great infusion of aid
into the war-devastated economies of western Europe came at a
critical moment. Today it seems obvious that liberal democracy could well
have faltered in postwar Europe were it not for the foresight of men like
George C. Marshall. By rebuilding Europe's economies, the Marshall Plan
restored a market for American goods and services and diminished communism's appeal. In so doing, the United States helped its friend Europe to
get back on its feet and alleviated the suffering of Europeans. The Marshall
Plan was a unique moment in the history of foreign aid when U.S. interests
and humanitarian concerns happily coalesced.

The more common scenario in the Cold War years that followed was
just the opposite. The interests of the United States and the humanitarian
needs of the people receiving its aid were often in stark conflict, rendering
foreign assistance a politically contentious issue. Reasonable people, after
all, could have different ideas of how one best gives the less fortunate a
hand. Anti-communists tended to see anything that thwarted the success of
foreign communist parties as inexorably advancing the common good. For
their opponents, propping up third-world dictators who served U.S. interests in the struggle with the Soviet Union was a road to neither justice nor
fairness.

Founded in 1961 as the linchpin of U.S. humanitarian foreign assistance, the United States Agency for International Development (USAID) quickly became a lightning rod for these political differences. USAID had been created to separate development from military/security aid, so its employees saw themselves involved in a long-term endeavor that had to be pursued despite short-term political pressures. This put USAID in perpetual conflict with strategic expediency. Since results were never immediate, no one was ever wholly satisfied with USAID performance, and reform movements were a permanent feature of the landscape.

Against this backdrop, the end of the Cold War was nothing short of an earthquake. At a stroke, the Soviet Union's collapse deprived foreign aid of its principal rationale as a bulwark against an encroaching enemy, and so transformed the playing field for U.S. aid efforts. At the same time, globalization dramatically expanded the potential realm of private sector action. Foreign direct investment flooded the post-Communist world, calling both the means and ends of traditional foreign aid into question. When Jesse Helms (R-North Carolina), then the chairman of the Senate Foreign Relations Committee, memorably equated aid with "throwing money down foreign rat holes" and called for the elimination of USAID in January 2001, the battle lines were clearly drawn.

Effectively absorbed by the State Department in 2006, and with its employee ranks decimated, USAID at the end of the Bush era was little more than a contract clearinghouse. In late 2008, three former USAID commissioners from both Democratic and Republican administrations urged the incoming Obama administration either to restore USAID's autonomous status or to consolidate all existing aid programs in a new Ministry of International Development, an institutional arrangement that has helped the United Kingdom punch above its weight in the development arena.[1] The enormous demands on government resources for development at home have only raised the stakes.

The Politics of Cold War USAID

When the creation of the United States Agency for International Development was under debate in 1961, most Americans felt that the verdict was still out on the Marshall Plan. The Kennedy administration had to persuade American taxpayers that sending their money abroad rather than using it to solve problems at home was a wise policy choice.[2] The Foreign Assistance Act of 1961, which launched USAID, was thus not an easy sell to the American people, even though it institutionalized and broadened the mandate of the Marshall Plan. What made all the difference was Soviet premier Nikita Khrushchev's unsettling "We Will Bury You" rhetoric. With both the Soviet Union and the People's Republic of China maneuvering for influence in the developing world, foreign aid was seen to advance national security objectives that resonated with Democrats and Republicans alike.

The creation of USAID was effectively a merger of existing programs with a mandate for future action. The new agency consolidated what had previously been a scattered collection of aid-dispensing bodies, and in so doing it seemed simultaneously to rationalize and advance development policies already in motion. At the time of its founding, the division of labor with other departments was relatively clear: USAID would oversee bilateral development aid, the Treasury Department multilateral aid, and the Department of Defense and the State Department military and other security-related programs.[3]

The birth of the new always ruffles the feathers of the old, and even the Marshall Plan had proved no exception. It is worth recalling that Marshall Plan aid had not been administered through U.S. embassies. Instead, in each country that received assistance, foreign economic aid missions were established to oversee the nuts and bolts of the plan, which inevitably raised the question of ultimate authority. A 1955 task force headed by the industrialist Henning W. Prentis Jr. makes it clear that these economic aid institutions, and the power bases that developed around them, had become a concern for the State Department, which at all costs wanted to avoid multiple voices claiming to represent the official position of the United States. As the report states, "In every country in the world, there should be only one voice speaking for the United States, and that voice should be the chief of the diplomatic mission to each country speaking on behalf of the State Department."[4]

The Prentis report concurred that the diplomatic missions were being weakened by the financial power of the foreign economic aid missions. It called for dissolving the Foreign Operations Administration, then overseen by the Pentagon, and reconstituting the body as a division within the State Department. In other words, the way to solve the problem of dual authority was to make the lines of supervision unmistakably clear on the organization chart by placing the State Department in charge. Right from the start, therefore, USAID would be challenged to define its distinctive contribution relative to State.

Both houses of Congress passed the Foreign Assistance Act by overwhelming margins: 287 to 140 in the House, and 66 to 24 in the Senate. As Rep. Morris Udall (D-Arizona) put it in 1961 in a special report on the bill, "The vote on mutual security was a unique test of that intangible quality, 'statesmanship.' I say this because those who receive our assistance do not vote in any congressional district; they have no lobby. Opposition to this program is 'popular' back home and an easy way to make votes, yet most congressmen know in their hearts that we would cripple our country in its fight against communism if we ended the program."[5] As the nature of Castro's revolution in Cuba gradually became clear, Congress's collective judgment seemed to be further vindicated. Passage of the Foreign Assistance Act did not resolve the enduring conflict between long-term development and short-term security, but it did create a consensus that it was prudent to separate development assistance from military aid. Founded as an independent agency, USAID was the institutional embodiment of that consensus.[6]

But was development assistance so effortlessly separated from security concerns? USAID, after all, was an arm of the U.S. government, so even had it pursued flawless policies, its motives would never be interpreted as wholly pure. Foreign Service officers served at every USAID mission just as they did at every U.S. embassy. Yet the belief that an agency of the U.S. government could serve the cause of development independent of strategic concerns was embedded in USAID's DNA. That faith set it up for being either the perpetual loose cannon of American foreign policy or the do-good agency, depending on one's perspective.

The unusually rich and publicly accessible USAID archives shed enormous light on the contours of Cold War debates over foreign assistance. At the most general level, the documents reveal that Congress engaged in a permanent struggle to rein in USAID and force it to be a better team player, and that USAID attempted to justify itself through an endless parade of task forces on its most vexing questions. Throughout the Cold War, every reform proposal from these task forces revealed an awareness that the private sector was a critical piece of the development puzzle, but none promoted private initiative to a position of real significance. Rather, the threat from Soviet expansion routinely elevated short-term reactions over long-term aspirations.

The stark dividing line that most people saw between domestic and foreign concerns in the early 1960s made it difficult for USAID to partner with other U.S. agencies such as the Treasury Department or the Department of Agriculture. USAID's partners in development in the early years were primarily the governments of developing countries or their universities, rather than international organizations, other government agencies, or American companies. Contracts with universities were increasingly used as a part of technical assistance programs, and outside evaluators applauded using contractors in this fashion.[7]

Not surprisingly, outside consultants, hired on contract, were among the most enthusiastic advocates of government outsourcing. But putting aside their own vested interests, the arguments they advanced in support of the cause deserve careful consideration. Booz Allen, the consulting company hired to assess the administration of USAID in 1965, argued persuasively for more contract employees and fewer direct hires, if only because contract employees were thought to work better and more efficiently. In Booz Allen's assessment, USAID also needed to decentralize and delegate its contracting authority to missions in the field, rather than micromanage from Washington. This advice fell on deaf ears at the time, but most of it would be adopted in later years. Efficiency arguments for privatizing aid were made from the start but were not perceived to be salient until globalization's imperatives grew too powerful to ignore.

The idea that the indigenous private sector in foreign countries must be engaged if development is to take off has a similarly long pedigree. In a 1969 speech to Congress, President Richard Nixon proposed the creation of an Overseas Private Investment Corporation (OPIC) and urged USAID to promote the development of the private sector in the countries where it was active. Nixon articulated a perspective that was ahead of its time. "No single government, no matter how wealthy or well-intentioned, can by itself hope to cope with the challenge of raising the standard of living of two-thirds of the world's people," he warned. "We must enlist the energies of the private sector. . . . We must emphasize innovative technical assistance. . . . We must induce other advanced nations to join in bearing their fair share."[8]

While Nixon was establishing OPIC, the World Bank was doing its own assessment of the past two decades of development assistance. In 1968, the bank's president, Robert McNamara, asked former Canadian prime minister and Nobel Peace Prize laureate Lester Pearson to chair a task force to review the World Bank's performance to date. With American public enthusiasm for foreign aid at a low point after the failures in Vietnam, and with official development assistance in decline for the first time, the Pearson Commission's report, titled "Partners in Development," was in many respects a watershed event for international aid. It maintained that there were two principal reasons for continuing aid: moral reasons, in that the more fortunate should help the less fortunate; and reasons of "enlightened national interest, whereby governments should recognize how their own futures are tied up with the fate of others."[9] The commission argued persuasively for expanding international assistance that focused on the complex interplay between trade, aid, and private investment.

The Pearson Commission's understanding of the most relevant partners focused almost exclusively on the relationship between governments

dispensing aid and those receiving it. When the West loses interest in foreign aid, the report argued, the inevitable results are embittered relations
between rich and poor. In focusing on multilateral institutions as well as
bilateral relations, the Pearson Commission framed a preliminary partnership approach. It proposed targets for foreign aid as a percentage of GDP,
and called for a global rather than nationalistic approach to world problems. It urged developing countries to pursue export-driven growth. Yet the
primary partners in the Pearson Commission vision were rich donors, either countries or multilateral organizations, and poor recipient governments. Multilateral institutions were the oversight institution of choice; bilateral programs were best placed in a "multilateral harness." Nonstate
actors, be they NGOs or businesses, barely merited a mention.[10]

The next major study, the 1970 product of a presidential task force
chaired by the president of Bank of America, Rudolph Peterson, recog-
nized the significant potential contribution of private voluntary organizations but noted that building the right policy to harness their potential was
no straightforward proposition because their contribution was unquantifi-
able. Echoing the findings of the Pearson Commission, the Peterson Commission argued that the developing countries themselves must stand at
the center of the international development experience, with international
lending institutions the primary channel for assistance. U.S. bilateral assistance should be provided within a framework set by international organizations, and contractors should be deployed whenever possible. Finally, all
U.S. foreign aid should be brought under one roof at the State Department, including the then autonomous USAID.[11]

The Peterson Commission's report gave aid and comfort to those arguing for reining in USAID. The Stern Report of 1971, USAID's self-
assessment of the challenges it faced, fanned the flames still further. We
were losing in Vietnam, and the search for scapegoats was already on. It
pointed out the lack of a clear sense of purpose about foreign aid, either
in government or among the public at large. In response, funding had been
reduced, while the basic delivery structure remained the same. Programs
had been rolled back but were overstaffed. The result was "over-regulation"
and "over-supervision."[12]

The Reagan administration looked at this state of affairs and charted a
distinctive course. It saw the road to development leading through the right
incentive structures, those provided by unfettered markets. The president's
1984 Task Force on Private Enterprise acknowledged a level of distrust between government and business and called for them to join forces to promote U.S. interests. Given that economic liberty was a necessary condition
for development, government interference in developing economies should

be seen as part of the problem rather than the solution. "Unless the less developed nations accept this, development assistance will fail."[13] The task force argued for the establishment of an Economic Security Council to elevate international economic policy to the level of national security, and urged that U.S. foreign aid be used to promote private enterprise and increased trade flows.[14]

Even the 1984 Kissinger Commission on Central America recommended overhauling USAID. Formed to evaluate American policy toward Central America after the 1979 Sandinista revolution in Nicaragua, the Kissinger Commission interpreted its task from the broadest possible perspective. Implementing the report's vision would require a brand new oversight body to work the seams of the development mission and properly channel USAID's energy. The panel's chairman, Henry Kissinger, envisioned a Central American Development Organization that would have representatives from the private sector in all seven countries and be chaired by the United States—and, if leadership had good sense, headed by Henry Kissinger.[15] Again, a new multilateral institution built on state representation was offered as the key to breaking up policy bottlenecks. The report concluded that the United States must respond to the security challenge caused by external intervention in the region while addressing the humanitarian issues. "This is one of those instances," the authors maintained, "in which the requirements of national interest and the commands of conscience coincide."[16] The report also noted the importance of harnessing market forces to the cause, urging "the greatest possible development of the private sector."[17]

The Task Force on Foreign Assistance, chaired by Rep. Lee Hamilton (D-Indiana), determined that foreign aid was still not delivering results. Its report, issued in February 1989, was the first to envision a future beyond the struggle between communism and the West. USAID, the task force wrote, "began with an emphasis on large resource transfers during the Marshall Plan, shifted toward technical assistance during Point Four, to infrastructure during the 1960s, to basic human needs during the 1970s, and finally to the role of markets and policy reform in the 1980s."[18] In the Hamilton group's view, continual redefinition had gradually amended the Foreign Economic Assistance Act of 1961 into an unworkable state.

The Hamilton task force proposed a radical solution: repeal the original legislation, jettison all its baggage, and replace it with a new international cooperation act. "U.S. foreign assistance needs a new premise, a new framework, and a new purpose to meet the challenges of today. It is time to start anew." The new international cooperation act would specify four main objectives: growth, environmental sustainability, poverty alleviation, and pluralism.[19] To implement the new vision, USAID should be dissolved and a restructured foreign aid agency be created to replace it. The Hamilton task force's conclusions were not subtle: Poor countries were not developing; USAID was beyond repair. A brand new approach was imperative.

The Hamilton report resulted in a new foreign assistance act that passed the House twice but never cleared the Senate.[20] It would be up to the USAID administrator to do what he or she could to put things right without the recommended assist from Congress. In response, USAID administrator Alan Woods proposed unleashing market forces on development problems as the foundation of a new understanding of foreign aid that could serve directly American and target country interests.[21] Something had not been working. Perhaps free market forces were the missing ingredient.

Less than a year after Hamilton's report, in November 1989 USAID assembled its own committee of employees to explore ways to improve agency efficiency. Chaired by assistant USAID administrator Walter Bollinger, the report echoed the reinventing foreign aid theme. Focusing on the role the private sector might play in attaining the goals of development, and on the obstacles that government can pose to developing private sector potential, Bollinger's group recommended the use of private contractors rather than service agreements with other agencies. It gave three reasons. First, since they are specified by contract, government can have greater control over the activities of private contractors. Second, contract employees are cheaper, especially when one avoids the double overhead of subcontracting (in other words, paying both agency and private sector overhead). Third, one avoids the turf battles that inevitably occur when government agencies try to coordinate. The Bollinger committee recommended a review to determine whether all such agreements with other agencies could be replaced with long-term contracts.[22] With the bipolar world in the process of unraveling, the Bollinger recommendations struck a chord.

Throughout the Cold War, therefore, two predominant themes, one obvious and the other less so, kept reasserting themselves on the matter of assessing USAID's contribution. First, both parties saw USAID as ineffective and in need of either a major overhaul or outright elimination. One could always point to a revitalized western Europe as evidence of the Marshall Plan's success, but USAID, for whatever reason, had no comparable development success story. Second, the power of the private sector was deemed critical for development, but there was significant disagreement over how its potential might best be actualized. The Soviet Union, while it existed, viewed American calls for expanded free markets abroad as a direct challenge to its interests. When it collapsed, the terrain suddenly looked very different.

The Means and Ends of Foreign Aid After the Cold War

There are at least three reasons why the demise of the Cold War order led bilateral development assistance to a crossroads. First, and perhaps most importantly, there has been a revolution in the idea of development itself. The concept of sustainable development has shifted policy attention from short-term humanitarian response to human progress over the longer term. With the changing of ultimate ends, there has been a parallel shift in thinking about optimal means. Second, the politics surrounding foreign assistance have created enormous legislative impediments to pursuing any particular strategic imperative. A dizzying array of earmarks (most country-specific) and set-asides tie the hands of even well-intentioned policymakers. Finally, globalization has remade the optimal means to long-standing desirable ends, so that the private sector now effectively implements and assesses USAID's agenda. If the private sector can move nimbly to address global problems when government cannot, it raises the question of why government-to-government programs are still necessary.

On the first point, the developed world's understanding of development itself has markedly changed over time. The initial fixation during the Cold War years was on economic growth as the foundation of a better future. But economic growth alone delivered neither equality nor social justice. Western development experts slowly learned that economic growth by itself could not guarantee that the gap between rich and poor did not grow alongside the expanding economy. In short, human development did not follow inexorably from economic development as the growth enthusiasts had expected. Some benefited from economic growth more than others, and that inequality became stubbornly entrenched. As the gap between society's haves and have-nots widened, economic development often erected substantial obstacles to societal betterment. Since development experts could see that efficiency was not cost-free, the key indicators for measuring development changed accordingly. Instead of tracking economic growth alone, they began to monitor the persistence of extreme poverty and social inequality as well.[23]

Today, rather than focusing exclusively on increased national income, according to Nobel Laureate Amartya Sen, development can be seen "as a process of expanding the real freedoms that people enjoy . . . if freedom is what development advances, then there is a major argument for concentrating on that overarching objective, rather than on some particular means, or some specially chosen list of instruments."[24] When development is perceived in this way, the best means of pursuing it is through unleashing the aspirations of individuals, who might choose very different roads to the same destination. In turn, top-down Western plans imposed on the developing world become part of the problem rather than the solution. In his controversial book *The White Man's Burden,* Bill Easterly surveys the history of foreign aid and finds that financial flows alone have not ensured local gain, and emerges with a simple maxim for the well-intentioned West: first, do no harm. "Aid cannot achieve the end of poverty," he writes. "Only homegrown development based on the dynamism of individuals and firms in free markets can do that."[25]

The collapse of the Soviet Union allowed the political aspects of development to be reconsidered without ideological blinders for the first time. With communist authority irreversibly compromised, it finally became possible for developing countries to pursue democratization without having to choose sides in an ongoing struggle of ideas and power. The paradigm of development as freedom thus facilitated a new focus on civil society and citizenship. USAID became the champion of civil society promotion in democratizing countries; it was their distinctive contribution.[26] A good example of this approach is encapsulated in former Harvard president (now head of the National Economic Council) Larry Summers's prescient focus on the status of women in the developing world. Since free societies are much more likely than unfree societies to want to educate women, Summers has argued, the most important indicator for human development in any given community is the level of female education.[27]

With respect to the second factor, those seeking to make a difference overseas in a radically changed world face a radically unchanged set of legal obstacles to action. The present incarnation of the 1961 Foreign Assistance Act requires USAID to labor under extraordinarily complex constraints to move any agenda item from point A to point B. Deciding what a given development situation demands is one thing; figuring out how to navigate the maddening web of earmarks, set-asides, and restrictions is another. While this obstacle had been noted repeatedly in assessments of USAID's shortcomings, little has been done to remove it.[28]

To address the third factor, actions that USAID took to adjust to post–Cold War development realities had the unexpected effect of undermining the case for USAID itself. Prior to its absorption by the State Department in 2006, USAID had dramatically redesigned the way it delivered government development assistance, relying whenever possible on partnerships with the private sector to get the job done. A few figures tell the story. During the 2004 Indian Ocean tsunami aid effort, the U.S. private sector contributed $1.9 billion to the effort, almost three times the official U.S. government assistance (including Pentagon spending) of $841 million.[29] Warren Buffett's $37 billion gift to the Gates Foundation empowered it to disburse $2.8 billion in grants in 2007; that amount exceeds what the Millennium Challenge Corporation, in its third year of operation, dispensed in the same period.[30] According to the Hudson Institute's 2008 Index of Global Philanthropy, U.S. private philanthropy in 2006—from voluntary organizations, the corporate world, religious institutions, and individual remittances—totaled four and a half times the level of official U.S. government assistance.[31] These private flows grew to dwarf Official Development Assistance (ODA) in part because American tax law favors philanthropic giving. But their sharp rise underscores the new opportunities for individual action that globalization has made possible.

Another way to understand the privatization turn is to examine direct hire statistics at USAID over time. The numbers are slippery, and contradictions exist within USAID's own publications, but the general trajectory is suggestive. In 1962, there were 8,600 direct hire personnel at USAID.[32] In 1968, the height of U.S. involvement in Vietnam, USAID had 17,500 employees. That number fell to 6,000 in 1980 and to 4,700 in 1988.[33] In 1990, USAID employed 3,262 individuals as direct hires, and by 2000 just 1,947, or a little over a tenth the number employed a generation earlier.[34] With need for humanitarian assistance certainly no less, contractors were deployed to plug this gap.

Changes in the international system and an expansion of the scope of contracting combined to turn USAID into a check-writing agency. Contracting had always been present, but USAID now contracted out new things: program design, management, and oversight.[35] As a result, the responsibility for implementing USAID's agenda slowly shifted from government employees to private actors. USAID became a fund-dispensing agency that provided only a marginal management role and relied almost exclusively on contractors and grantees to do the work.[36]

To summarize, the shape of foreign aid has undergone significant change over the past two decades. The idea of development moved from its original fixation on economic indicators and paternalistic strategies for meeting growth targets toward Sen's idea of development as freedom. The broadening of the development agenda in turn had powerful implications for the means and ends of foreign aid. Expanding the number of actors who can potentially be engines of development has created a dizzying array of new choices. It was no longer enough to specify the aim of foreign aid; one also had to think about the best vehicle for getting there. Development as freedom, in essence, levels the playing field for the private sector.

For NGOs and corporate initiatives alike, this has meant an expanded sphere of operation, with democracy promotion now part of the mix. For the U.S. government, it forces reflection on what government's particular contribution to meeting global challenges should be.

Reinventing Government at USAID

Neither the fall of the Berlin Wall nor the return of the Democrats to the White House in 1992 altered the snowballing consensus regarding USAID's shortcomings. After completing its own independent assessment in 1992, the General Accounting Office concluded that the troubled agency lacked a clearly articulated strategic vision. President George H. W. Bush convened yet another commission, this one chaired by investment banker George Ferris Jr., on the management of USAID programs. Its basic findings did not differ from those of the Hamilton task force: "USAID's basic management problems can never be resolved without a reappraisal of the objectives of foreign economic assistance."[37] This task force also concurred that the Foreign Assistance Act needed to be scrapped and drafted anew, and that USAID should be absorbed by the State Department. The Ferris team proposed a formal coordinating committee on foreign assistance to replace USAID, rather than a replacement agency.

The Ferris Commission's report was transmitted to Bush in December 1992, a year of multiple changes for USAID. The State Department was granted responsibility for U.S. foreign assistance programs in the former Soviet Union in 1992 (it had already been made the lead agency in central and eastern Europe in 1989). USAID took a back seat. Until 1992, the White House Office of Management and Budget had strictly enforced a rule stipulating that all foreign aid programs and spending had to go through USAID. Thereafter, it looked the other way, weakening USAID's hand. Congress had previously appropriated funds separately for each sector (agriculture, education etc.) by country; in 1992, for the first time some sector-specific designations were combined to encourage greater flexibility. This consolidation continued throughout the Clinton years. By 2004 just two sector-specific appropriations categories would remain: Development Assistance, and Child Survival and Health Programs. The global AIDS initiative is administered separately by the HIV/AIDS coordinator in the State Department.[38]

The immediate post–Cold War years were a period of great opportunity for those seeking change. In an effort to deal with USAID and other government entities mired in bureaucratic mazes not wholly of their own making, the Clinton administration unfurled the National Performance

Review in March 1993, a broad initiative to reinvent government. Just two months later, USAID administrator Brian Atwood designated his entire agency a laboratory for reinvention.

Reinventing government at USAID meant focusing on partnerships and private sector relationships as the keys to sustainable development. In a 2000 report summarizing the agency's accomplishments in eastern Europe over the previous eight years, the writers proclaimed that "USAID is modifying its approach in ways that will build lasting relationships that sustain and further progress long after formal assistance programs have ended. Simply put, USAID believes that partnerships between nations, communities, institutions and individuals are the best way to help this region overcome the isolation of the past and participate fully in international markets and institutions."[39] USAID would be rendered more efficient through privatization, and the cost savings would in turn make the agency's activities more palatable to Congress.

Meanwhile, globalization was empowering private actors to get involved in foreign assistance. Before the collapse of the Soviet Union, foreign governments had accounted for the overwhelming majority of international resource flows to developing countries. Once foreign direct investment began pouring into the financial markets of post-Communist Europe in 1992, private flows for the first time overtook official development assistance.

Resource flows continued to shift throughout the 1990s. In the previous decade, Official Development Assistance from the U.S. government had provided the majority of American aid to the developing world. By 2000, 60 percent of total development aid coming from the United States was from the private sector, and of the 40 percent coming from government a good portion was contracted out to private entities.[40] It is important to realize that those private aid figures do not refer to charity alone. They also include remittances from abroad (dollars earned by foreigners in the United States and sent back home) as well as scholarships for international students. For some countries, the impact of these two factors can be tremendous. For example, the prime minister of Lebanon once told USAID administrator Andrew Natsios that 25 percent of Lebanon's GDP comes from remittances from abroad.[41] American universities and colleges gave more to developing countries in foreign scholarships in 2000 than Australia, Belgium, Norway, Spain, and Switzerland each gave in official development assistance. In 2001, remittances from U.S. immigrants to their countries of origin exceeded Japan's official development assistance. Japan was the second largest provider (in dollars) of government aid to foreign countries in 2001.[42]

But which private actors were engaged in advancing USAID's agenda? The 1961 Foreign Assistance Act included provisions that extended the 1933 Buy American Act, designed to ensure that government agencies bought goods and services of American origin. That orientation had always shaped the perception of the desirable for contracting. Since USAID had long justified its existence to Congress by arguing that aid money channeled through the agency directly benefited domestic economic interests through contracts with U.S. firms and import programs for U.S. products, the agency contracted with those U.S.-based firms with which it already had relationships.[43] Supporters of the practice spoke of depending on reliable friends. Critics described the friends as "beltway bandits."

The steering of government funds to privileged U.S. firms always stands potentially in conflict with the overarching goals of development, when development is defined as freedom. For starters, the economic efficiency resulting from privatization depends entirely on a competitive market for contracts. When contracts are awarded on the basis of old relationships, the promised cost savings tend to evaporate. Rubén Berríos's 2000 assessment of USAID's experiment in reinventing government described the market structure for development aid as segmented and uncompetitive.[44] Even USAID's own promotional literature does not argue otherwise. An oligarchic and strictly American market for USAID contracts has negative effects beyond simple inefficiency. When U.S. firms are privileged, foreign entrepreneurship is not encouraged, and an opportunity to engage local forces in a partnership for their self-betterment is lost. While the "Buy American" provision does not extend to subcontractors, it still means that the American firms at the top of the contracting food chain are likely to profit most.

An especially pernicious consequence of outsourcing aid implementation follows directly from contracting norms themselves. USAID policy forbids disclosure of proprietary information about its contracts, which renders the financial details of any transaction totally opaque. There are legitimate security reasons for this secrecy in the more volatile parts of the world (Islamic states, for example), but USAID accounting has never distinguished between contracts that had to be hidden from public view and those that did not. All USAID contracts have been kept confidential, with troubling consequences for transparency.[45] In addition, outsourcing meant that reporting on the progress of projects depended on the perceptions of contractors, who by definition have a vested interest in reporting back good news.

Lack of transparency and uncompetitive bidding have always been a feature of contracting, but the new emphasis on outsourcing oversight as well has meant that a greater proportion of USAID's accounting is now veiled in secrecy. The 1989 Hamilton task force found the accountability of U.S. foreign assistance to be "extensive but ineffective. Accountability is focused on anticipating how assistance will be used, rather than on how effectively it is and has been used. It can take two and a half years to plan and approve a project, by which time conditions have changed and plans need to be revised."[46] These accountability problems remained a feature of USAID activities, even after it had been ostensibly reinvented. While privatizing aid permitted rapid response to humanitarian crises, it also rendered transparency and accountability all the more difficult. These problems only mushroomed over time.

The accountability problem is reflected in the ebbs and flows of USAID contracting. Figure 5 maps official USAID procurement data from 1995 through 2006. There is no explicable pattern whatsoever in the reported numbers. For example, procurements fell from $715.7 million in FY1996 to $34.6 million in FY1997. They jumped back up to $443.9 million in FY1998. While the contracting numbers from then presidential candidate Barack Obama's "Google for Government" are based on Federal Procurement Data Service (FPDS) data, the discrepancy between raw FPDS figures for 2005 and those presented on USAspending.gov when I visited the site on May 15, 2008, was a whopping $1.79 billion. There is no evidence to suggest that the spikes in spending captured in the chart below are attributable to counting large, multiyear contracts in one fiscal year only. The seemingly random walk can only be explained in two ways. Either USAID procurement decisions are indeed entirely random, with no underlying strategy, or in-house accounting practices have some very serious deficiencies.[47]

Despite the Clinton administration's efforts to reinvent it, USAID was still widely perceived as a mismanaged agency. By its own account, it was burdened with overly complex administrative procedures, low morale, and a public relations problem; it had not succeeded in persuading the general public of its own importance. In 1998, the Clinton administration took action to address the agency's critics. The Foreign Affairs Reorganization (Presidential Decision Directive 65) of 1998 brought the USAID director under the direct authority of the Secretary of State; Administrator Brian Atwood agreed to the change in order to keep USAID alive.[48] The reorganization that followed resulted in staff and budget cuts of 30 percent and the closing of twenty-eight country missions abroad.[49] USAID was hamstrung, but its problems remained.

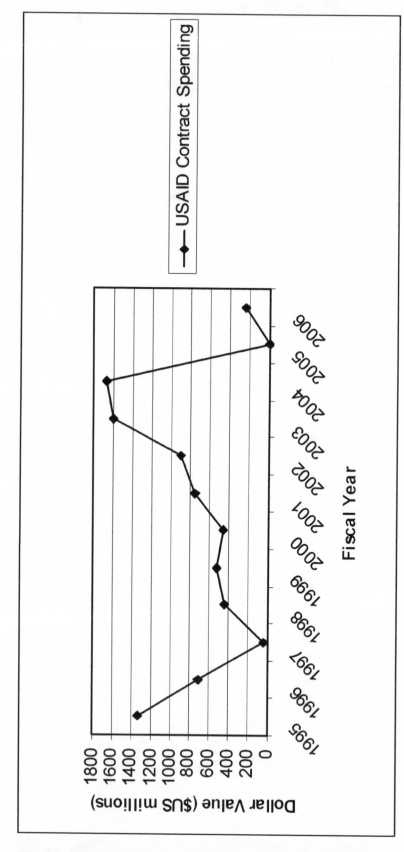

Figure 5. U.S. Agency for International Development contract spending, 1995–2006 (Source: Federal Procurement Data System. Graphic: Carolann Davis)

Transformational Development

By the end of the Clinton years, the private sector's role in foreign assistance had grown dramatically. There was a change in the "who" of foreign aid: beltway bandits or contractors, depending on your perspective, replaced USAID officers in the field. There was also a change in the "how": project-based aid replaced unrestricted aid to foreign governments.[50]

With respect to the "who," which is connected to the "how," the number of USAID employees overseeing contracts dropped nearly fivefold from 1997 to 2007. At the close of that period, there were just 109 USAID employees managing over $8.9 billion in aid funds, about $81 million per procurement officer. With respect to the "how" of aid, USAID contracted with both not-for-profit and for-profit organizations, but the Bush administration vastly preferred channeling money to businesses. For example, since the Iraq invasion, the top ten for-profits working for USAID have received almost $5.8 billion in contracts. That was more than twice as much as the top ten nonprofits, and ten times the amount that for-profits received in the preceding four-year span.[51]

Despite the unending discussion of the shortcomings of U.S. foreign assistance programs, the Bush administration's 2002 National Security Strategy elevated development for the first time to a pillar of national security, alongside the old standbys, defense and diplomacy. In his March 2002 speech on development, Bush argued that poverty does not by itself fashion terrorists; particular regimes create circumstances from which terrorists can emerge. From that premise, it followed that governance is of critical importance for national security, and promoting democracy and the rule of law is an integral part of the war on terror.[52] Development efforts should therefore focus on democracy as well as on free markets; development and democratization must go hand in hand.

Bush elaborated on the concept a week later at the International Conference on Financing for Development in Monterrey, Mexico, which saw the birth of the so-called Monterrey Consensus, a new vision of global financing endorsed by the major heads of state at the close of the conference.[53] Bush's pledge of support at Monterrey meant an immediate 50 percent increase in U.S. foreign aid allocations.[54] Forging a "new compact for global development," the administration promised both to ramp up U.S. foreign aid and to render it "smart" through the establishment of new institutions for administering it. The White House would seek to address foreign aid's inherent problems by effectively end-running USAID, first with the Millennium Challenge Account and shortly thereafter with the President's Emergency Plan for AIDS Relief.

As we saw in the last chapter, the Millennium Challenge Account was designed to reward best development practices by channeling money to those who had demonstrated a strong commitment to the right sorts of reforms. With this brand new institution devoted to administering the right sort of foreign aid, USAID's raison d'être grew ever more tenuous. The first five years of the twenty-first century saw a flurry of activity at that agency, spearheaded by its energetic new administrator, Andrew Natsios. As someone who had salvaged Boston's Big Dig debacle, Natsios was the sort of person USAID's existential angst seemed to demand. A long-time friend of the president's chief of staff, Andrew Card, Natsios had a direct line to the Oval Office. That a rival aid agency was formed on Natsios's watch shows how important it was to the Bush administration to demonstrate some big new initiative in international development.

For Natsios, USAID had to begin by learning from its past mistakes. Smart aid requires political will, competent policy reform, and plenty of partnerships to energize local leadership. Shortly after being sworn in on May 1, 2001, Natsios established four targets for USAID energy and resources: economic growth; agriculture and trade; global health; and democracy, conflict, and humanitarian assistance.

These goals would be pursued through the Global Development Alliance (GDA), an entity that Secretary of State Colin Powell had launched in 2001 "to promote public-private alliances that address development challenges." The idea was to connect USAID's international development expertise with the energy and resources of the private sector, bringing together like-minded people to tackle development problems. In USAID's own literature, reliance on partners "does not make USAID a pass-through organization." Instead, with the vital help from partners, USAID employees were well positioned to serve as the overseers, something the development process desperately needed.[55]

"We help countries balance their budgets," was how Natsios explained the USAID mission early in his tenure.[56] But getting the strategy right and the optimal alliances for change in place were only part of the problem. The elaborate web of legislation that still constrained USAID's activities remained a serious impediment to any genuinely new approach. According to Steve Radelet, a senior fellow at the Center for Global Development, the Foreign Assistance Act of 1961 "specifies a remarkable 33 goals, 75 priority areas, and 247 directives. These multiple goals are more than just an administrative burden; they make it very difficult for USAID to achieve clear results."[57] Radelet's judgments echo the conclusions of the Hamilton (1989) report.[58]

Natsios's remedy was to have another go at reinventing USAID, making sure to broadcast in explicit fashion what, precisely, had been rein-vented. USAID had to behave more like a business, he reasoned, if it was to survive direct challenges to its authority. It could accomplish that in three distinct ways. First, it could leverage its capacity by partnering with non-government forces committed to transformational development, both in the private and not-for-profit sectors. Second, the agency had to be re-branded. Finally, competitive sourcing would allay concerns about effi-ciency and cost-effectiveness.

The Clinton administration had also wanted to make partnerships a priority, but the new USAID ramped up the level of activity, seeking agreements with nontraditional partners. Between 2002 and 2005 it cre-ated 286 public-private alliances in sixty-five countries, deploying $1 billion in USAID resources to leverage over $3 billion in alliance partner contribu-tions. A new contracting instrument—the collaborative agreement—be-came operational in 2005. These agreements were designed to facilitate al-liances between the public and private sectors, providing an alternative to traditional grants.[59] A March 2005 USAID brochure proudly reported that the agency had collaborative relationships with 3,500 companies and over 300 U.S.-based private voluntary organizations.[60] Just one year later, the latter number had grown to 543.[61] According to Natsios, USAID should le-verage this "silent private financing" and channel it to good purposes.[62]

The global branding initiative ("From the American People"), officially undertaken in 2004, was perhaps the most controversial of the Natsios re-forms. All products of USAID assistance, regardless of their form, were now required to bear the USAID label. The idea itself was nothing new; goods distributed under the Marshall Plan had carried a label that read, "For European Recovery supplied by the United States of America."[63] Re-gardless of the contribution percentage of the agency to a given endeavor, branding the product in the language of the local population became a precondition for receiving aid.[64]

Unfortunately, the USAID branding initiative worked at cross-purposes with its stated goals. The idea was to let citizens of other countries know that the United States was on their side, but it also undermined any sense of pride of ownership that might otherwise have bloomed. It was one thing for USAID to brand a road, clinic, or bridge, but it was another thing en-tirely to tag a civil society group with "Brought to you by the American people." The blanket branding requirement made no effort to draw dis-tinctions among these different sorts of aid.[65] The initiative was also at odds with the stated objectives of transformational development, which were os-tensibly to promote local ownership and encourage local populations to collaborate for their own self-betterment. When USAID puts its label on

Colombian coffee because USAID dollars created incentives to grow coffee rather than coca, the accomplishment becomes a foreign achievement rather than an indigenous one. A visiting Colombian relative of mine grimaced when I noted the USAID label on a bag of Colombian coffee she had brought as a gift.

The final item on the Natsios reform agenda was a new emphasis on competitive sourcing. To confront charges of cronyism in contracting and hiring, as well as to improve mission performance and reduce costs, USAID would encourage competition for both contracts and in-house employment. Presumably competitive sourcing was also to apply to relationships forged abroad with indigenous groups, although just how this would work was not clearly articulated.[66] If development as freedom was the desired end, this was a step in the right direction.[67]

With the private sector increasingly involved in all realms of USAID activities, Natsios maintained, Official Direct Assistance had become an outdated way of measuring aid outlays. It no longer captured the significant impact of private flows and public-private partnerships on development, and by itself it cast the United States in a wholly undeserved negative light. For example, in 2000 the United States ranked last among industrialized countries in the percentage of its GNP devoted to direct assistance. But when private flows were counted as well, the United States rose to first place.[68] "Given the enormous growth of the private sector around the world," Natsios argued, "donors should reevaluate the measure."[69]

What this meant, in practical terms, was that the USAID dollar should never be the only one on the table. Whenever government funds are matched by private donors, the project has passed a market test that bodes well for its future. Traditional government-funded projects never have to pass such a test.[70] By expanding the range of permissible partners, local creativity and entrepreneurship could be more effectively rewarded and reinforced. By 2005, USAID spending had doubled since 2000 (to $14 billion), but the agency had added only 100 employees in that period (the total now numbered 2,400). Privatization filled the labor gap. Take the case of reconstruction in Afghanistan. In 2002 and 2003, for-profit companies won five of six major USAID contracts. A July 2005 GAO report found that the USAID mission in Kabul suffered severe personnel shortages; in 2004, it managed $11.2 million per Kabul staff member, compared to the worldwide norm of $1.3 million.[71]

To publicize its new look and agenda, USAID issued a blizzard of reports in the first term of the Bush administration, including a glossy primer,

"This is USAID," intended for new employees, Congress, and the public at large. "This is USAID" made it clear that USAID's core function had evolved from providing direct aid to managing contractors.[72] The new USAID, a government agency dressed up in corporate clothing, could not have been more clearly articulated or urgently needed. Yet this identity transformation was not cost-free. If USAID was now emulating a business, why was government even necessary?

Here the State Department, the nation's oldest foreign policy institution, stood poised to help. In 2003, USAID and the State Department issued their first ever joint strategic plan "to harmonize foreign policy and development goals" and build on the 2002 National Security Strategy.[73] In 2004, the State Department issued another call for more integrated management structures between the two institutions.[74] The writing on the wall was clear: USAID had valiantly made the case for its independent mission, but it was headed for further emasculation.

The slow loss of independence that had begun under Clinton reached its culmination. In December 2005, Natsios announced his resignation as USAID administrator to take a professorial post at Georgetown University. Secretary of State Rice used the occasion to confirm the end of an era. "The current structure of America's foreign assistance risks incoherent policies and ineffective programs," she remarked, "and perhaps even wasted resources. We can do better and we must do better."[75] The last vestige of USAID autonomy disappeared, and the agency was officially absorbed by the State Department. Rice announced a new leadership position, the director of foreign assistance; this person would also be the USAID administrator. The director of foreign assistance was given the task of transforming the American approach to foreign aid.

In March 2006, Randall Tobias took charge as the nation's first director of foreign assistance and administrator of the newly subordinated USAID. Although he had briefly served as Bush's global AIDS coordinator in 2003, Tobias had not followed the typical career path of a development administrator. He had been chairman and CEO of AT&T and later Eli Lilly. He believed that the ultimate focus of "transformational development" is local ownership, "helping to build and sustain democratic, well-governed states that respond to the needs of their people and conduct themselves responsibly in the international arena. . . . It's not about us; it's about them."[76] Creating hope through foreign aid required getting the optimum return on the government's investment. And how was that best done? In Tobias's view, "the short answer to that question . . . is remarkably similar to what it might be in the corporate world . . . you focus on performance, results, accountability. In foreign assistance, that means ultimately defining success as the ability of a nation to graduate from aid and become a full partner in international peace and prosperity." That, in turn, demanded a focus on investing in people, since "the majority shareholders in the future of any nation must be its own leaders."[77] As if to underscore the difference transformational development intended to make, the new chief economic adviser to USAID, Professor Arnold Horberger, was an outside contractor.[78]

Tobias's version of transformational development was never put to a real test. He was forced into early retirement by a sex scandal in May 2007. The *Washington Post* reported that Tobias had wanted to resign his position for the previous six months.[79] USAID limped on. The December 2007 report of the bipartisan HELP Commission (commissioned by Congress in 2003; the acronym stands for Helping to Enhance the Livelihood of People around the globe) on foreign assistance reform reached no consensus on USAID's future. It did embrace a bottom-up, partnership approach and urged the rewriting of the badly outdated and hopelessly compromised Foreign Assistance Act. Not one person who appeared before it endorsed the status quo; there was unanimous support for reform of foreign assistance. According to HELP commissioner Eric Postel, "the reason USAID has been a target for so many is that there are countless incidents where they just went their merry way despite the wishes of the administration. As a result, USAID is in a death spiral."[80]

The HELP Commission report also noted that the present broken system had created a vacuum that has been filled by DOD.[81] This additional responsibility is not DOD's cup of tea. In a September 2007 interview with the *New York Times*'s David Brooks, Defense Secretary Robert Gates said that two of our biggest mistakes after the Cold War were shrinking USAID and eliminating the United States Information Agency.[82] Something is amiss, Secretary Gates has argued, when the United States has more military marching band members than foreign service officers.[83]

Development in the Information Age

An American statesman once assessed American foreign assistance efforts in the developing world as accomplishing far too little; his words are worth quoting at length:

> For no objective supporter of foreign aid can be satisfied with the existing program—actually a multiplicity of programs. Bureaucratically fragmented, awkward and slow, its administration is diffused over a haphazard

and irrational structure covering at least four departments and several other agencies. The program is based on a series of legislative measures and administrative procedures conceived at different times and for different purposes, many of them now obsolete, inconsistent, and unduly rigid and thus unsuited for our present needs and purposes. Its weaknesses have begun to undermine confidence in our effort both here and abroad. . . . Although our aid programs have helped to avoid economic chaos and collapse, and assisted many nations to maintain their independence and freedom—nevertheless, it is a fact that many of the nations we are helping are not much nearer sustained economic growth than they were when our aid operation began. Money spent to meet crisis situations or short-term political objectives while helping to maintain national integrity and independence has rarely moved the recipient nation toward greater economic stability.[84]

Who penned these prescient words? Although the description would seem to fit the contemporary era perfectly, it wasn't President Bush, and it wasn't President Clinton. This was President Kennedy describing the landscape that the new USAID was intended to remake. That his words could just as well describe where we stand today should give us pause.

The Bush White House bears the lion's share of responsibility for leaving office with USAID's future status so uncertain. In establishing high-profile foreign assistance programs with no formal ties to USAID, such as the Millennium Challenge Corporation and the Office of the U.S. Global AIDS Coordinator, it presented the USAID leadership with a clear message. The Bush administration elevated "transformational development" to the same level as diplomacy and defense in its security strategy, but it did not want USAID to lead that effort.

USAID now finds itself in an unsustainable situation. Program funding for USAID increased and the number of countries with USAID programs has nearly doubled since the end of the Cold War.[85] USAID ramped up its presence in the world, backed by significant funding increases, while its direct-hire workforce did not increase proportionately. Small wonder that Tim Rieser, an aide to Sen. Patrick Leahy (D-Vermont), has called it "a check-writing agency."[86]

Opinions vary on how the gutting of USAID personnel came to pass.[87] Efforts by Congress to limit the size of government certainly played a significant role. According to Natsios, limits on the number of government employees were a driving force in the privatization of foreign aid. While continuing to allow increases in the budget for international programs, in 2002 Congress capped the international operating expenses account. The salaries and benefits of direct-hire government employees come out of that account, while contractors and grantees are paid from the programming budget. The congressional cap on operating expenses produced attrition in the number of Foreign Service officers available to administer USAID programs around the world, increasing the need for outsourcing.[88]

This suggests that USAID's transformation from an agency that administers programs to one that administers contracts was at least partly an unintended consequence. Congress capped operating expenses while letting the program expenses budget grow for straightforward political reasons. Every congressman with an NGO in his district wants more money for the programs budget. But there is no natural constituency for increased operating expenses. The result was predictable: anything that could be outsourced was, and Foreign Service officers who retired were not replaced.[89] Natsios told me in 2007 that, as USAID administrator, he pushed hard for more Foreign Service officers but couldn't get them.[90]

On the other hand, the president of the Professional Services Council, Stan Soloway, doesn't buy the idea that the growth in contracting has principally been caused by the reduction in the number of government employees. As he put it, "It's not that we don't have enough acquisitions officers. We don't have enough *properly trained* acquisitions officers."[91] The GAO assessed USAID's "human capital vulnerabilities" as involving "fewer and less experienced staff managing more programs in more countries." As a result, "USAID's ability to oversee the delivery of foreign assistance is becoming increasingly difficult."[92] Between 1998 and 2006, aid disbursement per USAID staff member grew by 46 percent, to $2 million annually, with most overseas managers implementing much larger programs.[93]

In theory, transformational development tipped its hat to private sector power and sought to harness it to the right agenda, and thus to serve both private and public interests. In Tanzania, for example, the USAID roads program helped to increase private sector involvement in road maintenance. As of 2002, 80 percent of Tanzania's roads were under private supervision. Concurrently, USAID endeavored to expand local involvement in road maintenance, a source of new jobs. Development by definition undermines tradition, which causes resistance. But properly conceived, as in Tanzania, development policy engages the local private sector to collaborate on pursuing shared goals that advance mutual interests. In that way, the gains can be made to outweigh the losses.[94] For strategy to match the context, ideas must emerge locally rather than be imposed from above.

Transformational development in Iraq, however, involved throwing money at the problem while shifting responsibility for reconstruction and development to the Pentagon. A textbook top-down operation, it should not be a model for the future.[95] Having the U.S. military coerce other countries to develop appropriately had little to do with the freedom of choice on which the Bush administration's concept of transformational development relied. The U.S. Assistance to Iraq program was the largest aid initiative since the 1948–51 Marshall Plan, but it is worth recalling that the Pentagon was not the Marshall Plan's lead agency.[96] In the end, transformational development came up short by the administration's own metric for success.

The gap between transformational development in theory and in practice raises one large question: In a world dominated by American military power, is the direct involvement of the U.S. government more likely to stunt development than to catalyze it? If the best solutions are designed locally to meet the challenges of particular situations, isn't a master puppeteer, especially one with a badly tarnished global reputation, more a hindrance than a help? When peer-to-peer microfinance via the Internet is a possibility, what is government's unique value-added?

One answer is that there can be bad privatization and good privatization, and government can ensure that the latter prevails. Bad privatization empowers the beltway bandits rather than building capacity and self-reliance in the developing world. According to the first Millennium Challenge Corporation chief, Paul Applegarth, USAID is an example of bad privatization in that it funneled money to American consulting firms rather than to indigenous organizations.[97] Natsios contested this characterization, since USAID subcontracts were usually local.[98] But it still seems appropriate to classify Iraqi reconstruction as an example of bad privatization. The Pentagon was the lead player for reconstruction, making what was to be a development project look indistinguishable from an occupation. No matter how one does the math, too few Iraqi citizens were involved in the work of rebuilding their own country. Corruption, waste, and the abuse of power were permanent features of the intervention.

Foreign aid's future as a government enterprise depends on getting privatization right, which demands the reinvention of oversight for the information age. It isn't just a matter of having enough U.S. government overseers. It matters who is being overseen. It is not enough to identify the right metric for development; the local population has to be a genuine stakeholder. Just as globalization has increased the opportunities for bottom-up innovation from the local population, the information revolution makes it possible to connect efforts on the ground with those funding them in unprecedented ways. Former USAID administrator M. Peter McPherson has argued that the clear separation of policymaking from implementation in foreign aid programming has itself become part of the problem.[99]

Good privatization understands that the how of policy is as important as the what.

If the aim is good privatization, ramping up the number of Foreign Service officers on the ground overseeing American aid programs or re-consolidating all existing aid programs in one large agency à la the Department of Homeland Security will not get us where we need to go. Both proposed solutions dodge the most important question: What should U.S. foreign aid look like when our principal enemy is no longer another state, development is defined as freedom, and all U.S. citizens are now capable of pursuing their own development policy through donations to private sector organizations from Kiva to Save the Children? In this new world, we need a proliferation of bottom-up initiatives and incentives from government to pursue them, rather than a proliferation of government programs. By it-self, consolidating existing programs in a brand new Agency for Global Development will not do the trick. After all, USAID was born of a similar effort to consolidate existing programs under one authority. Its history suggests that a reconstituted überagency will neither repair the oversight process nor ensure aid programs that can make a genuine difference. That is instead a task for creative individuals who are aware of the importance of local ownership and who might hang their hats at a government agency, an NGO, or a corporation.

Securing funds for development abroad is going to be increasingly difficult with pressing development needs at home. But make the case we must, since global development is legitimately a national security issue. Re-establishing an autonomous USAID or a brand new Ministry of International Development, however, is not a necessary condition for securing commitment to the fight against extreme poverty. Since all of the so-called three D's—Defense, Diplomacy, and Development—are now executed to an unprecedented extent by contractors, we must instead focus our attention on righting the imbalance in funding between defense and civilian agencies and improving government oversight of, and incentives for, public-private collaboration.

None of this is to say that government organization and personnel do not matter. They obviously do. But when we concentrate our energy on getting the architecture right, we are less likely to work on reorienting existing institutions toward information sharing, partnership, and transparency across the public-private divide. We are more likely to miss opportunities where government can make a difference right here and now. Founded in 2006 by leading nongovernmental institutions, Malaria No More today works in partnership with the President's Malaria Initiative; UNICEF; the American Red Cross; the Global Fund to Fight HIV/AIDS, Tuberculosis and Malaria; Millennium Promise; United Way of America; United Nations Foundation; and the Global Business Coalition. It is a successful bottom-up initiative that both government and the private sector have encouraged. It can be a model for the future, if only we can take the plunge and reimagine government itself.

7

Laissez-Faire Homeland Security

By dint of looking at a dubious object with a constructive imagination,
one can give it twenty different shapes.
—George Eliot, *Daniel Deronda*

The American homeland is the planet.
—*Report of the 9/11 Commission*

T HE SPECTACLE OF government paralysis after Hurricane Katrina
ravaged New Orleans in August 2005 is not easy to forget. Some
of America's most vulnerable citizens were in dire need, a major
American city was devastated and partly destroyed, and our federal government seemed incapable of responding. President George W. Bush debated
whether the crisis merited him cutting short his vacation. The Federal
Emergency Management Agency, under the newly constituted Department of Homeland Security (DHS), was so uninformed that it seemed not
even to be watching the reports on cable news. In contrast, private security
firms like Blackwater and DynCorp dropped everything and beat most federal agencies to the scene. A week later, they had secured multimillion-
dollar government contracts to provide security for reconstructing New
Orleans. Wal-Mart had 66 percent of its stores in the Gulf States operational just forty-eight hours after Katrina hit, providing critical supplies.[1]
But these efforts did not—could not—add up to a coordinated response,
and the entire episode raised a disturbing question: If government does not
exist to lead the nation in a time of crisis, what is government for?

A still more disturbing dimension of the government's failure in New
Orleans casts a dark shadow over America's future homeland security: the
DHS employees charged with keeping you safe hate their jobs. Morale at
DHS has been low from the department's inception. A 2005 independent
study showed that, out of the thirty largest federal agencies, DHS ranked
last in employee satisfaction. In the same survey done two years later, DHS
rose to twenty-ninth place, just beating out the Small Business Administra-

tion.[2] The House Committee on Homeland Security gave the agency a failing grade for employee morale in its 2007 annual report on the department. Why do DHS employees hate their jobs? DHS hired a consultant in 2008 to find out. A survey found that 55 percent of respondents believed pay raises did not depend on job performance, 45 percent did not believe promotions are based on merit, and 42 percent did not think creativity and innovation are rewarded.[3]

For a new agency in its first decade of existence assigned a task of the highest importance, the low morale is a red flag. Keeping the American homeland safer requires unprecedented cooperation between the public and private sectors, and demoralized employees are unlikely to be engines of initiative and collaboration. Yet DHS moved at lightning speed to privatize much of its operations. A December 2008 search of USAspending.gov, what Barack Obama has called "Google for government," showed that DHS contract spending grew from $4.2 billion in 2003 to $15.6 billion in 2006, a 271 percent increase. While numbers for 2007 and 2008 are not yet definitive and reliable, they map an unabated upward trajectory in DHS outsourcing.

The tortured tale of DHS's birth and early years highlights both the perils of a laissez-faire approach to contracting and the extent to which large bureaucracies are not the optimal vehicles for confronting security threats from nonstate actors. But DHS should not be singled out as the weak link in our self-defense; instead, its failures underscore just how little our national security architecture has adjusted to meet the new threats of the twenty-first century and the distinctive challenges of the information age. In the final reckoning, DHS is a mirror of larger systemic problems— an industrial-era security apparatus for a postindustrial age.

The Birth of DHS

After the September 11 attacks on New York and Washington, Bush established an Office of Homeland Security in the White House and appointed the governor of Pennsylvania, Tom Ridge, to head it. Critics like Sen. Joseph Lieberman (then D-Connecticut) argued that this was insufficient; the country needed a new government agency, subject to congressional oversight, to oversee domestic security.[4] Hostile to big government as the solution to any problem, especially when it was proposed by Democrats, the Bush administration stood firmly against creating a new agency even though Ridge himself argued in its favor. For nine months Bush publicly argued that creating more bureaucracy was the wrong response to the terrorist threat.[5]

But when it started to appear that the administration was obstructing the Democrats' good-faith efforts to serve the public interest, the president's position changed, first secretly and then publicly. In April 2002, White House chief of staff Andrew H. Card Jr. called together five mid-level staffers—the "Gang of Five," or G-5, as they liked to call themselves—to envision a new government department that would merge under one roof the disparate entities currently involved in homeland security. Nothing was off the table; the group even considered putting the FBI and the National Guard under the new department, but Secretary of State Rice thought a new department that included the FBI sounded too much like Germany's Federal Ministry of the Interior, and moving the National Guard was deemed too complicated.[6] The group's work culminated in a thirty-five-page bill nearly identical to the Lieberman proposal.[7] The most significant difference was that instead of passing through Congress as the Lieberman bill, the administration's plan would be voted on as the Homeland Security Act, identifying it with Bush instead of a Senate Democrat.[8]

In a speech to the nation on June 6, 2002, Bush did an official about-face and accepted Democratic congressional proposals to establish a Department of Homeland Security, saying that the government had to "be reorganized to meet the new threats of the twenty-first century." The new department would "unite essential agencies that must work more closely together," the president explained, and would involve "the most extensive reorganization of the federal government since the 1940s."[9] Supporting what had originally been the Lieberman initiative signified two things. First, the administration had accepted the argument that the country needed a permanent agency with budget authority to oversee its domestic preparedness, and that the existing Office of Homeland Security was simply too weak to get the job done. Second, and perhaps more importantly, the Bush team had realized the potential fallout should they allow the Democrats to paint them as uncommitted to taking dramatic action to meet the terrorist threat.[10]

Shortly after the 2002 midterm elections, the Homeland Security Act of 2002, a bill "To establish a Department of Homeland Security, and for other purposes," was passed in virtually its original form.[11] The Democrats, on the defensive after having lost control of the Senate in an election dominated by terrorism and security issues, wanted the bill to pass on what remained of their watch. And so Bush, ideologically committed to small government, presided over the creation of a new federal megabureaucracy. In testimony before the Senate two years later, John Hamre, president of the Center for Strategic and International Studies, described the result of

Congress's haste "to do something" on homeland security before the Senate changed hands as "a mess."[12]

The mess involved big organizational changes. Previously, writes the political scientist Donald Kettl, "the federal government had extraordinary expertise, but that expertise was highly compartmentalized."[13] To remedy that, DHS was given direct budgetary and supervisory control over twenty-two agencies and more than a hundred bureaus and subagencies, many of which had been relatively autonomous and had distinct cultures.[14] At a stroke the administration had created the federal government's third-largest agency, with no fewer than 170,000 federal employees. Despite a concerted effort to streamline and focus its purview, the new department was a complex and unwieldy behemoth. More than eighty different personnel systems had to be harmonized.[15]

Ridge was sworn in as the nation's first Secretary of Homeland Security on January 24, 2003. Bush pronounced him "a superb leader who has my confidence."[16] Four days later, Ridge learned from the president's State of the Union address that a new national intelligence center, which Ridge and his aides had seen as the linchpin of the DHS coordination mission, would not be under the new department's authority. Ridge had not been told of the decision before Bush's speech.[17] Since the Homeland Security Act had brought neither the FBI nor the CIA under DHS jurisdiction, oversight of the National Intelligence Center was essential if DHS was not to rely entirely on outside bodies for the information that was its lifeblood. Ridge's vision of how the new department would operate had been thwarted in his first week on the job.

Turning the Homeland Security Act from bill to reality was by all accounts a spectacularly ambitious undertaking. On paper, the department looked like an effective and powerful instrument for an urgently needed coordination of missions. The reality was something else entirely. Advised by representatives from Defense, Justice, and the CIA, the administration developed a blueprint that actually ensured that the new institution had quite limited authority. DHS was charged with overseeing a wide range of areas, from federal response to natural disasters to airline safety. But it had no authority over the counterterrorism activities of the CIA, the Pentagon, or the Justice Department, nor did it oversee any intelligence operations. The most critical players in domestic preparedness—those with the information necessary to prudent decision-making—were entirely beyond its purview. In practice, therefore, DHS had apparent vast responsibility with little authority to meet it.[18]

These factors weighed heavily against DHS from the start. John DiIulio, who resigned from his position as head of the White House Office of Faith-Based Initiatives after just eight months on the job, criticized the "remarkably slapdash" way in which "the most significant reorganization of the federal government since the creation of the Department of Defense" was pursued. In an on-the-record letter written to journalist Ron Suskind after his resignation and published in *Esquire* amid much controversy, DiIulio characterized the thoughtless DHS founding as "the administration's problem in miniature: Ridge was the decent fellow at the top, but nobody spent the time to understand that an EOP [executive office of the president] entity without budgetary or statutory authority can't coordinate over a hundred separate federal units, no matter how personally close to the president its leader is, no matter how morally right it feels the mission is, and no matter how inconvenient the politics of telling certain House Republican leaders we need a big new federal bureaucracy might be."[19]

And so the Department of Homeland Security was erected and appeared to be the locus of the country's future counterterrorism efforts. After spitting up this Leviathan-in-chains, Congress and the White House moved on to other more pressing matters. DHS leadership had no choice but to work things out on the fly with the odds stacked against them. But appearances and reality were badly aligned.

Branding DHS

With the founding of DHS, Washington entered uncharted territory. Neither the U.S. government nor the private sector had ever attempted such a huge merger involving so many different moving parts. The creation of the Department of Defense in the late 1940s bears some similarities, but it combined a much smaller number of more or less similar-minded entities. And getting the new Department of Defense right did not happen overnight; most experts would agree that only with the 1986 Goldwater-Nichols Act, which encouraged unity of effort through the mechanism of the Joint Chiefs, was the Pentagon's organization set right. Such a mechanism cannot work in the same fashion at DHS, as Ridge's successor, Homeland Security Secretary Michael Chertoff, emphasized, because civilians don't respond to orders in the same way that the military does: "You can't order them to move places they don't want to move; they quit."

Another big difference was timing. The Department of Defense was created after World War II, not during it. As Chertoff often pointed out, peacetime integration was no picnic for the newborn DOD.[20] The DHS merger had to be executed in a wartime environment, which meant that its constituent agencies had to focus simultaneously on waging war and on bureaucratic reorganization.[21]

Even if the transition had occurred in a peacetime environment, private sector experience shows that corporate mergers generally reduce productivity and effectiveness before increasing it. The first eighteen months are typically the most difficult: costs rise, performance declines, and many employees leave. When one corporation acquires another, it is clear which entity owns the assets and has the authority over daily activities. But when a merger takes place in the public sector, the ultimate boss, the U.S. government, ostensibly remains the same, leaving plenty of room for differences of opinion about authority. For DHS, this meant that expectations of what it could do were high precisely when they should have been the lowest.

Much like a CEO with a new acquisition, Secretary Ridge faced the enormous challenge of orchestrating a massive merger, but with the additional headaches of turf wars and anxiety-provoking daily colored threat assessments. If the new conglomerate of twenty-two federal agencies was to stand for something more than different-colored threat levels, it would have to forge a new identity that embraced all its various divisions. The newest cabinet agency sought to create that identity through a standard business tactic: it brought in marketing consultants.

Susan Neely, one of Ridge's closest aides, hired Landor Associates, inventors of the FedEx name and the British Petroleum sunflower, to rebrand DHS, which Landor described in a confidential briefing as "a disparate organization with a lack of focus." The *Washington Post*'s Susan Glasser and Michael Grunwald reported that Landor Associates produced a total makeover for the infant agency in 2003:

> They developed a new DHS typeface (Joanna, with modifications) and color scheme (cool gray, red and hints of "punched-up" blue). They debated new uniforms for its armies of agents and focus-group-tested a new seal designed to convey "strength" and "gravitas." The department even got its own lapel pin, which was given to all 180,000 of its employees— with Ridge's signature—to celebrate its "brand launch" that June.
>
> "It's got to have its own story," Neely explained.[22]

But this superficial exercise in branding did nothing to overcome bureaucratic inertia. The department's lack of clout within the administration was made obvious in one symbolic moment over Memorial Day weekend in 2004. U.S. attorney general John Ashcroft warned the public of a dangerous terrorist threat after Ridge had identified the same moment as relatively tranquil. Bush ordered Secretary Ridge to endorse the Justice Department's reading of the threat meter.[23]

The existential question might be posed another way. Where did the realm of homeland security begin and end? And what was "homeland security"? The Homeland Security Act of 2002 did not provide a definition, but it implied that defending the homeland encompassed much more than terrorism prevention and extended to emergency response to natural disasters.[24] Yet the official National Strategy for Homeland Security, unveiled in July 2002 after eight months of deliberation, offered a narrower view. In its second sentence it proclaimed the purpose to be "to mobilize and organize our nation to secure the US homeland from terrorist attacks," and on page fourteen it defined homeland security as "a concerted national effort to prevent terrorist attacks within the United States, reduce America's vulnerability to terrorism, and minimize the damage and recover from attacks that do occur."[25] In other words, homeland security was counterterrorism.

The first two prongs of homeland security, thus defined, appear to overlap with DOD's responsibilities. To establish a clear division of labor, DOD distinguishes homeland defense, the Pentagon's responsibility, from homeland security, the realm of DHS leadership. Yet maintaining that strict division is complicated. Testifying before the 9/11 Commission after the creation of DHS, Assistant Secretary of Defense Peter Verga reported in January 2004 that the Pentagon leadership itself decided, after lengthy internal assessment of the Posse Comitatus Act (the legislation limiting the use of military forces for law enforcement on U.S. soil), that the Act "does not unduly restrict the President's discretion to use the military as he deems necessary to respond to exceptional circumstances." The one critical caveat, Verga continued, is that the military may provide support only if that action does not adversely affect U.S. military preparedness at home and abroad. The distinction between homeland defense and homeland security, therefore, is ultimately a matter for presidential decision.[26]

What this means in practice is that any homeland security task can be assigned to DOD when the president deems it desirable. But how, then, are DOD and DHS to collaborate on a routine basis? The DOD currently pursues a three-point strategy for homeland defense: the DOD should "lead, support, and enable."[27] "Enable" refers to helping other agencies get better at what they do. To that end, the DOD has organized attendance at DOD schools for DHS personnel.[28] Beyond that, however, DOD and DHS officials do not regularly interact outside the formal interagency process, which by law is overseen by the president's national security advisor.

The artificial line drawn between the realms of homeland security and homeland defense inevitably left plenty of gray area, as the new institution sought to establish its realms of jurisdiction. As retired DHS and Immigration and Naturalization Service official Joe Cuddihy put it, "I wish I had a nickel for every time I heard someone from DHS headquarters say, 'Is that ours?'"[29]

None of this is to suggest that proper backing from the White House would have solved all of DHS's problems. But there could have been greater awareness that announcing a new department does not automatically produce a team committed to shared goals. Absent proper support at the highest levels, Secretary Ridge could not possibly have consolidated the integration of the department or asserted its prerogatives in competition with other departments. Secretary Ridge had no choice but to fight the Global War on Terror while simultaneously overseeing a merger of unprecedented proportions. The Government Accountability Office designated DHS's transformation a high-risk area in 2003 and continued to deem it such in 2005, maintaining that "significant management challenges remain."[30]

The one thing on which everyone could agree is that the current homeland security system wasn't working. In November 2002 Congress and the president created the National Commission on Terrorist Attacks upon the United States—the 9/11 Commission. They assigned it the task of examining the facts and context of the September 11 attacks, identifying the lessons, and issuing recommendations that might prevent a repetition of such an event. The 9/11 Commission's 2004 final report aptly described America's foreign policy infrastructure as having been "designed generations ago for a world that no longer exists." It may be true that "good people can overcome bad structures," the report warned, but "they should not have to."[31]

In the 9/11 Commission's recommendations, the new Department of Homeland Security was not singled out as a prominent player in the unity-of-effort agenda. National defense was first and foremost the responsibility of the Department of Defense.[32] In fact, what is most striking in hindsight about the 9/11 Commission report is the secondary role DHS was to play in securing the nation's citizens. The impression created in the eyes of the public at the time of the new department's creation could not have been more different. The 9/11 Commission's successor organization, the 9/11 Public Discourse Project, issued a report card in December 2005 evaluating the administration's progress on implementing the recommendations the commission had issued in 2004. The administration received no grade higher than a B, and it was given D's and F's in seventeen of the forty-one areas the commission assessed.[33]

Taken together, the three reports depicted a nation still asleep at the wheel. The *National Journal* examined fourteen of the seventeen D or F grades in the commission's report card to determine why the government had failed to implement so many of the recommendations. The major obstacles to realizing the 9/11 Commission's vision, it found, were "a Congress resistant to institutional change; a bureaucracy that bucks new ideas; lack of money; lack of leadership; special interests that have the ear of Congress or the White House; and, finally, an inability to accurately see how the United States is perceived abroad."[34]

One example of how these recommendations were undermined is Congress's program to help train and equip police officers, firefighters, and other emergency personnel. After the attacks on the World Trade Center and the Pentagon, Congress created several grant programs for training these personnel in emergency response to acts of terrorism, an idea that made sense. But rural states such as Wyoming and Alaska received more money per capita than did New York, a state with more likely targets. The 9/11 Commission recommended simply revamping the funding formula, calling this reform a "no-brainer." But the change was repeatedly blocked in Congress, as every district wanted its share of the pork. To be sure, homeland security should be devoted to the protection of all American citizens, but if money is to be deployed effectively, the flow of dollars must be guided by some assessment of risk.[35]

The commission's recommendation to create one joint bicameral intelligence panel with both authorization and appropriation power provides another good example of how the protection of turf undermined badly needed reform. House and Senate appropriators did not support the reform for a variety of reasons, but the one that united them was that it would have taken some of their power and given it to the new bicameral body. After the intelligence reform bill passed in 2004, recommendations for declassifying the intelligence budget were staunchly opposed by the Pentagon. Why? Declassifying this budget would have strengthened the new national intelligence director at the expense of the secretary of defense.[36]

The same fate befell the commission's recommendation that the CIA and FBI improve information-sharing. Most experts agree that the CIA and FBI could have caught the 9/11 plotters before they boarded their various planes had the two services shared information. Yet the commission gave the government a D on improving information-sharing. Turf protection partly explained this failure, but lingering Cold War thinking about national security also played a role. During the Cold War, information had to be compartmentalized to keep it from the Soviets. A strict domestic/foreign division prevailed for intelligence, with the FBI in charge of the former and the CIA the latter. With the Soviet Union long gone and an information revolution in full swing, such strict barriers became counterproductive, yet they persisted because powerful institutions had been defined around them.

DHS's ongoing accountability problems were made worse by dysfunctional congressional oversight. Congress has yet to establish clear lines of authority for homeland security authorization and appropriations. The Justice and Defense Departments have had those clear lines, but Homeland Security, with its diverse conglomeration of agencies with multiple interwoven purposes, still does not have the same for its dealings with Congress. DHS currently answers to no less than one hundred congressional committees and subcommittees, which means that DHS is a far cry from dealing with a single authorizing committee. Until that is in place, Congress cannot fairly ask the secretary of homeland security whether the department has adequate resources to protect against terrorist attacks or hold the secretary responsible for its performance.[37]

The common denominator of all of these problems is the power of entrenched bureaucratic interests to undercut badly needed reforms. Those who hold power fear losing any of it through reform. Founding an enormous new bureaucracy was one way of combating vested interests. But absent a clear White House vision of how the new configuration was to function, the result was only further dysfunction. The same forces that stymied the implementation of the 9/11 Commission reforms also thwarted efforts to render DHS effective. The issues surrounding terrorism prevention are so complicated and multidimensional that it is easy enough for those with power to construct reasonable arguments as to why reforms that threaten institutional or personal self-interest are not vital. The 9/11 Commission and its successor organization fought valiantly to overcome this dynamic, but ultimately failed.

Assessing this history with the benefit of hindsight, one cannot help but wonder whether the costs of mounting DHS outweighed the anticipated benefits. The desire to do something is understandable, but was unveiling another large bureaucracy the right thing to do? It only exacerbated existing turf wars and increased political maneuvering. The irony is that if the Bush administration had stood by its ideological convictions and resisted adding another bureaucracy to the mix, perhaps greater attention could have been focused on the real task at hand: engaging the American people in the cause of protecting themselves and their homeland.

Homeland Security Beyond the Beltway

Secretary Ridge had a daunting set of turf wars to fight inside the beltway, but keeping America safe from another terrorist attack demanded that he focus attention on action beyond the beltway. When our principal enemies are no longer other states, the means to national security must change accordingly. Since 70 percent of the nation's critical infrastructure is in private hands, the homeland simply cannot be secured without extensive public-private collaboration, as well as vertical cooperation between federal and state/local authorities.

The overarching goal was clear: to prevent another terrorist attack on U.S. soil. The way to make that happen, however, could take many forms. For instance, at the Los Angeles/Long Beach port complex—the country's busiest seaport and hence a prime target for terrorists—no less than fifteen different federal, state, and municipal agencies and dozens of labor unions and private firms all play vital roles in terrorism prevention and emergency response, yet no one body is in charge of them all. Coordinating their activities presents a three-dimensional challenge for integration. DHS had to encourage horizontal collaboration across federal agencies; vertical collaboration between federal bodies and their state and local counterparts; and public-private collaboration. This process must be duplicated at many thousands of different facilities, all with different needs and governance structures, across the country.[38]

Not that the will to work together was lacking. The comptroller general of the United States, David A. Walker, reported to Congress in April 2002—before DHS was created—that federal agencies, state and local governments, and the private sector were all eagerly awaiting guidance on how best to coordinate their mission and make a contribution to enhanced security. With the memory of September 11 still fresh, citizens and public officials alike were primed to be led. Walker stressed the importance of defining "homeland security" and clarifying the appropriate roles of federal, state, and local government in the president's national strategy for homeland security to ensure accountability and prevent duplication of effort. Partnerships with the private sector would be critical to the successful achievement of these goals.[39] Yet the clear definition Walker called for remained elusive.

Effective public-private cooperation relies on government having a clear understanding of what only government can do well, the so-called inherently governmental functions. The creation of the Transportation Security Agency (TSA) in November 2001 provides a good example of Congress drawing a clear line and declaring a category of work to be inherently governmental. Before 9/11, the screening of passengers and baggage at airports was not a federal responsibility but belonged to airports and airliners operating under Federal Aviation Administration oversight. They typically contracted the work out to the lowest bidder. The Department of

Transportation inspector general had already determined that security was lax at major airports. In establishing the TSA immediately after 9/11, the November 2001 Aviation and Transportation Security Act mandated that all screeners at airports be federal employees and required them to clear a series of hurdles to qualify for the job: they had to speak and read English, be U.S. citizens, have no criminal record, have a high school diploma, and complete a course of classroom instruction and on-the-job training.[40]

Putting together the new sixty-thousand-person TSA workforce from scratch was a significant challenge. To get the job done, the Department of Transportation hired contractors in 2002 to help them do the hiring and to help them assess optimal placement of security checkpoints at individual airports. With that extra help, the TSA workforce successfully met the demands of Congress by the end of the calendar year.

As a result, while the individuals who check documents at American airports are usually contractors, those at the security checkpoints screening baggage and body are all federal employees.[41] Interestingly, even though Europe in general carves out a bigger realm of authority for its public sector, the screeners at European airports are typically contractors.[42] In March 2003, the newly staffed TSA became a component of the equally new DHS.

The 2006 Dubai Ports World scandal brought another congressional revolt against privatization. When there is an enormous gap between how elites and the American public see the line between public and private action, the public will generally prevail. Ports are frequently owned or operated by private parties, a circumstance that caused little concern until a United Arab Emirates state-owned company, Dubai Ports World, tried in February 2006 to purchase ports in New York and New Jersey from a British company. A public outcry erupted at the thought of an Arab country running American ports, placing Bush, who had supported the deal, in the hot seat. Since the Coast Guard and DHS would oversee port security, and only the port's operation would be outsourced, the administration did not see a problem. Congress disagreed. On March 8, 2006, The House Appropriations Committee voted 62–2 to block the deal. A Fox News poll showed that 69 percent of Americans agreed with the committee.[43] With the Senate threatening a similar vote and the president poised to veto the legislation, Dubai Ports World backed out of the deal and announced it would sell its American holdings and turn over operation of the ports to an American entity.

When Congress speaks through a vote, as it did on airport screeners and the Dubai Ports World deal, it is clear where accountability resides. But these two examples were exceptions to the rule. Most realms of homeland security lacked such clear authority. The ideal DHS would be a model of networked governance, leading federal/state-local, interagency, and public-private collaboration. The trick for DHS was to render that web of action transparent, so that every node in the network knew its role and relationship to others. Transparency and accountability are necessary conditions for effective public-private collaboration; outsiders need to know what particular piece of government they should partner with to get the job done.[44]

Instead, haphazard contracting carried the day. When Congress did not explicitly declare a function inherently governmental, DHS tended to assume that it wasn't and to outsource whenever possible. In its first year of operations the DHS spent $3.5 billion on federal contracts. By 2006, this spending had grown to $15.1 billion, an increase of 337 percent. From 2005 to 2006 alone, procurement spending at DHS increased by 51 percent.[45] Figure 6 captures the explosive growth of contracting related to homeland security.

Data for 2007 and 2008 was still a moving target and hence unreliable as this book went to press. For example, the aggregate numbers gleaned from the FPDS reporting system used in the chart below do not match those from USAspending.gov. These glaring discrepancies show that the federal government still has considerable work to do in rendering its accounting practices fully transparent and its reporting accurate. But the growth trajectory is the same, regardless of the data source. All numbers currently available indicate that this exponential growth in contracting has continued unabated.

The logic fueling the contracting frenzy is easy to understand. Homeland security cannot be commanded; it must be inspired. The private sector and local authorities are critical to this effort. Therefore, DHS can appear to be advancing its agenda by simply channeling funds to the private sector and local government. That reasoning for what needs to be done is sound, but how the money was spent and who got to spend it should have mattered as well. In the wholly understandable rush to get things done, it didn't.

Laissez-Faire Homeland Security

It is impossible to know how well DHS might have managed the consolidation of its many constituent parts without the backdrop of concurrent wars in Afghanistan and Iraq and the administration's Global War on Terror. The challenge of managing a merger of this magnitude while waging war was formidable. But the department's actual performance, especially given

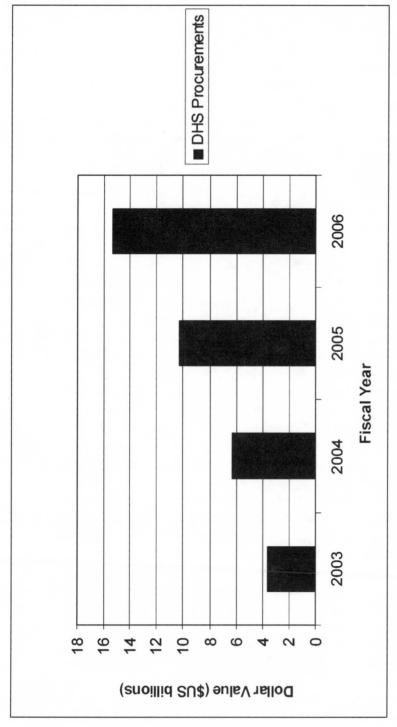

Figure 6. Department of Homeland Security procurements, 2003–2006 (Source: Federal Procurement Data System. Graphic: Carolann Davis)

the seriousness of its mission, was scandalous. Billions in federal funds flowed into DHS, but since neither the original Patriot Act nor the legislation establishing DHS ever made reference to relative risk, billions of dollars flowed out with neither risk assessment nor planning.

The mix of a well-funded new bureaucracy with the antigovernment ethos of the Bush White House was nothing short of toxic. Laissez-faire homeland security caused lots of raised eyebrows. The District of Columbia used part of its DHS money to buy leather jackets for government employees and to send sanitation workers to self-improvement seminars. The city of Newark, New Jersey, purchased air-conditioned garbage trucks with homeland security grants. Columbus, Ohio, bought body armor for its fire department dogs.[46] The fire department of Princeton, New Jersey, invested in Nautilus exercise equipment, free weights, and a Bowflex exercise machine.

Yet the department's spending has been closely monitored, and no audit has ever found evidence of systematic fraud or abuse. That is because purchases such as the ones listed above were within the guidelines that DHS dispensed with the funds. For some reason, the federal government did not set preparedness standards to require state and local governments to deploy federal funds effectively. Perhaps this is because DHS leadership was distracted by the other challenges on its plate and simply wanted to get federal funds put to use as soon as possible. Perhaps Ridge wanted to devolve decisions on how the money was to be spent down to those closest to particular threats. Neither explains why locations like Columbus and Princeton were receiving large grants from the federal government for terrorism prevention in the first place. What really drove this less-than-strategic deployment of federal funds was that Congress had provided every state with a guaranteed level of grant money regardless of the degree of risk, with the result that less-populated areas received disproportionate funding. Of the top ten grant recipients through 2005, only the District of Columbia also appeared on the top ten list of areas at risk.[47]

Not surprisingly, accountability problems were a persistent feature of DHS contracting. According to former DHS inspector Clark Kent Ervin, the DHS procurement office had "so few people expert in contract procurement, the private sector was able to take the department for a ride."[48]

The most glaring example of outsourcing without sufficient oversight was the Deepwater scandal. Launched in 2002, the Coast Guard's Deepwater program is a twenty-five-year, $24 billion plan—the most comprehensive in the service's history—to modernize and update its fleet of boats and aircraft. Several things about the Coast Guard's approach raised Gov-

ernment Accountability Office concerns from the start. First, the program
was a performance-based acquisition, which means that it was structured
around results rather than processes. Without appropriate oversight, GAO
warned, performance-based acquisition is a recipe for cost overruns and
poor-quality outcomes.[49]

More disturbing still, since results trumped process, the Coast Guard
delegated overall management of the project to a contractor. Integrated
Coast Guard Systems (ICGS), a joint venture of Lockheed Martin and
Northrop Grumman, was assigned oversight of both the deployment of
federal funds and general assessment of their impact. In other words, ICGS
was assigned the task of choosing who should perform the work as well
as the task of evaluating itself. Not surprisingly, ICGS chose Lockheed
and Northrop to do the lion's share of the work. Captain Kevin Jarvis,
commander of the Coast Guard's Engineering and Logistics Center when
the program was launched, described the unprecedented arrangement to
CBS's *60 Minutes* in the following way: "People say that this is like the fox
watching the henhouse. And it's worse than that. . . . It's where the government asked the fox to develop the security system for the henhouse. Then
told 'em, 'You're gonna do it. You know, by the way, we'll give you the security code to the system and we'll tell you when we're on vacation.'"[50]

After its failures were reported by the *New York Times,* the Deepwater
program became a poster child for outsourcing gone awry. The Government Accountability Office's concerns had been on target. The first phase
of the Deepwater modernization program involved converting rusty
110-foot patrol boats into more versatile 123-foot cutters. But that enterprise
was cancelled after the first eight ships produced were found to have hull
cracks and engine failures that essentially made them unseaworthy. In another piece of the contract, plans to build a new class of 147-foot ships with
an innovative hull were halted after design flaws were discovered. And the
first completed national security cutter, a $564 million venture unveiled in
November 2006, turned out to cost double what had been originally projected and to have structural weaknesses that both threatened its safety and
limited its life span. Four years into the program, the Coast Guard had
fewer operational boats and ships than it had when Deepwater was first
launched.[51] These snowballing problems turned what had originally been a
$17 billion program to a $24 billion one—and the prospect of additional
cost overruns loomed large. Anthony D'Armiento, a systems engineer who
had worked on the project, told the *New York Times* in December 2006,
"This is the fleecing of America. . . . It is the worst contract arrangement
I've seen in all my 20 plus years in naval engineering."[52] In another first,

former Lockheed Martin project manager Michael DeKort claimed that corruption was so rife that his only recourse was to post a whistle-blower video on YouTube.[53]

Some of Deepwater's shortcomings followed from the politics of congressional appropriations. Large firms like Lockheed and Northrop have powerful lobbying arms, which helped the Coast Guard obtain full funding for Deepwater that it might not otherwise have obtained. A close look at the program's strongest supporters in Congress reveals a quid pro quo chain that suggests other factors besides homeland security at work in the Deepwater vision. Democratic congressman Gene Taylor of Mississippi and Republican congressman Frank LoBiondo of New Jersey formed the Congressional Coast Guard Caucus in the late 1990s with four members. By 2006, it had seventy-five. Taylor's district is home to Northrop Grumman's shipyard in Pascagoula, Mississippi. LoBiondo's district is home to the Coast Guard's national training center, and he is also one of the top congressional recipients of Lockheed contributions.[54]

In April 2007 the Coast Guard announced that it was taking over the role of lead systems integrator from Integrated Coast Guard Services, much to the embarrassment of Lockheed and Northrop. Admiral Thad W. Allen, the Coast Guard commandant, told the *New York Times,* "We understand all too well what has been ailing us within Deepwater for the past five years. . . . We've relied too much on contractors to do the work of government as a result of tightening budgets." A spokeswoman for ICGS answered that the Coast Guard had always been in charge of Deepwater.[55] Yet since the original decision to outsource had resulted from a lack of capacity and expertise in-house, simply ending the contract did not resolve the problems the Deepwater program brought to light.[56]

These deficiencies led to maddening job conditions at DHS and astonishing homeland security–related business opportunities. Naomi Klein's book *The Shock Doctrine* gives a partial list:

> John Ashcroft, former attorney general and prime mover behind the Patriot Act, now heads up the Ashcroft Group, specializing in helping homeland security firms procure federal contracts. Tom Ridge, the first head of the Department of Homeland Security, is now at Ridge Global and an advisor to the communication technology company Lucent, which is active in the security sector. Rudy Giuliani, the former New York mayor and hero of the September 11 response, started Giuliani Partners four months later to sell his services as a crisis consultant. Richard Clarke, counterterrorism czar under Clinton and Bush and an outspoken critic of the administration, is now chairman of Good Harbor Consulting, specializing in

homeland security and counterterrorism. James Woolsey, head of the CIA until 1995, is now at Paladin Capital Group, a private equity firm that invests in homeland security companies, and a vice president at Booz Allen, one of the leaders in the homeland security industry. Joe Allbaugh, head of FEMA on September 11, cashed out just eighteen months later to start New Bridge Strategies, promising to be the "bridge" between business and the lucrative world of government contracts and investment opportunities in Iraq. He was replaced by Michael Brown, who bolted after only two years to start Michael D. Brown LLC, specializing in disaster preparedness.[57]

Yes, you've read that right: the same Michael Brown who headed the Federal Emergency Management Agency (FEMA) when Hurricane Katrina struck now serves as a private sector consultant for disaster preparedness. Tom Ridge accepted a job advising TechRadium on Immediate Response Information System (IRIS) technology in January 2008.[58] Small wonder that the exit ramp from DHS to the private sector is heavily congested just six years after the department's creation.

What Hurricane Katrina Revealed

With the revolving door between DHS and the private sector spinning at an unprecedented rate, DHS was put to its first official test in late August 2005 and was found lacking. Because government officials had not stressed the storm's likely severity, evacuation and other preparations were delayed and incomplete.[59] The result was devastating. The world looked on in disbelief at televised images of New Orleans's most vulnerable citizens struggling to survive in what had become an anarchic war zone. Such chaos was familiar in the developing world, but to see it in a major city of the world's most powerful nation was truly shocking. Faced with the possibility of a like-sized disaster in the political realm, even Bush was finally forced to speak out against FEMA and remove Brown from his post in September 2005.

FEMA's chaotic rescue efforts were well documented and publicized throughout the world. The problems that turned Katrina into a catastrophe—an unclear chain of command, lack of an incident management center, incompatible or unavailable communications, lack of hospital space and supplies, and a resettlement plan plagued by waste, fraud, and abuse—were symptoms of more general problems within DHS.[60] While DHS's and FEMA's roles in disaster relief had never been properly articulated in the homeland security strategy, they were clearly meant to be the key players, yet they seemed powerless to seize control of the emergency situation. What had gone wrong?

According to a White House review commission, chaired by the president's homeland security advisor, Frances Fragos Townsend, the failure to act decisively was a product of current institutional arrangements. "At the most fundamental level," The Townsend Commission argued in its February 2006 final report, "the current system fails to define federal responsibility for national preparedness in catastrophic events."[61] Though FEMA was ostensibly within the DHS fold, it hadn't been clear who was to lead coordination efforts in a national emergency, the head of FEMA or the secretary of homeland security. In addition, many employees had left FEMA following the DHS merger, which had taken away the FEMA director's cabinet secretary status. The Townsend Commission thought the emergency response responsibility should reside with DHS and traced a vision of command and control for homeland security that would mirror what was already in place for national security.[62] Creating the requisite unity of effort required the reinforcement of the secretary's authority as the government's "preparedness and incident manager," something he had possessed on paper but not in practice.[63]

The Townsend Commission's report concluded with a call for "Transforming National Preparedness," a companion volume of sorts for both transformational diplomacy and transformational development. Getting that job done required setting two urgent priorities: "We must institutionalize a comprehensive National Preparedness System and concurrently foster a new, robust Culture of Preparedness."

But just who was "we"? The White House report is astonishing for the questions it avoided answering directly. First, who was to blame for the Katrina debacle? Wasn't it the job of the head of the Federal Emergency Management Agency to manage emergencies? If not, did that authority belong to the secretary of homeland security? Was an administration that presided over the creation of an enormous new bureaucracy responsible for having failed to articulate how the new structure was to interact with the old? Second, if the right reforms could be instituted, who should lead on national preparedness? Should it be the national security advisor, the homeland security advisor (Townsend), or the secretary of homeland security? In the end, the White House simply urged all the players to do better without mapping out how that might best be done and without really fingering anyone for having dropped the ball.

The Townsend Commission was clear on what it did not want. It warned against relying on Defense to be the critical player in homeland security. While Hurricane Katrina demonstrated DOD's responsiveness under fire, as it stepped up to fill the gap DHS inaction created, the lesson of Katrina cannot simply be, "Let the Pentagon do it."[64] Yet the Pentagon took away lessons of its own from the Katrina experience, pursuing a range of reforms to address perceived shortcomings, especially with respect to handling information flows during an emergency.[65] Homeland security secretary Chertoff publicly endorsed the findings of the White House report and announced that DHS had already begun to take action on its recommendations.[66]

While DHS never issued its own account of what went wrong, the House of Representatives also established a bipartisan committee to explore the Katrina catastrophe. "The preparation for and response to Hurricane Katrina," the committee's executive summary in February 2006 argued, "show that we are still an analog government for a digital age." Many of the problems that well-intentioned institutions and individuals encountered stemmed from "information gaps." The committee's 363-page report was titled "A Failure of Initiative," and the biggest cause of this failure was information deficits.[67] The executive summary is worth perusing online, if only for its bizarre structure. Rather than listing points for reform, it relates its argument in a series of sentence fragments, as though its authors were writing a poem.

The House report made DHS its scapegoat and also faulted the president for being slow to get involved.[68] The disaster was not due to some individual failure, the report proclaimed, but to "organizational and societal failures of initiative. . . . We are left scratching our heads at the range of inefficiency and ineffectiveness that characterized government behavior before and after the storm."[69] The congressional investigation called for greater collaboration and unity of purpose, without hinting at how these virtues might best be cultivated.

Some things actually went right in the response to Hurricane Katrina, and there are lessons in both sorts of stories. By all accounts, the private sector rose to the challenge with little prompting. While giving low marks to the federal response, the Townsend report praised the response of such companies as Wal-Mart and Home Depot, which helped transport badly needed supplies to victims.[70] According to the House Bipartisan Committee, charitable organizations like the Red Cross "performed heroically."[71]

Yet the companies that cleaned up Katrina were also familiar faces from the Iraq occupation. Right after the levees broke, Blackwater received a no-bid contract from DHS: $409,000 for guarding the temporary morgue in Baton Rouge. More contracts followed. By June 2006, Blackwater had received a total of $73 million for its hurricane cleanup assistance.[72] As Naomi Klein wrote, "Within weeks, the Gulf Coast became a domestic laboratory for the same kind of government-run-by-contractors that had been pioneered in Iraq. The companies that snatched up the biggest contracts were the familiar Baghdad gang: Halliburton's KBR unit had a $60 million gig to reconstruct military bases along the coast. Blackwater was hired to protect FEMA employees from looters. Parsons, infamous for its sloppy Iraq work, was brought in for a major bridge construction project in Mississippi. Fluor, Shaw, Bechtel, CH2M Hill—all top contractors in Iraq —were hired by government to provide mobile homes to evacuees just ten days after the levees broke. Their contracts ended up totaling $3.4 billion, no open bidding required."[73]

Hurricane Katrina ultimately revealed that in the areas of infrastructure protection and emergency response DHS had failed to take even the most basic steps toward the necessary reforms. As Chertoff commented in June 2007, "The greatest lesson of Katrina was the day before the storm hits, if you don't have the plans and the training and the exercising done, you're lost. No matter how good you are, you're going to have problems, because people will simply never have worked together."[74] Yet even without optimal government leadership, many private organizations and the Pentagon performed admirably. Partly this was because top military officials relied on news reports for information to plan and deploy resources—the same news sources that were readily available to private citizens.[75] Though it had access to the same sources, DHS did not rise to the challenge.

To be sure, the federal and state civilian response teams were short-handed during the crisis and depended on private contractors as well as on the Pentagon to assist the relief effort. The National Guard, too, was a vital part of Mississippi and Louisiana's recovery project.[76] Yet the response of the executive branch in the storm's aftermath did not focus on civilian institutions. Instead, Bush declared: "It is now clear that a challenge on this scale requires greater federal authority and a broader role for the armed forces—the institution of our government most capable of massive logistical operations on a moment's notice."[77] In a pattern that became all too familiar, when the president needed an efficient response, the Pentagon became our nation's go-to institution. Whether DOD wanted the additional responsibility or not, laissez-faire homeland security strengthened the hand of an already powerful Pentagon.

The Urgency of Collaboration

From the start of the debates over the shape and function of DHS, the Bush administration insisted that it would not endorse security regulations that would impose costs on American business. The private sector would voluntarily increase security, the White House reasoned, both to protect its assets and to reduce insurance costs. This blind faith in the goodwill and capacity for long-term thinking of business seems utterly naïve today. Not surprisingly, spontaneous private sector activity to secure its infrastructure was slow in coming. The years since September 11 have clearly shown that, absent strong government leadership, the private sector will pursue business as usual, and our nation's infrastructure and citizens will remain at serious risk.

The most important reason that bolstering homeland security is so daunting follows directly from its status as a public good. As the economist Amartya Sen defines it, public goods are things that people consume together rather than separately; governments cannot rely exclusively on market mechanisms to deliver them reliably.[78] The "tragedy of the commons" tells us that laissez-faire approaches to homeland security will always come up short. Without government intervention, firms have no incentive to take individual action, since investing in protective measures for the part of the infrastructure that they own places them at a competitive disadvantage vis-à-vis those who do not do the same.

Realizing that homeland security is a public good is a necessary prerequisite for devising policies that will actually enhance national preparedness. Instead of fostering collaborative mechanisms for transcending the tragedy of the commons, the hands-off approach of the Bush administration created an arena for corruption and self-enrichment that did little to improve the protection of vital infrastructure. The concept of homeland security as a public good that could be eroded by business's pursuit of its short-term interest did not make even a cameo appearance in the national homeland security strategy. Neither did the idea that the private sector has an important role to play. Instead, the Bush White House erected an enormous bureaucracy, which implied just the opposite: that the federal government can, all on its own, meet the terrorist threat, and that DHS is responsible for all of homeland security.[79] That action conveyed the sense that the right commands, issued with the right degree of government authority to the right government entities, will keep us safe. But just as the laissez-faire approach to public-private partnerships will not get us where we need to go, top-down commands will not deliver what we need. As strategist Thomas Barnett points out, "Our homeland is only as secure as every other homeland to which it is connected."[80]

With the White House failing to define homeland security properly, partnerships with the private sector proved difficult to forge. Well before 9/11, the Clinton administration had actually begun to define a security role for the private sector when it created the Commission on Critical Infrastructure Protection in 1998 to recommend a national strategy for protecting critical infrastructure from physical and cyber threats.[81] But two issues in particular have slowed progress on this front. First, the specter of antitrust litigation arises whenever business and government explicitly cooperate. In the information age, as Microsoft discovered, the cost of these cases in public perception vastly exceeds the legal expenses. Second, business will always be reluctant to be candid about potential security vulnerabilities within its operations, since it does not want to be liable in the event of some terrorist exploiting them. In sum, companies answering to their stockholders can ill afford to expose their vulnerabilities publicly or set themselves up for antitrust actions.

To remove these obstacles, the Council on Foreign Relations' Hart-Rudman Commission in 2002 proposed enacting an "Omnibus Anti-Red Tape Law" that would give three big exemptions to public-private collaboration on homeland security. A fast-track security clearance process would be created so that "secret-level" classified information could be shared with the private sector; a Freedom of Information Act exemption would be granted to leaders in critical infrastructure industries if they agreed to share information with government about security vulnerabilities; and those leaders from the private sector who participated in business-government task forces would be exempt from antitrust legislation.[82]

Most homeland security experts agree that business still has not been engaged to rise to the challenge. The title of a March 2006 Council on Foreign Relations special report on the topic "Neglected Defense" captures the government's lack of progress to date on mobilizing the private sector in support of common interests. The Council on Foreign Relations report noted that the federal reorganization that produced DHS had actually made it *more* rather than less difficult for the private sector to cooperate with the federal government on security. It also pointed out that information sharing and overall investment in private sector initiatives had been modest, and that Washington had failed to provide either incentives for cooperation or standards for securing critical infrastructure. This is unfortunate, as government and business often share an interest in securing standards; when standards produce a more predictable business climate, they are in the best interests of business.[83] In an earlier evaluation, the Progressive Policy Institute found that the Bush administration's homeland security strategy had failed to harness the American entrepreneurial spirit to the cause; it gave the administration a D grade for its overall efforts.[84]

While progress on business-government collaboration has been limited, there have been several promising initiatives that involve cooperation with foreign governments. The Container Security Initiative (CSI) is a good example of a homeland security effort that builds on cooperation with foreign governments. Under CSI, U.S. customs and border protection officials can prescreen U.S.-bound shipping cargo at the foreign port from which it departs. This venture is built on reciprocity; foreign customs agencies that participate in CSI are allowed to send their own officials to the United States to inspect cargo bound for their home countries. Ships coming from ports that meet CSI minimum-security requirements, of which there are currently fifty worldwide, face less stringent inspection standards on arrival in the United States. The lesser likelihood of security delays means that shipping companies are more likely to choose CSI ports, which in turn encourages non-CSI ports to improve security to attract business.[85] With CSI fully operational, U.S. customs can focus its attention on cargo arriving from non-CSI ports.

DHS has established other promising programs as well. The Customs-Trade Partnership Against Terrorism (C-TPAT), which works in concert with CSI, focuses on persuading private transport companies to improve their own security in exchange for shorter waits at U.S. borders. C-TPAT also works with foreign customs agencies and the World Customs Organization to create uniform security standards. Operation Safe Commerce helps shipping companies find cost-effective security improvements. The Smart and Secure Trade Lanes Initiative uses global positioning system (GPS) technologies to track container ships.[86] In general, the idea of swapping private investment in security for gains in efficiency is a model that might be easily replicated in other sectors of homeland security, such as transportation.[87]

Some DHS officials understand what is needed. When Michael P. Jackson, deputy secretary of homeland security, addressed potential bidders on the Secure Border Initiative in 2006, he told them they were receiving an unusual invitation: "We're asking you to come back and tell us how to do our business."[88] Yet resources have not been allocated to support a radically new approach. DHS opened an Office of the Private Sector, headed by Alfonso Martinez-Fonts, assistant secretary for the private sector, in November 2005.[89] The Web site for the Office of the Private Sector is impressively inviting, but in June 2007 the office comprised all of twenty people: thirteen federal employees, two Boren scholars, three contract employee economists, and one intern.[90] The DHS Web site also features an "Open for Business" section, which is supposed to centralize information "to let every business in America know how to work with the Department of Homeland Security."[91] In short, a basic foundation is in place for harnessing private sector energy and resources, but it is still viewed as one area among many, not as the umbrella issue it should rightfully be.

This shortcoming is not unique to DHS. Taken as a whole, America's national security architecture is not designed to generate productive public-private partnerships. National security and homeland security have become indistinguishable, yet the homeland security and national security budget accounts remain completely different tracks—an arrangement that ensures that debates will preempt shared purposes. As homeland security expert Steve Flynn has pointed out, no other country in the world approaches national security in such a bifurcated fashion. Rather, national security is first and foremost about protecting the homeland, and secondarily for defending interests abroad. The American division of labor, which assigns the federal government responsibility for the struggle abroad, and state and local government and the private sector the job of protecting American citizens at home—the laissez-faire approach—is not only anomalous but completely inadequate.[92]

Proposals aimed at integration emerge from a sense that excessive complexity in the U.S. national security architecture has impeded progress in meeting the terrorist threat. Our sprawling current architecture treats as discrete issue areas that are in reality overlapping jurisdictions. These arrangements discourage cooperation across all the public/private, foreign/domestic, and federal/state-local government divides. Adding a brand new bureaucracy and a Homeland Security Council to the mix further complicated matters. The first national strategy for Homeland Security articulated a broadly inclusive vision of partnership for homeland security, but, on every conceivable measure, our industrial-era institutions and budgetary structures have hindered the attainment of that goal. As a witness at a Senate hearing noted, "The most important challenge for the Department of Homeland Security is to weave ever greater levels of security into the fabric of American society."[93]

So how might this circle be squared? The trick is to get the federal government as a whole to embrace a wholly new approach that exploits the power and initiative of private actors. Government must acknowledge that it cannot attain its objectives unilaterally but must instead leverage the power and ingenuity of nongovernment employees. In so doing, government must accept full responsibility for the provision of public goods such as security, even though optimal solutions can no longer be devised by government alone. While much of its work can be outsourced, government must never outsource oversight.

A good place to start is to realize that, in the Internet world, much of the security ordinary people rely on isn't governmental at all. For example, corporations and individuals alike routinely depend on private-sector devised solutions for network security. In such a world, the traditional, hierarchical government mindset simply does not serve the cause of homeland security well.[94] The story of DHS is ultimately a metaphor for the overarching challenge of American security in the information age: how to reinvent and sometimes transcend industrial-era government bureaucracy that often thwarts innovation and saps commitment.

Even if DHS had been optimally organized and integrated like the Pentagon after Goldwater-Nichols, it still wouldn't have been able to do its job, because command and control is ill-equipped to meet twenty-first century security challenges. With the majority of the homeland in private hands, you can't have homeland security without extensive public-private cooperation, and cooperation cannot be proclaimed. The requisite innovation will not follow when people are told what they need to do, regardless of particular context or the personalities involved. Like development, homeland security is best conceptualized as a bottom-up process that the federal government must facilitate but can never mandate or control. That means we need more privatization, not less. But it must be good privatization, where government takes full responsibility in partnership with the private sector, rather than privatization in which government turns over critical tasks to the private sector and then is nowhere to be found when things go wrong.

8

A Postindustrial Foreign Policy

And who will deny that a world in which the wealthy are powerful is still a
better world than one in which only the already powerful can acquire
wealth?
—Friedrich von Hayek, *The Road to Serfdom*

The free development of each is the condition for the free development
of all.
—Karl Marx, *The Communist Manifesto*

Established to confront threats no longer salient, the core institutions of American foreign policy were quietly transformed as they endeavored to adapt to the information age. The preceding chapters have mapped the rise of outsourcing at the State Department, the Pentagon, USAID, and the Department of Homeland Security. These departments' approaches to diplomacy, defense, development, and security ranged widely, but they had one feature in common. Private actors, both for-profit and not-for-profit, increasingly played roles that were once the exclusive preserve of government—so much so that a February 2007 story in the *New York Times* called contractors "a fourth branch of government."[1] A single individual can now make a significant difference in these areas without being on the U.S. government payroll. The proliferation of hybrid organizations that do not fall neatly into the government, business, or nonprofit categories is the institutional manifestation of this new reality.[2]

While reliance on contractors has been especially prominent in the Iraq and Afghanistan interventions, Republicans and Democrats alike have contributed to turning outsourcing into business as usual; what started as a Republican ideal has since been embraced by Democrats. The Clinton administration's campaign to reinvent government implicitly relied on private actors to pick up the slack for a leaner bureaucracy. It was during Clinton's second term that Halliburton nearly doubled the value of its contracts with the federal government, from $1.2 billion to $2.3 billion; those years also happen to be when Dick Cheney was Halliburton's CEO.[3] While the contrast between George W. Bush's foreign policy and Bill Clinton's could not be starker, both pursued their objectives through the private sector as well as through government. Thus, contracting is not a partisan issue. We cannot address the serious problems this book has illuminated simply by restoring Democrats to power.

While it was not a creation of the Republican Party alone, the revolving door between business and the private sector spun far more rapidly in the Bush years, and revelations of corruption and fraud seemed unending. This was no coincidence. The Bush administration's wildly ambitious overseas agenda and its belief that government itself is the problem combined to fuel what I have called laissez-faire outsourcing. Laissez-faire outsourcing meant that government footed the bill and got out of the way. Business was effectively given a blank check to pursue its interests, and the results were nothing short of devastating.

Such laissez-faire contracting undermined American power, but contracting itself was not the cause. Wealth can be put to work in a variety of ways that serve the interests of the United States, with or without direct government involvement. In many instances, keeping government at a distance may be the most prudent strategy. Thus, while the face of government necessarily changes as more governmental functions are outsourced, American global influence and legitimacy need not be a casualty, provided that government assumes its rightful position as chief custodian of the public interest.

Extending America's reach in ways that enhance rather than undermine our prestige and security depends on getting privatization right. This requires us to jettison foreign policy frameworks that celebrate the omnipotence of the state; these frameworks no longer fit the way government actually works. Instead, we need a postindustrial foreign policy, one that dispenses with the notion that the keys to wealth and power are access to natural resources and territory. We need a foreign policy that sees power flowing to the entrepreneurs and opinion shapers, and that sees the future as belonging to those who can harness innovation to serve the common good.

The means of restoring American standing in the world becomes apparent only when the real nature of American strength is properly understood. Because of globalization, firms operating in a highly competitive global environment now need to behave differently. Why should it surprise us that the same is true for states? The number of actors and entities that today conduct America's relations with the world has risen dramatically. We have yet to come to terms with the implications of this development.

The Bush administration behaved as though the United States had a monopoly on power, when that monopoly was confined to just one dimension of power—military might. The country's overall position consequently suffered, in the same way that any firm's position is compromised when it misunderstands its position in the marketplace.

How American Foreign Policy Was Militarized

The principal misconception at the heart of the Bush administration's foreign policy was that it could advance American interests by behaving like a traditional empire—endeavoring to dictate outcomes to the world—rather than upholding the very different enterprise that is the true source of American power and prosperity. The problem was not only hypocrisy—that imperial tactics contradicted the Bush team's stated goals of transformational development and diplomacy—but also a failure of vision. The Bush administration, to all appearances, believed that free individuals are more likely to unleash the creative forces that fuel economic growth but genuinely did not see that its unilateralism was at odds with the very values it sought to promote.

Old-fashioned imperialism pursued in a postimperial milieu had significant consequences for the traditional division of labor between the State Department and the Pentagon. But again, the tale does not begin with the presidency of George W. Bush. America's engagement with the world had grown increasingly militarized long before the wars in Afghanistan and Iraq began. For example, the Clinton administration's policy of engagement and enlargement was spearheaded by military leaders rather than civilian ones, with the military taking on tasks that had previously been delegated to civilian agencies.[4] According to Clinton's former central command chief, General Anthony Zinni, Secretary of Defense William Cohen fully endorsed the military's more active role in engaging the world. Col. Lawrence Wilkerson, who was chief of staff to Colin Powell when he was secretary of state, commented that "when General Zinni was commander, people from the State Department would come to him to get appointments with foreign leaders."[5]

Less inclined to empower the combatant commanders in this fashion, engagement became a dirty word at the Rumsfeld Pentagon.[6] Yet the Pentagon's power relative to civilian agencies continued to grow. By FY 2007, U.S. defense spending was $578 billion while the nonmilitary dimensions of engagement with the world received just $35 billion. Defense spending exceeded civilian spending by more than eighteen to one. The gap further widened in FY2008. DOD's 2008 budget was more than twenty-four times as large as the combined budgets of the State Department and USAID ($750 billion versus $31 billion).[7] In Iraq and Afghanistan, civilian agencies are responsible for just 1.4 percent of U.S. intervention outlays.[8] The proposed 2009 Pentagon budget, the largest in real terms since World War II, was more than 30 percent bigger than when Bush took office.[9]

As these figures collectively demonstrate, the United States has stunning organizational capacity to execute a war, but it does not possess the same capacity for reconstruction.[10] In Iraq, DOD took on roles that had previously been the exclusive domain of the State Department.[11] The Provisional Reconstruction Teams (PRTs) in Iraq and Afghanistan were intended to restore the State Department's role in reconstruction, but since the State Department could not staff them, it remained unclear how pivotal the department could become.[12] And so the allure of just having DOD continue to fill the operational gap became all the more powerful despite the unusual spectacle, in November 2007, of the secretary of defense forcefully urging significant increases in funding for State.[13]

These exhortations notwithstanding, the Pentagon's role shows no signs of diminishing. The 2006 Quadrennial Defense Review, the Pentagon's strategic blueprint, for the first time included stability operations (meaning development), long the purview of USAID, as a core Pentagon mission.[14] One indirect consequence of these new responsibilities has been the concurrent militarization of intelligence. When Congress established the post of director of national intelligence, it meant to integrate and harmonize the sixteen agencies involved in America's intelligence gathering. The effect has been just the opposite: the position has created endless turf wars. To fill the gap, the Pentagon quietly stepped up its own independent intelligence activities.[15] Whenever getting a job done efficiently is the priority, absent a clear vision of limits, the work will devolve to the action department of choice, the Department of Defense.

This book shows how we arrived at the present state of affairs. Assigned tasks traditionally seen as outside its purview and for which it had no relevant expertise, the Pentagon adopted outsourcing as its tool of choice. And since outsourcing is assumed to bring cost savings, why not stretch the taxed budget by letting private actors take care of more and more tasks? Thus, the forces of globalization that have fueled the privatization of American power increased the attractiveness of outsourcing, upsetting established diplomatic practice, which in turn encouraged further outsourcing. The impulse to circumvent government gridlock and turf wars when a job needs to get done can be irresistible. Pentagon primacy has thus gone hand in hand with an expanded role for contractors.

That problem has been further exacerbated by the use of supplementals (extrabudgetary financing) to provide funding for the continuation of the war. Whenever Congress appropriates through supplementals, Wilkerson points out, oversight is compromised. Government money is typically appropriated in discrete categories, and those categories have built-in mechanisms for accountability. But when money is appropriated in supplementals, Congress gives it directly to the department seeking funding, which must then oversee its own activities.[16] Since no department has much incentive to audit itself, supplementals further exacerbate the accountability problems created by outsourcing. Small wonder, then, that five months into FY2008 the Bush administration had yet to make public the Pentagon's FY2006 and FY2007 procurement figures.

This state of affairs helps no one but the contractors. Unless there is a ground-up reconceptualization of what the United States is trying to accomplish in the world and why, the militarization of nonmilitary functions will continue. Like the private sector, the DOD can be relied on to execute. Being wholly subordinate to the U.S. government, the Pentagon will continue to do what it is told to do, regardless of whether it actually serves American interests for the Pentagon to be doing it. The United States will continue to lead with its military so long as the American people and civilian authorities give their tacit support to the idea that promoting American interests at the barrel of a gun is a prudent policy objective.

Since "people don't give reliable feedback at gunpoint,"[17] it is precisely that core assumption that must be challenged if the United States is to stop unwittingly undermining the very values that are its greatest asset. Militarizing our public posture through Pentagon leadership of our engagement with the world does not play to American strengths, for at least three reasons. First, the price tag for an assertive posture is simply unsustainable. We damaged the country's fiscal health to pursue the quixotic dream of a democratic Middle East. Second, our hubristic stance alienated all but our staunchest allies. To pursue globalization through coercion is the surest way to undermine everything positive about it. Third, a militaristic posture effectively hides the universal values that have made America a beacon to all corners of the globe. Our diplomacy and development agendas became hopelessly compromised, and by fueling the hatred of our enemies we weakened both our security and our capacity for world leadership.[18] For all of these reasons, the militarization of American foreign policy is a problem, not a solution.

Does this mean that President Eisenhower's 1961 warning about the military-industrial complex has become reality? Films such as the disturbing 2005 documentary *Why We Fight* suggest that it has, but they misstate the causes of our present predicament. America's policies are indeed distorted by the influence of a military-industrial complex, but the cause is misguided government priorities, not capitalist greed run amok. Large corporations reaping enormous profits from government contracts have very little to do with the vitality of free markets. But since every Pentagon contract represents jobs in some congressman's district, nothing will change until the American people insist that their government allocate resources in a more enlightened way.

Yet it is also important to realize how privatization and outsourcing have transformed the military-industrial complex since Eisenhower's time. For Eisenhower, the military-industrial complex was a result of annual spending on the military exceeding the total net income of U.S. corporations. That is no longer the case. Even at today's record highs, defense spending is dwarfed by the net income of U.S. corporations. In 2002, the United States budgeted $344.9 billion for defense and the military, and the net income of all U.S. corporations that year came to $1.08 trillion.[19] Eisenhower could not foresee the wholly unprecedented ways in which globalization would empower the private sector and transform the calculus of government power.

Demilitarizing American foreign policy does not necessarily mean cutting the defense budget. It does mean channeling defense dollars to the right sort of postimperial research and development. For example, the Pentagon may have a positive role to play in the quest for alternative energies, if only because the fuel needs of the U.S. military are astronomical ($12 billion in FY2007 alone) and the costs of defending oil resources are unsustainable.[20] Is it naïve to think that the Pentagon might lead us to a better future? Not at all. The Internet grew out of an earlier network called DARPANET, a project of the Defense Advanced Research Projects Agency.

Why Contractors Aren't the Problem

A March 2007 front-page article in the *Wall Street Journal* asked, "Is the Government Outsourcing Its Brain?"[21] and essentially answered yes. On its face, this sounds disturbing. Yet the metaphor is misleading. Government never had one brain to outsource, so the vision of a headless monster, while attention-grabbing, does not describe the current situation. Still, as we have seen, the relative contribution of government direct hires to policy formulation has certainly changed profoundly over time, in ways both good and bad.

On the one hand, government no longer has the in-house capacity to match the private sector in a range of highly technical issue areas. In that sense, government has indeed outsourced its intellectual power. But this trend began long ago and explains the rise of the Washington think tank. During the Woodrow Wilson administration, Robert S. Brookings came to Washington convinced that business techniques could be applied to government and founded the Brookings Institution, an organization dependent from the start on government outsourcing. The Brookings Institution contributed substantially to the ideas for the Office of Management and Budget, the Marshall Plan, the presidential transition process, and the Great Society initiatives, to name a few prominent examples. In turn, the proliferation of think tanks initiated a countertrend within government of building in-house policy planning staffs.[22] The point is that contracting and private sector/NGO involvement in the business of government has a long history largely because of the results it has delivered.

On the other hand, under the Bush administration government oversight was all too often outsourced along with the mandate to innovate. The result, according to John Hamre, president of the Center for Strategic and International Studies, is a very skilled and aggressive contractor community that receives suboptimal guidance from government.[23] It is one thing for government to solicit recommendations from private entities; it is another thing entirely when government asks the private sector to assume decision-making authority, as it did with the Coast Guard's Deepwater program. This can be a fine line to negotiate, as contractors and grantees often possess expertise that should contribute directly to the decision-making process. Thus, while farming out projects to private bodies increases the number of good ideas and the efficiency with which they can be implemented, it also makes accountability an ever-present concern. When layers of subcontractors enter the picture, transparency becomes all the more elusive.[24] There are ways of countering that natural trend (see below), but suffice it to say that any form of networked governance will need to spend much of its time fostering the transparency on which good oversight relies.

Serious consequences can follow when government effectively delegates oversight to contractors. All of them are on full display in Iraq. In 2008 Rep. Henry Waxman (D-California) launched a major punitive effort for the misuse of taxpayer money for Iraq reconstruction. His efforts focused on three sins in particular. First, the Bush administration relied too heavily on cost-plus contracts, which do not encourage contractors to control costs. Second, many of the contracts were sweetheart deals with familiar partners such as Halliburton and Bechtel rather than open competitions. This too does little for cost-effectiveness. Finally, in the immediate aftermath of the war, the United States did not make good use of Iraqi companies, which often offered services at lower cost. As Waxman wrote, "Millions of Americans want to help Iraqis, but they don't want to be fleeced."[25]

Waxman's investigation into contracting abuse wisely focused on the dearth of proper oversight and transparency. But it also implies, at least implicitly, that contractor greed is in part responsible for what has gone wrong. Take, for example, the often cited matter of gasoline and diesel fuel for American forces in Iraq. Halliburton brought the fuel from Kuwait at a much higher price than the Iraqi oil company Somo had offered. Why, Waxman asked, did the government sign a contract with Halliburton to deliver the fuel rather than accept a cheaper price from a company that also provided jobs for Iraqis?[26] One explanation might be the cozy relationship between Vice President Cheney and Halliburton, but it is far from satisfactory. The Iraqis could have contracted to provide the fuel for less, but since Somo was incapable of bringing in supplies from Turkey or Kuwait, buying from that company would have made the American presence in Iraq wholly dependent on the stability of the Iraqi oil supply. Rather than accept the constant risk of disruption by the insurgency, the army gave the job to Halliburton. At a much higher cost—the result of additional transportation costs, the requirement of meeting U.S. safety standards, carrying liability insurance on their fuel trucks, and their need to apply Federal Acquisition Regulation rules in fulfilling the contract—Halliburton brought an uninterrupted stream of fuel in from Kuwait. In addition, the deal pleased the State Department, which had wanted to reward Kuwait for the use of their airfields during the war.[27]

Perhaps above all, this story illustrates the danger of deriving contracting-first principles from the lessons of Iraq. Since the security situation deteriorated rapidly in ways that no one had anticipated, a good deal of expense that some have attributed to contractor greed simply followed from the dangerous environment in which companies had to operate. For example, KBR was instructed to cook meals in Baghdad for every single member of the U.S. contingent throughout Iraq, simply because of the presumed security risk should word leak out regarding precisely how many individuals needed feeding in Baghdad. Moreover, if conditions on a particular day make work too dangerous, companies still have to pay workers for being present. It was simply an unprecedented undertaking to fight a war and also take care of infrastructure development, health care, and education all at once. Many things went wrong. While it may feel good to blame "business" for cost overruns, the truth is vastly more complicated.

Business offers what the government requests. Scapegoating contractors means that government is not forced to reflect on whether it has requested the right things.

It is all too easy to find examples of contracts with cost overruns, contracts that were forged without proper competition, or contracts granted through close personal ties. Government, media, and the public must be ever vigilant in monitoring the business-government relationship. But one of the built-in advantages of contracting versus doing things in-house is that performance and assessment standards can be built into the contract. Outsourcing produces a division of labor: the contractor performs and the government assesses that performance on the basis of whether or not the contract was fulfilled. Technology permits a range of new models for evaluation that government has only just begun to exploit. Our system of checks and balances provides myriad ways for government to oversee itself, but conflicts of interest and the negative consequences of partisan politics are always a stone's throw away. Contracting, in contrast, does not raise the same conflicts of interest, but other problems emerge elsewhere, primarily near the revolving door between business and government employment.

While there is plenty of room for improvement in the writing and overseeing of contracts, our focus has not been on the legal aspects of procurement and acquisitions, which are rightly the realm of experts, but on the larger questions that privatization raises. It is easy but unproductive to find horror stories and generalize from them to identify self-interested contractors and corrupt officials as the cause of ineffective policy. Contractors aren't the problem, and privatization is not a creation of any single administration. But the Bush administration took us into uncharted territory with its laissez-faire outsourcing practices, which amounted to an abdication of government responsibility. It is the job of the president, not business, to preserve, protect, and defend the Constitution of the United States. Government, not business, must enforce appropriate norms of conduct and punish those who betray society's trust.

In addition to creating incentives for collaboration, there are at least three other ways in which government might facilitate more extensive cooperation across the public-private divide. First, government can intervene directly in markets. It can impose standards that guide companies' behavior along the desired pathways. Standards are negative incentives, and they are most likely to be effective when business itself is involved in devising them. Second, government can foster innovative forms of oversight through advisory councils that include the full range of stakeholders. Finally, government can provide financial support for promising solutions that bubble up from below; this is the creative spark at the heart of the Millennium Challenge Corporation. What all of these share is an interest in fostering collaborative long-term thinking on common problems.

In his first inaugural address Ronald Reagan said, "Government is not the solution to our problem; government is the problem." Reagan got many things right, but on this he was very wrong. Business can be hired to solve problems, but there are some problems that only government can solve, since business absent good government will always sacrifice sustainability to short-term gain.

The How Is as Important as the What

In addition to raising accountability challenges, the privatization of American power blurs the formerly clear divisions between the public and private sectors, and between the "what" and the "how" of policy. In the past, the operative assumption was that the government made policy and told the private sector how to implement it. Within government, some groups devised policy (the "what") and others dealt with the politics of securing policy aims ("the how").

Neither firewall is holding up well. The volume of transactions has simply grown too large for the U.S. government to monitor without instituting new oversight procedures that take advantage of the information revolution. The wars in Iraq and Afghanistan are good examples: contracting activity grew to the point where the line between policy and implementation effectively dissolved, and the private sector found itself making policy right alongside government. For example, the contractor Aegis was hired to coordinate the activities of other contractors in Iraq (see chapter 5). Whenever things need to be done immediately and there is no time to ask the proper authority for guidance, the line between the how and the what tends to dissolve.

Moreover, for many policies, the implementation defines the substance. Both transformational development and transformational diplomacy, as we have seen, sought to harness liberty and entrepreneurship, both as means to a valuable end (liberal democracy) and as ends in themselves. In both instances, the implementation virtually is the policy, since innovation and contextual problem-solving cannot be had by simply issuing a government or World Bank command.

Both of these factors combine to make the standard government solution, expanding bureaucracy to deal with an ever more complex world, part of the problem. Privatization is ultimately a revolt against bureaucracy, against giving inputs and processes precedence over outcomes. But this is not the same thing as a revolt against government, since government need not by definition be bureaucratic in the traditional sense.[28] We need government whose form and modus operandi is suited to the information age and global economy. Above all, the private sector cannot replace government, since there will always be instances where public and private interest are in conflict, and government must both adjudicate and set up the right system of incentives for the public interest to prevail. The profound changes in the information environment only make inherently governmental functions more important.

That the how of policy has risen in stature means that the U.S. government is not the only entity whose actions have policy impact. In the twenty-first century, NGOs, socially responsible (or irresponsible) corporations, and hybrid organizations can all make policy. Even when the U.S. government is not a majority funder, Western NGOs serve American interests by advancing globalization. It is no accident, as the Soviets used to say, that Putin's Russia today finds NGOs, regardless of their focus or funding sources, threatening to its interests. It feels the same way about foreign business interests. Both present obstacles to the institutionalization of authoritarian governance and economic organization, and remind the world of the ways in which Russia's political and economic liberties are currently circumscribed and threatened. Smart government will ally with the private forces that share its interests.

The firewall between policy and implementation will continue to hold where crisis diplomacy and war are concerned, but in the everyday business of crisis prevention—the lion's share of America's interaction with the world—the barrier has effectively dissolved. The sooner our policymakers acknowledge that Team America extends beyond the government alone, the sooner the United States will be able to stop outsourcing proper oversight over how American foreign policy is actually delivered. Disconnects between strategy and practice can be bridged by mechanisms that allow the private sector to share knowledge and best practices with government. Strengthening that feedback loop should be a top priority. Simply put, in the information age, the how of policy is every bit as important as the what.[29]

Paying attention to the how of foreign policy, in turn, highlights the economic foundations of American security and the extent to which militarizing America's public face undermines our long-term interests. American national security was conceived in militaristic terms during the Cold War, but, as Walter Russell Mead has pointed out, the Cold War was an anomaly in American history.[30] The Marshall Plan was enormously successful at advancing American national security, and it wasn't a military operation. For its success it depended on extensive collaboration between business and government.[31] To be sure, there is some economic benefit in maintaining the world's most powerful military machine, especially when military demands spur the invention of broadly applicable technologies. But keeping that pump primed has made us the most leveraged democracy on the planet. There must be a reason no other Western state today imitates our strategy for success.

None of this is to argue that government should simply stand aside and let markets work their magic. Globalization demands the active involvement of both business and government. Markets are occasionally going to fail, and the private sector on its own will not intervene to address market failure unless government prods it to do so. The challenge for twenty-first century governance is twofold: to discover new ways of encouraging private actors to shoulder their share of the burden of system maintenance, and to forge new forms of government oversight consistent with the realities of networked governance. The standard pattern, where government doesn't know how to do things quickly and so hands its responsibilities off to the private sector, in effect end-running itself, must stop. The problem is that we lack an Archimedean point from which to manage our government today. As a result, our government is faltering. As the Partnership for Public Service's CEO Max Stier put it, government failure is "rust that creeps up on you. You don't know what is happening until the entire structure falls apart."[32]

Approaching the subject of shadow government from the unusual perspective of foreign policy can show us that missing Archimedean vantage point. Our foreign policy apparatus is in dire need of revitalization. The first step is to meet head-on the challenge of getting talented people to work in government. Government needs employees who are capable of seeing beyond their immediate domain to forge networks among seemingly disparate spheres. In his book *The Tipping Point,* Malcolm Gladwell identifies these individuals as "connectors." Connectors have a foot in many different worlds and a knack for bring those worlds together.[33] They can forge the teams that can imagine innovative solutions to challenging problems. New forms of innovative and tech-savvy government oversight simply will not emerge if the nation's best and brightest continue to seek career fulfillment only outside of government.

The private sector's relative gain in prestige and power need not be the public sector's loss, but it requires government to articulate and defend the things that only government can do well. The outsourcing issue is a perfect place to start. It focuses our attention on the way the world has changed, and on the way in which government has and has not adapted to cope with those changes. It forces us to consider anew the question of what government is for. Government's first function is to ensure the security of its citizens, but this is no longer the work of government alone. And ensuring security involves much more than simply deploying military force at the right time.

The democratization of information, technology, and finance has radically redefined the global milieu in which U.S. security policy must be devised. Traditional imperial methods no longer produce traditional imperial results. When the United States behaves as though it were an empire of old, it undermines the main sources of its strength. Washington must acknowledge what the twenty-first century corporation has already been forced to accept: the how is now as important as the what.[34] Knowing the context in which you are operating is every bit as important as knowing where you want to go.

In his thought-provoking book *Are We Rome?* Cullen Murphy sees profound similarities between the Rome of old and the contemporary United States.[35] But striking though those similarities are, the differences are far greater. Destroying the Roman Empire meant defeating the Roman legions. Eradicating the empire of the willing is not so straightforward a proposition. As Nayam Chanda wrote, "Calls to shut down globalization are pointless, because nobody is in charge."[36] The lifeblood of the Roman Empire may have been patron-client relations, but the lifeblood of the empire of the willing is the freely negotiated contract between equals in which both parties possess full information.

The United States can choose to amplify that difference between itself and Rome, or to minimize it. But that is up to us—and by us, I ultimately mean all of us as citizens of the free world. The final unprecedented feature of the empire of the willing is that it need not be led by the United States to endure. In fact it is more likely to realize its full potential when the United States collaborates with others. When it comes to leadership in the twenty-first century, the how, it turns out, must take center stage as well.

Markets and Virtue

In the short run, the market rewards those who are quickest to convert ideas into commodities, without concern for their impact on the public good. In the long run, however, the market must somehow be encouraged to produce sustainable outcomes if it is to continue to function at all. For example, the world's environmental predicament is very much the product of a myopic capitalist dynamic. The unintended consequences of the struggle for short-run gain are but one dimension of the challenge that laissez-faire policies have always posed. The political economist Karl Polanyi called this capitalism's "double movement": the commodification of nature and man that capitalism demands produces profound social disloca- tion and environmental degradation, requiring active government inter- vention to address the consequences of free markets in land and labor. We can see Polanyi's double movement at work in world history, first in the emergence of the welfare state and today in the form of policies to address global poverty and avert environmental ruin.[37]

In addition to the free market's social and environmental costs, there are purely economic costs that follow from the unenlightened pursuit of monetary gain. As we saw in the financial meltdown of 2008, today's global economy runs largely on trust. Even the perception of corruption endan- gers a fragile and astonishing system. Thus, for social, environmental, and economic reasons, liberal government for the information age exists to pro- tect us when the market fails. To advance the public interest, government must actively cultivate what David Vogel has insightfully called "the market for virtue."[38]

Virtue through the centuries has meant the moral excellence of indi- viduals, but Vogel uses the term to encompass the behavior of organiza- tions as well. The market for virtue exists if and when companies and indi- viduals alike see it in their interest to forsake short-term gain to contribute to the solution of global problems.[39] It does not matter what ulterior mo- tives might lie behind the ostensibly virtuous behavior. What matters is that virtuous behavior is perceived to pay off in the long term.

Vogel's contribution is to remind us that the market for virtue cannot flourish without the active involvement of government.[40] It is in everyone's interest to have uncorrupt judicial institutions and a secure homeland, but neither is likely to develop spontaneously. The raison d'être for government in the twenty-first century is to ensure that public goods continue to be delivered. Given the dramatic changes in the distribution of power, smart government will create new incentives for the private sector to help it at- tain its ends. Efforts to right inequalities, protect nature, and quantify or institutionalize trust deserve the active support of government, regardless of where those initiatives originate. Rather than do these things all on its own, government can best serve its citizens by harnessing and channeling the energies of nongovernmental actors.

In this sense, government must promote and bolster Tocqueville's fa- mous doctrine of self-interest properly understood. Tocqueville considered this doctrine the unifying creed in America, where virtue is pursued not for its own sake but because it is in the long-term self-interest of the vir- tuous. In *Democracy in America* Tocqueville writes, "The doctrine of self- interest properly understood does not inspire great sacrifices, but every day it prompts some small ones. . . . If it does not lead the will directly to virtue, it establishes habits which unconsciously turn it that way." Tocqueville saw in this distinctly American approach to virtue something new and powerful. He drew a direct connection between the wholly self-interested drive to make money and its potential to spawn virtuous circles of action. When virtue pays, individuals and organizations alike will be inclined to be virtuous.

The best way to understand the corporate social responsibility movement is as the globalization of Tocqueville's doctrine of self-interest properly understood. Corporate social responsibility is addressed to two audiences: consumers and company employees. With respect to the former, since revenues fall after a product has been identified with corporate ruthlessness, it should not surprise us to see businesses striving to be seen as socially responsible. With respect to the latter, according to Bob Fisher, board chair of The Gap, corporations also strive for social responsibility so as to hire the best employees in a competitive labor market. People want to work for a company that stands for something beyond mere profit.[41] A business can also find that it pays to be virtuous when access to foreign markets is at stake. In 2007 Rep. Charles Rangel (D-New York) included private sector measures to raise labor and environmental standards around the world as part of a new trade bill. The response of the business community was unprecedented; they were willing to do whatever was needed to get the bill passed.[42]

People like Rangel (though he, it turns out, had other issues), Bono, and my students at Middlebury College understand that when business has signed on to this Tocquevillian understanding of virtue, it can be a formidable partner for positive change. But government has been slow to exploit this capacity, in part because that is the nature of bureaucracies, but also because it possesses an antiquated sense of its own purpose. A central objective of this book has been to map the responses of the major foreign policy institutions to a changed world so that government and citizens alike can recognize the extent to which American power has been privatized— and adapt accordingly. Only then will the United States truly harness the private sector's creative capabilities, both producers and consumers alike, to the common cause of sustainable security. In a word, government needs to cultivate the emerging market for virtue.

One possible objection to the call for increased business-government collaboration is that it will create a military-industrial complex even more monstrous. That peril is ever present. Outsourcing what were once military functions, after all, does create a moral hazard: an industry that profits most when America is at war. Yet the cartel relations on which Eisenhower's iron triangles rely are incompatible with transparency and free markets. With these as operative principles, government can uphold the public interest when the pursuit of profit might threaten it. A military-industrial complex can flourish only with secrecy and the active support of government. As U.S. comptroller general David Walker argued, what we need are political leaders who are willing to challenge the status quo to get government back on track.[43]

If we remain true to our founding principles and attentive to fostering the market for virtue, public-private partnerships that leverage government influence can proliferate instead of iron triangles that, by definition, close down free markets and innovation. The iron triangle, after all, becomes a social network when free competition and transparency prevail.

Another potential objection to business-government collaboration is that it calls for co-optation of the virtuous by the privileged. By celebrating the market we only undermine the scope of other-oriented action. But since co-optation can exist only when a realistic alternative vision of the good exists, this objection presupposes some antiglobalization alternative that has proven to work. Is there such a thing? Surely a world order based on simple self-interest is a more likely and desirable proposition than one that demands altruism from human beings in order to function. From the Tocquevillian perspective, it does not matter what motivated Milton Hershey during the Depression when he provided the employees of his chocolate company with free medical care and paid off the mortgages of every church in town. Whether he acted from enlightened self-interest or altruism is less important than that suffering was alleviated and the business survived. Debates on motives are beside the point. The late Chinese leader Deng Xiaoping was right: it doesn't matter whether a cat is black or white, so long as it catches mice.[44]

Others might object that the call for accountability through radical transparency is ultimately undemocratic, since the overseers are ultimately self-appointed. This argument presupposes that elections are the only way of holding the powerful accountable. It is easy enough to see how that was once so. Is it still the case today—are elections even a reliable mechanism of accountability any more? Bolstering the market for virtue will require remaking the incentive structure that every member of Congress presently faces. When elected officials must fund-raise incessantly to stay in office, guess whose interests will be best represented? Moneyed special interests will continue to distort our politics so long as it is so easy to buy influence. We need to change the entire system. The catalyst for such reform obviously cannot come from within Congress but must be promoted from without.

What we need is enlightened collaboration for the public good that minimizes conflict of interest. The key to securing that goal will always be a commitment to radical transparency. In the age of instant information, as Google CEO Eric Schmidt notes, "No falsehood can last."[45] The powerful may seek to manipulate the powerless in time-honored ways, but the Internet is the new weapon of the weak. Cyber-lawyer Lawrence Lessig and Joe Trippi, Democratic political operative and former national campaign manager for Howard Dean's 2004 presidential run, founded Change Congress, which is premised on this understanding. Change Congress addresses the problem of crony capitalism through a Wikipedia approach that maps the culprits, one member at a time. Citizens can distinguish the corrupt from those committed to reform—and, Lessig and Trippi hope, vote accordingly. In January 2009, Change Congress launched a "donor strike." Citizens pledged "not to donate to federal candidates until they support legislation making congressional elections citizen-funded, not special-interest funded."[46]

As to the charge that the empire of the willing is a utopian notion, I would point to the sweep of human history. When viewed from thirty thousand feet, human progress has unfolded through the gradual (if intermittent) expansion of identity and empathy from local to ever more encompassing structures. Human beings can be challenged to behave differently. We once kept slaves, forced young children to work in factories, and accorded lesser rights to minorities and women. Now most of the world's legal systems recognize these as wrongs. Calling for the globalization of self-interest properly understood is no radical break with the past but instead a step forward in a progression initiated long ago.

The Way Forward

What does it mean, in concrete terms, to cultivate the emerging market for virtue? There is no one-size-fits-all, top-down answer, but instead as many answers as might emerge from the creativity of free individuals. Indeed, top-down thinking is precisely the framework we must abandon if we are to get this century's foreign policy right. But some good bottom-up examples are in order. All of them involve government engaging the private sector in new ways. There are ten points of departure to consider.

The most important call to action, one that unites all the others, is the promotion of radical transparency in all government financial transactions, especially those between business and government. President Obama's first Presidential Memorandum on Transparency and Open Government could not have been more on target. But so much work remains to be done. In theory, the information age has made transparency easy. Simply posting on a public Web site all relevant contracts and a clear record of how funds were expended—the aim of USAspending.gov—advances the cause. For national security matters, there are ways to restrict access on a need-to-know basis, but that basis should be defined as broadly as possible across government. In practice, ensuring transparency involves breaking down information partitions and getting once autonomous entities to cooperate in a consolidated data-sharing effort. Since transparency is a power resource, the incentives for collaboration need not be elusive.[47] Sometimes governments assert that they cannot disclose information because it violates business confidentiality, but the citizen's right to know should trump any such claims.[48] It is up to us and government, however, to insist that be so.

On the government side, several promising transparency initiatives are already in motion. For example, great strides have been made to meet the requirements of the 2006 Federal Funding Accountability and Transparency Act (FFATA), spearheaded by then Sen. Obama, but much still remains to be done. It is not enough to post agency-reported numbers on a user-friendly Web site; those numbers must also capture financial flows accurately, clearly indicating when a given fiscal year has closed out. To fulfill the spirit of FFATA, many federal agencies need to revise their internal accounting practices. Most importantly, it will not be enough to bring only prime contracts into full sunlight. The chain of subcontracting must become transparent as well, as the letter of FFATA demands. USAspending.gov must become the indisputable go-to portal for accurate and timely information on how taxpayer money is spent. Getting new systems in place that successfully exploit technology to enhance the transparency of all government transactions will take time, but it is crucial.

In addition to government efforts to render its relationships with the private sector more transparent, there are private strategies that can be pursued over the heads of both business and government. The new Wikileaks initiative demonstrates the unprecedented power that the Internet places in the hands of ordinary citizens. Wikileaks is developing a searchable Wikipedia for untraceable document leaking and analysis. Whistleblowers worldwide can anonymously post evidence of corruption or dishonesty on the Internet, in any language, and the relevant user community can then collaborate on providing interpretation. Wikileak's beta site stated its core principles: "We believe that it is not only the people of one country that keep their government honest, but also the people of other countries who are watching that government. . . . We propose that every authoritarian government, every oppressive institution, and even every corrupt corporation, be subject to the pressure, not merely of international diplomacy or freedom of information laws, not even of quadrennial elections, but of something far stronger: the individual consciences of the people within them."[49]

Second, government must strive to promote virtue in its departing employees. While it can serve positive purposes, the revolving door between government and the private sector is an invitation to corruption. We do not need to shut this door, but we need to limit its use. Banning cabinet officials from migrating to jobs where they lobby the administration they have recently served, as Obama's first executive order mandated on his first full day on the job, is a straightforward way of encouraging interaction likely to further the public good. But rules are effective only if they are enforced, and this will require constant vigilance. Here ample room exists for a nonprofit watchdog organization to post information on public-private migrations in a searchable and publicly available database. Those with nothing to hide need not fear their actions being publicized. The aim is to maximize the flow of talent between business and government while minimizing conflicts of interest. There is no conflict of interest inherent in the very idea of employees leaving government for the private sector—and vice versa. Smart government needs that sort of movement and should distinguish between lobbyists for small, nonprofit organizations and those working on behalf of large, for-profit companies.

Third, the grip of special interests on American politics must be loosened so that our elected officials can legislate in ways that serve the public interest. To do that, the iron triangle that binds Congress, lobbyists, and agencies that contract out—the Department of Defense being most prominent—must be transformed. There are many bad ways to do this, but the right path involves changing the incentive structure that currently exists for any member of Congress. So long as staying in office requires raising large sums of money, the temptation to trade votes for campaign donations will be ever present, and suspect appropriation choices and corruption scandals will continue to undermine the trust of the American people in the system itself. Campaign finance reform that favors citizen financing can revitalize our democracy while restoring integrity to the contracting process on which our national security currently relies.

Fourth, as the deepening financial crisis has revealed, we must reimagine regulation and oversight. Contractors feature so prominently in our governance and foreign policy, yet there is no governmentwide body specifically dedicated to upholding the long-term integrity of the business-government relationship. We want the very best and brightest to serve as guardians, but how do we make such service attractive? An idea was floated at Davos in January 2009 to pay bonuses to the watchdogs for nailing violators.[50] But this presents an obvious moral hazard. To be sure, regulators should be better paid, as they are in Singapore, but might it not be a better idea to offer prestige, job security, and the chance to make a difference instead? We need something akin to a National Trust for Oversight, whose members would be appointed for life, much like Supreme Court justices, and for similar reasons. Life-time appointment would eliminate potential conflicts of interest, since there would never be an opportunity to benefit in the private sector from favors granted to others while in public service. These Jedi knights of oversight would be digital warriors, partnering with watchdog organizations like Wikileaks, OMB Watch, and the Sunlight Network to enlist the energies and creativity of the American people in ensuring our security.

Fifth, to fuel innovation, the United States needs a better human capital strategy, both for attracting the best talent to service in government and for encouraging the brightest from other countries to call America home. Embracing the free market makes sense only when government helps its citizens acquire the right skills to compete well in it and grants full competition rights to the individuals most likely to make major contributions to social progress. These are areas where the interests of the public and private sector coincide, so collaborative initiatives in education, especially in helping Americans acquire better foreign language skills, should be the wave of the future. In addition, both business and government have an interest in revamping our immigration policy, currently based almost entirely on a vision from 1952 and made more restrictive after 9/11, to make it easier for those who have the most to contribute to work on U.S. soil.[51] It makes no sense whatsoever to educate foreign nationals and then actively discourage them from becoming Americans. Globalization has made both education and immigration major foreign policy issues. Supporting the market for virtue demands attention to both.

Sixth, government can encourage corporate leaders and stockholders to rethink the manner in which company performance is evaluated and rewarded. Robert Pozen has argued persuasively for eliminating quarterly earnings indicators, which keep corporate attention myopically focused on the short term.[52] Compensation that richly rewards short-term gain, such as spectacular investment bank bonuses on risky subprime mortgage bonds, is similarly problematic.[53] Some Wall Street executives voluntarily gave up their bonuses in 2008, a gesture that merits government encouragement. Imagine how many more would have done the same if bonuses were required by law to be publicly disclosed? Self-interest properly understood cannot flourish without attention to the long run. Government must do all that it can to encourage businesses, as stewards of the country and planet, to shoulder their rightful share of this responsibility.[54] Holding the powerful fully accountable for their choices is a good place to start.

Seventh, America compromises its future by conducting national security discussions as though relative costs were wholly irrelevant. As the Government Accountability Office has emphasized repeatedly, "The nation's current fiscal policy path is unsustainable."[55] To continue in this fashion only increases the probability that we will eradicate our core strengths in the process of securing the republic. It should not dishonor the heroic efforts of the U.S. military to point out that both the Pentagon and its relative share of the budget were forged during the Cold War to combat an enemy state bent on our destruction; meeting the challenge of a more amorphous enemy demands a different configuration. Unlike companies, countries cannot go out of business when they behave in fiscally irresponsible fashion, but that is not a license for ignoring costs entirely. The market for virtue suffers when government itself does not take a longer view.

Eighth, government should restrict the use of no-bid contracts, save in situations of national emergency. While it is not clear whether contracting saves money, clearly it will not do so in the absence of competition. Besides, as a core American value, fair competition makes moral claims as well. It is never prudent for business or government to operate as though fairness were beside the point. Generally speaking, there is also great room for improvement in the writing of contracts themselves. Arizona State University law professor Laura Dickinson examined the sixty publicly available Iraq contracts as of 2005 and found that not one contained provisions requiring contractors to obey human rights, anticorruption, or transparency norms.[56] To have an incentive to write restraint into contracts, of course, policymakers must first acknowledge the extent to which American foreign policy has been outsourced.

Ninth, to the extent that is practical, American foreign policy must be demilitarized. While this is an internal government matter, it is also a goal that can be pursued by directly engaging the private sector, whose interests are often directly threatened by the anti-American sentiment created by our coercive overseas ventures. The market for virtue cannot be made to flourish at gunpoint. The threat to America's well-being has changed, and unilateral state power is no match for it. Since Osama Bin Laden is waging war on globalization, not on the United States, the best way to fight his network is to reinforce globalization's networks, both public and private. This is best done by revitalizing the ties that bind the world's established and nascent liberal democracies while acknowledging that the empire of the willing's vitality is compromised by ill-conceived wars.

One good place to begin would be to forbid the use of armed contractors in conflict zones where the United States is an occupying force. The ban would make the appropriate distinction between hiring private security as an auxiliary force in peaceful areas and using hired guns to bolster American military force projection overseas. Such a move would be modest compared to what other governments have done. In 2006, South Africa's parliament passed a Prohibition of Mercenary Activities Act that prevents any South African citizen from "participating as a combatant for private gain in an armed conflict" or from involvement in "any act aimed at overthrowing a government or undermining the constitutional order, sovereignty, or territorial integrity of a state." South Africans now need a license to seek employment with private security firms, and they are banned from serving in foreign armies if the South African government was opposed to that country's involvement in a conflict.[57]

Finally, the United States must take full advantage of our unique capacity for innovation and constantly seek ways to continue to exploit our technological advantage. Smart power knows how to utilize soft and hard power judiciously.[58] But smart power, above all, requires smart government, which understands that the nature of power has changed and innovative technology is its weapon of choice. Google's partnerships with the states of Arizona, California, Utah, and Virginia to make it easier to search for public information on state government Web sites provide a template that might be easily replicated elsewhere.[59] Productive partnerships that bridge the public-private divide will not flourish, however, until the obsolete notion that government solves public problems while business simply focuses on a quick buck is officially retired. Both business and government have a vested interest in thinking strategically about globalization's future.[60]

Does this mean that the right blueprint for institutional reform of our national security infrastructure is the key to success? The one thing on which all foreign policy experts seem to agree is that the present foreign policy process is broken; every person I interviewed concurred on this. But while institutional reform is desperately needed, we would be unwise to focus the bulk of our energy on it. Getting the right institutions in the mix is less important than government's rediscovering its purpose in a networked world where command solutions neither inspire confidence nor produce results, and American power extends well beyond the confines of government mandates. The best institutional reforms will realign and streamline government, not make it more complex. In this regard, the separation of national security from homeland security is highly problematic. Policy complexity should follow from the multiplicity of collaborative networks involved in its creation and promulgation; it should not follow from counterproductive turf wars within government.

Tearing down the outdated budget barriers between national security, foreign policy, homeland security, and energy policy and creating a unified national security budget is a good place to start.[61] Rather than funding defense, diplomacy, and homeland security from different lines, there should be one national security budget. Rather than having a homeland security, national security, and economics council, there should be one body with appropriate diverse representation to advise the president on security more broadly conceived.[62] Taking down budgetary walls is always a daunting task. Exceptional leadership will be required to encourage all players to see the change as being in their best interest; the Goldwater-Nichols reorganization of the Defense Department provides a promising model of how this might be done.

None of this will be easy, but it must be done. Some crises will still demand traditional statecraft and direct government involvement. But other situations, the simmering cauldron of global problems that will one day boil over if left unaddressed, require a radically different orientation. We need to separate the abuse of American power from its true character to see that American power has not been irretrievably undermined but both misused and privatized. Coming to terms with the privatization of American power is a necessary condition for the restoration of America's reputation in the world.

Since power now flows from new sources, we must think about the conduct of foreign policy in a wholly different way. If government simply pursues business as usual, throwing its problems to the private sector without asserting its position as chief defender of the public interest, it could privatize itself out of business. We need a postindustrial foreign policy that starts with a networked world of self-interested entities sharing a common interest—the sustainability and improvement of the present system—and turns it to the advantage of liberty and social justice. The empire of the willing has unprecedented potential to endure, provided a new paradigm for global leadership is embraced, one in which the public and private sectors join forces to confront global problems that threaten our freedom, peace, and prosperity.

Notes

CHAPTER ONE. THE NEW WORLD

1. Michael Barbaro, "Wal-Mart Chief Offers a Social Manifesto," *New York Times,* January 24, 2008.

2. Harriet Rubin, "Google Offers a Map for Its Philanthropy," *New York Times,* January 18, 2008.

3. James Risen, "Use of Iraq Contractors Costs Billions, Report Says," *New York Times,* August 11, 2008.

4. Roya Wolverson, "Beltway Bandits," *Newsweek,* December 3, 2007.

5. Glenn Kessler, "Iraq Embassy Cost Rises $144 Million Amid Project Delays," *Washington Post,* October 7, 2007.

6. Leslie Wayne, "A Growing Military Contract Scandal," *New York Times,* October 8, 2004.

7. Eric Schmitt and Ginger Thompson, "Top Air Force Official Dies in Apparent Suicide," *New York Times,* October 16, 2007.

8. James Glanz, "Official at Saudi Company and Ex-Employee at Halliburton Unit Accused in Kickback Inquiry," *New York Times,* March 24, 2006.

9. Philip Shenon, "Army Says It Will Withhold $19.6 Million from Halliburton, Citing Potential Contract Breach," *New York Times,* February 8, 2007.

10. CNN News, *Contractor for Military Committed Serious Violations,* Special Investigations Unit, November 24, 2008.

11. Michael Hirsh, "Watchdogs Are Warning That Corruption in Iraq Is out of Control," *Newsweek,* October 16, 2007.

12. James Risen, "2005 Use of Gas by Blackwater Leaves Questions," *New York Times,* January 10, 2008.

13. Deborah Avant, "What Are Those Contractors Doing in Iraq?," *Washington Post,* May 9, 2004; Lynda Hurst, "The Privatization of Abu Ghraib," *Toronto Star,* May 16, 2004.

14. Siobhan Gorman, "CIA Likely Let Contractors Perform Waterboarding," *Wall Street Journal*, February 8, 2008.

15. Betsy Stark, Lara Setrakian, and Teri Whitcraft, "Peace Through Paypal?," http://abcnews.go.com/print?id=3244120.

16. Bill Gates, "Creative Capitalism" (speech presented at the World Economic Forum, Davos, Switzerland, January 24, 2008).

17. Ibid.

18. Ibid.

19. David Pogue, "Laptop with a Mission That Widens Its Audience," *New York Times*, October 4, 2007.

20. One Laptop Per Child, "One Laptop Per Child: A Low Cost Connected Laptop for the Worlds' Childrens' Education," OLPC, http://laptop.org/.

21. International Campaign to Ban Landmines, "International Campaign to Ban Landmines," http://www.icbl.org; and Robert Keohane and Joseph Nye, "Power and Interdependence in the Information Age," in *Democracy.Com? Governance in a Networked World*, ed. Elaine Kamarck and Joseph Nye (Hollis, New Hampshire: Hollis, 1999).

22. U.S. Department of State, "U.S.-Palestinian Partnership," Bureau of Public Affairs, Washington, D.C., January 14, 2008, http://www.state.gov/documents/organization/99505.pdf.

23. Joseph Stiglitz, *Making Globalization Work* (New York: W. W. Norton, 2006), 187–88.

24. David Rothkopf, *Superclass: The Global Power Elite and the World They Are Making* (New York: Farrar, Straus and Giroux, 2008), 31.

25. Ibid., 32.

26. Eugene Steuerle, "'Creative Capitalism': Can It Meet the Needs of the World's Poor?," (Washington, D.C.: Hudson Institute Center for Global Prosperity, 2008).

27. Robert D. Hormats, *The Price of Liberty: Paying for America's Wars* (New York: Times Books, 2007).

28. James Glanz and Riyadh Mohammed, "Premier of Iraq Is Quietly Firing Fraud Monitors," *New York Times*, November 17, 2008.

29. Alexis Tocqueville, *Democracy in America*, ed. J. P. Mayer, trans. George Lawrence (New York: HarperPerennial, 1988), 693.

CHAPTER TWO. THE UNITED STATES OF MARKET VALUES

1. Scott Shane and Ron Nixon, "In Washington, Contractors Take on Biggest Role Ever," *New York Times*, February 4, 2007.

2. Tim Weiner, "Lockheed and the Future of Warfare," *New York Times*, November 28, 2004.

3. David Rothkopf, *Superclass: The Global Power Elite and the World They Are Making* (New York: Farrar, Straus and Giroux, 2008), 204.

4. U.S. House of Representatives Committee on Oversight and Government Reform, "Dollars, Not Sense: Government Contracting Under the Bush Administration," June 2006, http://oversight.house.gov/Documents/20060711103910–86046.pdf;

NOTES TO PAGES 14-19

and "More Dollars, Less Sense: Worsening Contracting Trends Under the Bush Administration," June 2007, http://oversight.house.gov/features/moredollars/.

5. Donald Kettl, *Sharing Power: Public Governance and Private Markets* (Washington, D.C.: The Brookings Institution, 1993), 41.

6. Kenneth Waltz, "Globalization and American Power," *The National Interest* (Spring 2000).

7. Dwight D. Eisenhower, Farewell Address, January 17, 1961.

8. Office of Management and Budget, "Circular Number A-76: Performance of Commercial Activities," OMB, http://www.whitehouse.gov/omb/circulars/a076/a076.html.

9. Quoted in Paul Light, *The True Size of Government* (Washington, D.C.: Brookings Institution, 1999), 146.

10. Government Accountability Office, "Implementation of O.M.B Circular Number A-76 at Science Agencies," Briefing for Congressional Staff, March 16, 2007.

11. Ibid.

12. Jason Peckenpaugh, "Definition of 'Inherently Governmental' Could Change," *Government Executive Daily News Service*, June 8, 2001, http://www.govexec.com/dailyfed/0601/060801p1.htm.

13. Stan Soloway, in discussion with author, March 27, 2007.

14. Paul Verkuil, *Outsourcing Sovereignty: Why Privatization of Government Function Threatens Democracy and What We Can Do About It* (New York: Cambridge University Press, 2007).

15. Paul Starr, "The Meaning of Privatization," *Yale Law and Policy Review* 6 (1988).

16. Michael Hardy, "Defense Bill Would Halt A-76 Competition," *Federal Computer Weekly*, May 15, 2008, http://www.fcw.com/online/news/152543–1.html.

17. Office of Management and Budget, "Budget of the United States Government (Historical Tables)," White House, Washington, D.C., 2008, http://www.whitehouse.gov/omb/budget/fy2008/pdf/hist.pdf; John Palguta, in discussion with author, June 6, 2007.

18. Numbers were adjusted for inflation using the Consumer Price Index (CPI) inflation calculator of the Bureau of Labor Statistics: http://data.bls.gov/cgi-bin/cpicalc.pl.

19. Walter Pincus, "U.S. Cannot Manage Contractors in Wars, Officials Testify on Hill," *Washington Post*, January 5, 2008.

20. Private Sector Council, "Creating Momentum in Contract Management: The Acquisition Innovation Pilot Handbook," Partnership for Public Service, Washington, D.C., November 2006, http://ourpublicservice.org/OPS/publications/viewcontent-details.php?id=46.

21. Paul Light, *The New Public Service* (Washington, D.C.: Brookings Institution, 1999), 8.

22. Stephen Goldsmith and William D. Eggers, *Governing by Network: The New Shape of the Public Sector* (Washington, D.C.: Brookings Institution, 2004), 123.

23. Ibid., 155.

24. Pincus, "U.S. Cannot Manage Contractors in Wars."

25. James Glanz, "Iraq Spending Ignored Rules, Pentagon Says," *New York Times*, May 23, 2008.

26. Andrew Natsios, in discussion with author, June 7, 2008; Light, *The True Size of Government*.

27. Soloway, in discussion with author, March 27, 2007.

28. Paul Starr, "The New Life of the Liberal State: Privatization and the Restructuring of State-Society Relations," in *Public Enterprise and Privatization*, ed. John Waterbury and Ezra Suleiman (Boulder, Colorado: Westview, 1990).

29. Paul Applegarth, in discussion with author, January 19, 2007.

30. Government Accountability Office, "Improvements Needed to F.P.D.S.-N.G.," GAO, Washington, D.C., 2005, http://www.gao.gov/new.items/do5960r.pdf.

31. See FAQ section of Office of Management and Budget, "Fedspending.Org," http://www.fedspending.org/.

32. Robert Shea, e-mail message to author, May 21, 2008.

33. Stanley Trice, in discussion with author, June 5, 2007.

34. Allison Stanger, "Your Tax Dollars at Work—If You Can Find Them," *Washington Post*, May 18, 2008.

35. They wrote letters to the editor, which the *Washington Post* chose not to publish. Gary Bass, e-mail message to author, May 19, 2008; Shea, e-mail message to author, May 21, 2008.

36. Paul Light, "The Real New Size of Government," *Organizational Performance Initiative, Research Brief,* no. 2 (2006): 1.

37. Private Sector Council, "Creating Momentum in Contract Management."

38. General Services Administration, "Federal Procurement Data System-Next Generation [F.P.D.S.-N.G.]," https://www.fpds.gov/.

39. Office of Management and Budget, "Fedspending.Org."

40. Adam Hughes, in discussion with author, April 9, 2008.

41. The same trend line pertains for the number of actions, though a change in accounting systems that took place in FY2004 makes the most recent data more difficult to interpret comparatively. See http://www.fpdsng.com/downloads/FPR_Reports/2005_fpr_section_I_total_federal_views.pdf (4), and http://www.fpdsng.com/downloads/FPR_Reports/2005_fpr_section_I_total_federal_views.pdf (5).

42. http://www.fpdsng.com/downloads/FPR_Reports/2005_fpr_section_I_total_federal_views.pdf; see, also, http://www.fpdsng.com/fpr_reports_fy_81–99.html.

43. Alexander Tabarrok, "The Rise, Fall, and Rise Again of Privateers," *Independent Review* XI, no. 4 (2007).

44. Verkuil, *Outsourcing Sovereignty*, 103.

45. Herb Fenster, in discussion with author, March 28, 2007.

46. Milton Friedman, *Why Government Is the Problem* (Palo Alto, California: Hoover Institution Press, 1993), 6.

47. Donald Rumsfeld, tribute to Milton Friedman, May 9, 2002, http://www.defenselink.mil/Speeches/Speech.aspx?SpeechID=216.

48. Amanda Dory, in discussion with author, March 26, 2007.

49. Peckenpaugh, "Definition of 'Inherently Governmental' Could Change."

50. Ibid.

51. Megan Scully, "Bill Would Bar Contractors from Running Defense Programs," *Government Executive.com* (May 16, 2007), http://www.govexec.com/story_page.cfm?articleid=36940.

52. David Walker, in discussion with author, June 4, 2007.

53. Ibid.

54. Anthony Zinni, in discussion with author, January 18, 2007.

55. Goldsmith and Eggers, *Governing by Network: The New Shape of the Public Sector,* 32.

56. Allison Stanger and Omnivore, "Foreign Policy, Privatized," *New York Times,* October 5, 2007.

57. Lawrence R. Jacobs and Benjamin I. Page, "Who Influences US Foreign Policy?," *American Political Science Review* 99, no. 1 (2005).

58. U.S. House of Representatives, *Testimony of Jacob Hacker (Professor of Political Science, Yale University) Before Committee on Education and Labor,* January 31, 2007, http://edlabor.house.gov/testimony/013107JacobHackertestimony.pdf.

59. Jacob Hacker, *The Great Risk Shift: The Assault on American Jobs, Families, Health Care, and Retirement—and How You Can Fight Back* (New York: Oxford University Press, 2006).

60. Jacqueline Williams-Bridgers, in discussion with author, March 27, 2007.

61. For the pilot program on subcontracts, see General Services Administration, "Electronic Subcontracting Reporting System (E-Srs)," http://www.esrs.gov/index?cck=1.

62. Barry C. Lynn, *End of the Line: The Rise and Coming Fall of the Global Corporation* (New York: Doubleday, 2005), 11.

63. "More Dollars, Less Sense."

64. Figures accessed from USAspending.gov on May 22, 2008.

65. Robert Gates, remarks delivered to the Association of the United States Army, Washington, D.C., October 10, 2007, http://www.defenselink.mil/speeches/speech.aspx?speechid=1181.

66. Government Accountability Office, "High-Risk Series: An Update," 2007.

CHAPTER THREE. STATE POWER IN A PRIVATIZED WORLD

1. Michael Crowley, "The Stuff Sam Nunn's Nightmares Are Made Of," *New York Times Magazine* (2007).

2. Muhammed Yunus, "Grameen: Banking for the Poor," Grameen, http://www.grameen-info.org/index.html; Muhammed Yunus, *Creating a World Without Poverty: Social Business and the Future of Capitalism* (New York: Public Affairs, 2008).

3. Ashoka, "What Is a Social Entrepreneur? Ashoka.Org," Ashoka: Innovators for the Public, http://www.ashoka.org/social_entrepreneur.

4. "Schwab Foundation for Social Entrepreneurship," Schwab Foundation, http://www.schwabfound.org/.

5. Acumen, "The Acumen Fund," Acumen, http://www.acumenfund.org/.

6. "Omidyar Network," Omidyar Network, http://www.omidyar.net/.

7. Kiva, "Kiva: Loans That Change Lives," http://www.kiva.org/.

8. "Global Giving: Donate to Grassroots Projects, Education, Health, Microfinance," GlobalGiving, http://www.globalgiving.com/index.html.

9. Inge Kaul and Pedro Conceição, ed., *The New Public Finance: Responding to Global Challenges* (New York: Oxford University Press, 2006).

10. Nicholas D. Kristof, "Do-Gooders with Spread Sheets," *New York Times,* January 30, 2007.

11. Jodie Morse, "Charity Without the Checks," *Time,* October 28, 2001, http://www.time.com/time/magazine/article/0,9171,181571,00.html.

12. Katie Hafner, "Philanthropy Google's Way: Not the Usual," *New York Times,* September 14, 2006.

13. Sebastian Mallaby, "The Slate 60," *Slate,* February 20, 2006, http://www.slate.com/id/2136384/.

14. Adam Smith, *The Wealth of Nations* (New York: Bantam Classics, 2003), book IV.

15. David Bornstein, *How to Change the World: Social Entrepreneurs and the Power of New Ideas* (New York: Oxford University Press, 2004).

16. Henry Kissinger, *Does America Need a Foreign Policy?* (New York: Simon and Schuster, 2001).

17. Anne-Marie Slaughter, *A New World Order* (Princeton, NJ: Princeton University Press, 2004).

18. Robert Keohane and Joseph Nye, *Power and Interdependence,* 3d ed. (New York: Longman, 2000).

19. Tony Blair, "Check Against Delivery," speech presented at Georgetown University, Washington, D.C., May 26, 2006, http://www.number10.gov.uk/Page9549.

20. Robert Keohane and Joseph Nye, "Globalization: What's New? What's Not? (and So What?)," *Foreign Policy,* no. 118 (2000).

21. Francis Fukuyama, "After Neoconservatism," *New York Times Magazine,* February 19, 2006, 67; Francis Fukuyama, *America at the Crossroads: Democracy, Power, and the Neoconservative Legacy* (New Haven: Yale University Press, 2007).

22. Anatol Lieven and John Hulsman, *Ethical Realism: A Vision for America's Role in the World* (New York: Pantheon, 2006).

23. Peter Beinart, *The Good Fight: Why Liberals—and Only Liberals—Can Win the War on Terror and Make America Great Again* (New York: Harper Collins, 2006).

24. John Ikenberry and Anne-Marie Slaughter, "Forging a World of Liberty Under Law: US National Security in the Twenty-first Century (Final Report of the Princeton Project on National Security)," Princeton, NJ, Woodrow Wilson School, 2006.

25. Stephen Goldsmith and William D. Eggers, *Governing by Network: The New Shape of the Public Sector* (Washington, D.C.: Brookings Institution, 2004), vii.

26. Thomas L. Friedman, *The Lexus and the Olive Tree: Understanding Globalization* (New York: Anchor, 2000); Thomas L. Friedman, *The World Is Flat: A Brief History of the Twenty-first Century* (New York: Farrar, Straus, Giroux, 2006).

27. Ronald Coase, "The Nature of the Firm," *Economica* 4 (1937).

28. United States Agency for International Development, "Tsunami Assistance One Year Later," USAID, http://www.usaid.gov/press/factsheets/2005/fs051221.html.

29. Jessica Matthews, "Power Shift," *Foreign Affairs* 76, no. 1 (1997).

30. Max Weber, "Politics as a Vocation," in *From Max Weber: Essays in Sociology,* ed. H. H. Gerth and C. Wright Mills (New York: Oxford University Press, 1958), 77–78.

31. David Rothkopf, *Superclass: The Global Power Elite and the World They Are Making*, (New York: Farrar, Straus and Giroux, 2008), 36.

32. Samuel Palmisano, "The Globally Integrated Enterprise," *Foreign Affairs* 85, no. 3 (2006): 129.

33. Ibid., 132.

34. Zygmunt Bauman, *Globalization: The Human Consequences* (New York: Columbia University Press, 2000).

35. Tony Blair, "A Battle for Global Values," *Foreign Affairs* 86, no. 1 (2007).

36. John Robb, *Brave New War: The Next State of Terrorism and the End of Globalization* (New York: Wiley, 2007).

37. Alexander Motyl, "Empire Falls: Washington May Be Imperious but It Is Not Imperial," *Foreign Affairs* 85, no. 4 (2006).

38. Joseph Nye, "The Dependent Colossus," *Foreign Policy* (March–April 2002).

39. Anne-Marie Slaughter, *The Idea That Is America* (New York: Basic, 2007).

40. Michael Walzer, "Is There an American Empire?," *Dissent* (Fall 2003).

41. Geir Lundestad, *The United States and Western Europe Since 1945: From 'Empire' by Invitation to Transatlantic Drift* (Oxford: Oxford University Press, 2003).

42. Charles S. Maier, *Among Empires: American Ascendancy and Its Predecessors* (Cambridge, MA: Harvard University Press, 2006).

43. Martin Walker, "America's Virtual Empire," *World Policy Journal* 19, no. 2 (2002).

44. William E. Odom and Robert Dujarric, *America's Inadvertent Empire* (New Haven: Yale University Press, 2004).

45. John Ikenberry, "Illusions of Empire: Defining the New American Order," *Foreign Affairs* 83, no. 2 (2004).

46. Walzer, "Is There an American Empire?"

47. Antonio Gramsci, *The Antonio Gramsci Reader: Selected Writings, 1916–1935* (New York: New York University Press, 2000).

48. Ivo and James Lindsay Daalder, "American Empire: Not 'If' but 'What Kind,'" *New York Times*, May 10, 2003.

49. Michael J. Sandel, *Liberalism and the Limits of Justice* (New York: Cambridge University Press, 1998).

50. Anne-Marie Slaughter, "America's Edge in a Networked World," *Foreign Affairs* 88, no. 1 (2009).

51. Ibid.

52. Livy, *Livy, with an English Translation*, trans. B. O. Foster, 13 vols., vol. 4, The Loeb Classical Library (London: Heinemann; New York: Putnam, 1919), 56–57. In the original Latin: "Certe id firmissimum longe imperium est quo oboedientes gaudent."

53. Fareed Zakaria, *The Future of Freedom* (New York: W. W. Norton, 2003).

CHAPTER FOUR. THE END OF STATESMANSHIP

1. Henry Kissinger, *A World Restored: Metternich, Castlereagh and the Problems of Peace, 1812–1822* (Weidenfeld and Nicholson, 2000).

2. George Packer, "Knowing Thy Enemy," *New Yorker*, December 18, 2006.

3. Christine Hauser and Taghreed El-Khodary, "Blair Is Appointed Mideast Envoy," *New York Times,* June 27, 2007.

4. George F. Kennan, "Diplomacy Without Diplomats? (75th Anniversary Issue)," *Foreign Affairs* (75th Anniversary Issue) 76, no. 5 (1997): 199–200.

5. Ibid., 202.

6. David J. Rothkopf, *Running the World: The Inside Story of the National Security Council and the Architects of American Power* (New York: Public Affairs, 2005), 391.

7. Anthony Quainton, in discussion with author, January 15, 2007.

8. Kennan, "Diplomacy Without Diplomats?," 206.

9. Quainton, in discussion with author, January 15, 2007.

10. Ibid.

11. Ibid.

12. Anthony Lake, in discussion with author by phone, June 14, 2007.

13. Helene Cooper, "U.S. Is Urging Blair to Be Lead Mideast Envoy "*New York Times,* June 21, 2007.

14. David E. Sanger, "The Reach of War: News Analysis," *New York Times,* April 12, 2007.

15. For two well-written examples, see George Packer, *The Assassin's Gate: America in Iraq* (New York: Farrar, Straus, and Giroux, 2005), and Rajiv Chandrasekaran, *Imperial Life in the Emerald City: Inside Iraq's Green Zone* (New York: Knopf, 2006).

16. Packer, "Knowing Thy Enemy."

17. Stewart Patrick, "The U.S. Response to Precarious States: Tentative Progress and Remaining Obstacles to Coherence," 2007, http://www.cgdev.org/content/publications/detail/14093/.

18. White House, "National Security Presidential Directive/NSPD-44," December 7, 2005, http://www.fas.org/irp/offdocs/nspd/nspd-44.html.

19. Stewart Patrick, in discussion with author, March 30, 2007; J. Anthony Holmes, "Where Are the Civilians? How to Rebuild the U.S. Foreign Service," *Foreign Affairs* 88, no. 1 (2009): 155.

20. Robert Oakley, in discussion with author, January 15, 2007.

21. Thomas D. Boyatt, "Managing Secretary Rice's State Department: An Independent Assessment," Foreign Affairs Council Task Force, Washington, D.C., 2007.

22. Robert Blackwill, in discussion with author, March 26, 2007.

23. Andrew Natsios, "American Fortresses," *Weekly Standard,* May 15, 2006.

24. Quainton, in discussion with author, January 15, 2007.

25. Nicholas Wood, "Rebellious Diplomat Finds Work as Envoy of the Voiceless, *New York Times,* March 3, 2007; Carne Ross, *Independent Diplomat: Dispatches from an Unaccountable Elite* (Ithaca, NY: Cornell University Press, 2007).

26. Brian Hocking, "Privatizing Diplomacy," *International Studies Perspectives* 5 (2004).

27. "A New Diplomacy for the Information Age," United States Advisory Commission on Public Diplomacy, Washington, D.C., 1996, 6.

28. Charles MacCormack (CEO, Save the Children), in discussion with author, April 7, 2006.

29. Strobe Talbott, "Globalization and Diplomacy: A Practitioner's Perspective," *Foreign Policy,* no. 108 (1997).

30. U.S. House of Representatives, Committee on Oversight and Government Reform, "Dollars, Not Sense: Government Contracting Under the Bush Administration," June 2006, http://oversight.house.gov/Documents/20060711103910-86046.pdf; and "More Dollars, Less Sense: Worsening Contracting Trends Under the Bush Administration," June 2007, http://oversight.house.gov/features/moredollars/.

31. Anthony Quainton, "Diplomacy for the Twenty-first Century," in *Global Challenges in the Twenty-first Century* (Chesterton, MD: Literary House Press, Washington College, 2000).

32. John Broder and David Rohde, "State Department Use of Contractors Leaps in 4 Years," *New York Times,* October 24, 2007.

33. Jeffrey Lunstead (former U.S. Ambassador to Sri Lanka), in discussion with author, January 28, 2007.

34. Marc Grossman, "Are We Ready for 21st Century Diplomacy?" (paper presented at "A New American Diplomacy: Requirements for the 21st Century," Belmont Conference Center, Elkridge, MD, October 2, 2000).

35. Robert Oakley, in discussion with author, January 15, 2007.

36. Condoleezza Rice, "Transformational Diplomacy" (speech presented at Georgetown University, Washington, D.C., January 18, 2006).

37. Julian Borger, Ewen MacAskill, and Jonathan Watts, "Special Report: How the Balance of Power and Influence Is Changing: New Diplomatic Priorities Offer Snapshot of Changing World Order: US Moves Resources from Europe to Asian Giants: Global Context Changed, Says Foreign Office," *Guardian,* March 4, 2006.

38. Ibid.

39. Tony Blair, "Check Against Delivery," speech presented at Georgetown University, Washington, D.C., May 26, 2006, http://www.number10.gov.uk/Page9549.

40. Quainton, in discussion with author, January 15, 2007.

41. Karen Hughes and Office of Private Sector Outreach, "Public Diplomacy Update," ed. State Department (October 2006).

42. Business for Diplomatic Action, "America's Role in the World: A Business Perspective on Public Diplomacy," BDA, New York, NY, 2007, 4.

43. Keith Reinhard, letter to Karen Hughes, December 5, 2005.

44. Business for Diplomatic Action, "America's Role in the World," 14; U.S. House of Representatives, *Keith Reinhard (president, Business for Diplomatic Action), Testimony Before the House Subcommittee on National Security, Emerging Threats, and International Relations,* August 23, 2004, http://www.businessfordiplomaticaction.org/action/written_testimony.pdf.

45. Peter G. Peterson, "Public Diplomacy and the War on Terrorism," *Foreign Affairs* 81, no. 5 (2002).

46. Pete Peterson, "Privatizing U.S. Public Diplomacy," *Financial Times,* January 21, 2004.

47. Discover America Partnership, "Discover America Partnership—the Power of Travel," Discover America Partnership Online, http://www.poweroftravel.org/default.aspx.

48. South Asia Earthquake Relief Fund, "South Asia Earthquake Relief," South Asia Earthquake Relief Fund, https://www.southasiaearthquakerelief.org/. Visitors to the Web site for South Asia Earthquake Relief in March 2007 discovered the frame for

a bilingual page that has yet to be fleshed out; the Urdu link reloaded the English version. In October 2007, the Urdu version was available.

49. United States Agency for International Development, "Press Release: U.S.AID Announces Partnership with Procter & Gamble for Pakistan Earthquake Survivors," USAID, Washington, D.C., 2005, http://www.usaid.gov/press/releases/2005/pr051020.html.

50. U.S. Department of State, "U.S.-Lebanon Partnership," Bureau of Public Affairs, http://www.state.gov/documents/organization/79536.pdf.

51. The Web site for the organization, however, speaks volumes about the distance still to be traveled in engaging the world in language it can understand. The site was clearly designed to be accessible in two languages—both Arabic and English. Much like the Web site for the South Asia Earthquake Relief Fund, however, while the skeleton for full bilingual presentation is in place, a click on the Lebanese flag in March 2007 yielded just the English language version, freshly reloaded. For some reason, the translation into Arabic was slow to materialize. The shortcomings of both initiatives demonstrate the glaring need for speakers and writers of Arabic and other less commonly taught foreign languages if the aspirations of transformational diplomacy are to be properly realized.

52. U.S. Department of State, "Middle East Partnership Initiative—Outreach," http://mepi.state.gov/outreach/index.htm.

53. Ibid.

54. Hughes and Outreach, "Public Diplomacy Update."

55. Condoleezza Rice, remarks at the 2006 Awards for Corporate Excellence Ceremony, Washington, D.C., November 6, 2006.

56. "The New Diplomacy: Utilizing Innovative Communication Concepts That Recognize Resource Constraints," United States Advisory Commission on Public Diplomacy, 2003.

57. Felix Rohatyn, in discussion with author, November 4, 2007.

58. Rice, remarks at the 2006 Awards for Corporate Excellence Ceremony.

59. George L. Argyros, Marc Grossman, and Felix G. Rohatyn, "The Embassy of the Future," Center for Strategic and International Studies, Washington, D.C., 2007.

60. "Private Sector Summit on Public Diplomacy: Models for Action," U.S. State Department and the PR Coalition, Washington, D.C., 2007.

61. Rothkopf, *Running the World*, 410.

62. Blackwill, in discussion with author, March 26, 2007.

63. Oakley, in discussion with author, January 15, 2007.

64. U.S. House of Representatives, Appropriations Committee, Subcommittee on Foreign Operations, Export Financing and Related Programs, *Testimony of Ambassador Randall L. Tobias, U.S. Director of Foreign Assistance and U.S.Aid Administrator: FY 2007 Budget Hearing for U.S.Aid*, 109th sess., April 26, 2006, http://www.usaid.gov/press/speeches/2006/ty060426.html.

65. George W. Bush, speech presented to the Inter-American Development Bank, March 14, 2002.

66. Jamie Drummond, in discussion with author, June 23, 2008.

67. Lorne Craner et al., "U.S. Aid Should Be Earned," *New York Times*, December 20, 2008. The four authors were the citizen appointees to the MCC board.

68. Andrew Natsios, in discussion with author, March 26, 2007.

69. John Hewko, in discussion with author, January 17, 2007; Paul Applegarth, in discussion with author, January 19, 2007.

70. Lex Rieffel and James Fox, "The Brookings Institution Policy Brief #145," Brookings Institution, Washington, D.C., 2005; Lex Rieffel and James Fox, "The Millennium Challenge Corporation: An Opportunity for the Next President (Working Paper 30)," ed. Center for Global Economy and Development, Brookings Institution, 2008.

71. Hewko, in discussion with author, January 17, 2007.

72. Ibid.; Applegarth, in discussion with author, January 19, 2007.

73. Rieffel and Fox, "The Brookings Institution Policy Brief #145."

74. Applegarth, in discussion with author, January 19, 2007.

75. Derek Chollet and James M. Goldgeier, "The Faulty Premises of the Next Marshall Plan," *Washington Quarterly* 29, no. 1 (2005–2006): 8.

76. Martin Kady, "When Good Intentions Meet Budget Realities in the Millennium Challenge Program," *CQ Weekly* (2005).

77. Celia Dugger, "Bush Aid Initiative for Poor Nations Faces Sharp Budget Cuts and Criticism of Slow Pace," *New York Times*, June 17, 2005.

78. Ibid.

79. Condoleezza Rice, "Tenure of Paul Applegarth at the Millennium Challenge Corporation," speech presented on the occasion of Paul Applegarth's resignation, Washington, D.C., June 17, 2005.

80. George W. Bush, remarks delivered at the Swearing-In Ceremony of the CEO for Millennium Challenge Corporation, Washington, D.C., December 20, 2005.

81. "U.S. Foreign Policy: Missteps, Mistakes, and Broken Promises (an Interview with Tom Daschle)," *Harvard International Review* 28, no. 1 (2006).

82. John Danilovich, "Remarks by MCC CEO John Danilovich at a Center for Global Development Conversation with Steve Radelet" January 13, 2009.

83. *New York Times* editorial, "A Timely Departure," June 19, 2005.

84. Lael Brainard, in discussion with author, March 28, 2007.

85. Steve Radelet, in discussion with author, March 30, 2007.

86. Jim Vermillion, in discussion with author, June 6, 2007.

87. George Ingram (President, U.S. Global Leadership Campaign), in discussion with author, March 26, 2007. Radelet, in discussion with author, March 30, 2007.

88. Radelet, in discussion with author, March 30, 2007; Sheila Herrling and Sarah Rose, "Will the Millennium Challenge Account Be Caught in the Crosshairs? A Critical Year for Funding," *MCA Monitor Analysis, Center for Global Development* (March 30, 2007), http://www.cgdev.org/content/publications/detail/13398; John Hewko, e-mail messages to author, June 4, 2008, and January 5, 2009.

89. Radelet, in discussion with author, March 30, 2007.

90. Hewko, in discussion with author, January 17, 2007.

91. Randall Tobias, "Advancing the Message That Foreign Assistance Works," remarks at the U.S. Global Leadership Campaign, Washington, D.C., June 26, 2006.

92. William Langewiesche, "The Mega-Bunker of Baghdad," *Vanity Fair* (2007).

93. Packer, *The Assassin's Gate*, 227.

94. Ibid., 242.

95. Eric Schmitt and David Rohde, "Reports Assail State Dept. On Iraq Security," *New York Times,* October 23, 2007.

96. Philip Zelikow, e-mail messages to author, October 6 and 8, 2007.

97. Edmund Hull, in discussion with author, January 15, 2007.

CHAPTER FIVE. THE PRIVATIZATION OF DEFENSE

1. Doris Kearns Goodwin, *Team of Rivals: The Political Genius of Abraham Lincoln* (New York: Simon and Schuster, 2005).

2. *Frontline,* "Private Warriors," PBS.

3. Associated Press, "180,000 Private Contractors Flood Iraq," *New York Times,* September 19, 2007.

4. Renae Merle, "Census Counts 100,000 Contractors in Iraq," *Washington Post,* December 5, 2006.

5. Steve Vogel, *The Pentagon: A History* (New York: Random House, 2007).

6. John Hamre, "The Privatization of National Security," remarks at the Rohatyn Center for International Affairs, Middlebury College, Middlebury, VT, October 9, 2004.

7. "Improving the Combat Edge Through Outsourcing," U.S. Department of Defense, March 1996.

8. "Report of the Defense Science Board Task Force on Outsourcing and Privatization," Defense Science Board, Washington, D.C., 1996, http://www.dtic.mil/cgi-bin/GetTRDoc?AD=ADA316936&Location=U2&doc=GetTRDoc.pdf.

9. William Cohen, speech presented to the Business Executives for National Security Eisenhower Awards Dinner, Washington, D.C., May 6, 1997, http://www.defenselink.mil/releases/release.aspx?releaseid=1250.

10. Linda D. Kozaryn, "Gore Lauds DOD Reforms," American Forces Press Service, Washington, D.C., 1997, http://www.defenselink.mil/news/newsarticle.aspx?id=41528.

11. Donald Rumsfeld, "Bureaucracy to Battlefield," speech presented at the Pentagon, Washington, D.C., September 10, 2001, http://www.defenselink.mil/Speeches/Speech.aspx?SpeechID=430.

12. Donald Rumsfeld, "Twenty-first Century Transformation," remarks at the National Defense University, Fort McNair, Washington, D.C., January 31, 2002, http://www.defenselink.mil/speeches/speech.aspx?speechid=183.

13. Anthony Zinni, in discussion with author, January 18, 2007.

14. Theresa Whelan, in discussion with author, January 17, 2007.

15. P. W. Singer, "Lessons Not Learned: Contracting Out Iraqi Army Advising," Brookings Institution, Washington, D.C., 2008, http://www.brookings.edu/opinions/2008/0512_iraq_singer.aspx.

16. Paul Light, "The Real New Size of Government," *Organizational Performance Initiative, Research Brief,* no. 2 (2006): 9.

17. Susan Yarwood, in discussion with author, June 10, 2007.

18. Center for Public Integrity, "Making a Killing: The Business of War," Washington, D.C., 2002, 10.

19. Government Accountability Office, "Defense Acquisitions: Tailored Ap-

proach Needed to Improve Service Acquisition Outcomes," GAO, Washington, D.C., 2006.

20. Paul Verkuil, *Outsourcing Sovereignty: Why Privatization of Government Function Threatens Democracy and What We Can Do About It* (New York: Cambridge University Press, 2007).

21. Ayelish McGarvey, "Outsourcing Private Ryan (an interview with Peter Singer)," 2004, http://www.prospect.org/cs/articles?article=outsourcing_private_ ryan.

22. David M. Walker (Comptroller General of the United States), *Testimony Before the Committee on Government Oversight and Reform, House of Representatives, "Rebuilding Iraq: Reconstruction Progress Hindered by Contracting, Security, and Capacity Challenges,"* February 15, 2007, http://www.gao.gov/new.items/d07426t.pdf.

23. U.S. House of Representatives Committee on Oversight and Government Reform, "More Dollars, Less Sense: Worsening Contracting Trends Under the Bush Administration," June 2007, http://oversight.house.gov/features/moredollars/.

24. David M. Walker (Comptroller General of the United States), *Testimony Before the Sub-Committee on Defense, Committee on Appropriations, House of Representatives, "D.O.D. Acquisitions: Contracting for Better Outcomes,"* September 7, 2006, http://www.gao.gov/new. items/d0680ot.pdf.

25. *Frontline,* "Private Warriors."

26. Peter W. Singer, *Corporate Warriors: The Rise of the Privatized Military Industry* (Ithaca, NY: Cornell University Press, 2003).

27. Kellogg, Brown and Root (KBR), a blend of two previously distinct entities, Kellogg and Brown &Root, became a wholly-owned subsidiary of Halliburton in March 2002. See http://www.halliburton.com/about/history_new_phase.jsp.

28. Tim Spicer, *An Unorthodox Soldier: Peace and War and the Sandline Affair* (Edinburgh, U.K.: Mainstream, 1999), 24.

29. Quoted in Jason Vest, "State Outsources Secret War," *Nation,* May 23, 2001.

30. "Private Military Companies: Options for Regulation," London, The House of Commons, 2002.

31. Laura Peterson, "Privatizing Conflict: The New World Order," Center for Public Integrity, Washington, D.C., 2002.

32. *Frontline,* "Private Warriors."

33. Peterson, "Privatizing Conflict."

34. Dan Guttman, "The Shadow Pentagon: Private Contractors Play a Huge Role in Basic Government Work—Mostly out of View," Center for Public Integrity, Washington, D.C., 2004.

35. Linda Robinson and Douglas Pasternak, "America's Secret Armies," *U.S. News and World Report,* November 4, 2002.

36. Jason Vest, "Dyncorp's Drug Problem," *Nation,* July 11, 2001.

37. Jonathan D. Tepperman, "Can Mercenaries Protect Hamid Karzai?," *New Republic,* November 18, 2002.

38. Stephen Fidler, "Private Security: Operating in a Troubling Legal Vacuum," *Financial Times,* May 6, 2005.

39. P. W. Singer, "The Law Catches Up to Private Military and Embeds," http:// www.defensetech.org/archives/003123.html.

40. James Surowiecki, "Army, Inc.," *New Yorker,* January 12, 2004, 19; David Isenberg, "A Fistful of Contractors: The Case for a Pragmatic Assessment of Private Military Companies in Iraq," in *British American Security International Council (BASIC) Research Report,* 2004.

41. Donald Rumsfeld, "Budget Testimony Before the Senate-House Armed Services Committee," February 17, 2005, http://www.defenselink.mil/speeches/speech.aspx?speechid=56.

42. Owen West, "Private Contractors Aren't the Answer to the Army's Problems," http://slate.msn.com/id/2104305/entry/2104507/.

43. David Shearer, "Private Military Force and Challenges for the Future," *Cambridge Review of International Affairs* 13, no. 1 (1999): 83. Ed Soyster, in discussion with author, January 16, 2007.

44. For further details on the use of PMCs in Latin America and the Balkans, see Allison Stanger and Mark E. Williams, "Private Military Companies: Benefits and Costs of Outsourcing Security," *Yale Journal of International Affairs* 2, no. 1 (2006).

45. Theresa Whelan, remarks to the IPOA Dinner, Washington, D.C., November 19, 2003.

46. General Accounting Office, "Contingency Operations: Army Should Do More to Control Contract Costs in the Balkans," GAO, Washington, D.C., 2000, http://www.gao.gov/new.items/ns00225.pdf.

47. Erik Eckholm, "Excess Billing by Halliburton Is Put at $108 Million in Audit," *New York Times,* March 15, 2005; Joel Brinkley and Eric Schmitt, "Halliburton Will Repay U.S. Excess Charges for Troops' Meals," *New York Times,* February 3, 2004.

48. Neil King Jr., "Pentagon Questions Halliburton on $1.8 Billion in Work," *Wall Street Journal,* August 11, 2004.

49. Neely Tucker, "A Web of Truth," *Washington Post,* October 9, 2005.

50. Donald Rumsfeld, speech presented on the future of Iraq, Johns Hopkins School of Advanced International Studies. Baltimore, MD, December 5, 2005.

51. KBR's cost projections were based on their experience in Bosnia and Kosovo, which turned out to be a flawed assumption for estimating costs in Iraq. Unlike Bosnia and Kosovo, Iraq remained a war zone even after victory had been declared, which has made the provision of the same services a more costly proposition. Such knowledge should make us leery of facile assertions that KBR is gouging the American taxpayer. "It is perfectly feasible, and it happens all the time, for contractors to lose money on cost-reimbursement contracts." See the interview with Steve Schooner, *Frontline,* "Private Warriors."

52. I am indebted to conversations with Thierry Warin and Jeff Carpenter of the Economics Department at Middlebury College for the insights in the analysis that follows.

53. Anthony Bianco and Stephanie Anderson Forest, "Outsourcing War," *Business Week,* September 15, 2003.

54. Isenberg, "A Fistful of Contractors."

55. Walter Pincus, "Increase in Contracting Intelligence Jobs Raises Concerns," *Washington Post,* March 19, 2006.

56. Government Accountability Office, *Testimony of David M. Walker, "D.O.D. Acquisitions: Contracting for Better Outcomes,"* http://www.gao.gov/new.items/d0680ot.pdf.

57. "Contractors' Support of US Operations in Iraq," Congressional Budget Office, Washington, D.C., 2008, 16–17.

58. Whelan, remarks to the IPOA Dinner.

59. *Frontline*, "Private Warriors."

60. Whelan, remarks to the IPOA Dinner.

61. Rajiv Chandrasekaran, *Imperial Life in the Emerald City: Inside Iraq's Green Zone* (New York: Knopf, 2006), 13.

62. The CPA report also made it clear that most contractors do not work directly for the U.S. government. Instead a web of subcontracting prevails, one that all too quickly becomes impossible to map. Isenberg, "A Fistful of Contractors."

63. John Broder and James Risen, "Death Toll for Contractors Reaches New High in Iraq," *New York Times*, May 19, 2007.

64. Isenberg, "A Fistful of Contractors"; Matthew Quirk, "Private Military Contractors," *Atlantic Monthly*, September 2004.

65. Chandrasekaran, *Imperial Life in the Emerald City*, 273.

66. Borzou Daragahi, "In Iraq, Private Contractors Lighten Load on U.S. Troops," *Pittsburgh Post-Gazette*, September 28, 2003.

67. P. W. Singer, "Nation Builders and Low Bidders in Iraq," *New York Times*, June 15, 2004.

68. Pratap Chaterjee, "Private Contractors and Torture at Abu Ghraib, Iraq," Democracy Now, http://www.democracynow.org/2004/5/12/private_contractors_and_torture_at_abu.

69. Singer, "Nation Builders and Low Bidders in Iraq."

70. Source Watch, "Erinys International Ltd.—Source Watch," Source Watch: A project of the Center for Media and Democracy, http://www.sourcewatch.org/index.php?title=Erinys_International_Ltd.

71. *Frontline*, "Private Warriors."

72. Ibid.

73. Chandrasekaran, *Imperial Life in the Emerald City*, 288.

74. T. Christian Miller, "Private Contractors Outnumber U.S. Troops in Iraq," *Los Angeles Times*, July 3, 2007.

75. Ray Jennings (USAID Contract Specialist), in discussion with author, March 29, 2007.

76. Jason Aplon (USAID Team Leader), in discussion with author, March 29, 2007.

77. Doug Brooks (President, IPOA), in discussion with author, January 16, 2007.

78. Lawrence Wilkerson (former State Department chief of staff for Colin Powell), in discussion with author, March 28, 2007.

79. Neil MacDonald, "Billions Pour into Iraqi Reconstruction Efforts," *Financial Times*, December 7, 2005.

80. Roger Cohen, "The MacArthur Lunch," *New York Times*, August 27, 2007.

81. James Boxell, "Competition Hits Security Groups in Iraq," *Financial Times*, November 5, 2005.

82. David Sanger, "The Reach of War: News Analysis; Amid Hints Bush Will Change Policy, Clues That He Won't," *New York Times*, December 4, 2006; James Baker and Lee Hamilton, *Iraq Study Group Report* (New York: Random House, 2006).

83. Naomi Klein, *The Shock Doctrine: The Rise of Disaster Capitalism* (New York: Metropolitan, 2007), 356.

84. Joseph Stiglitz, "Markets Do Not Belong in a War Zone," *Financial Times,* November 23, 2004.

85. Government Accountability Office, "Military Operations: High Level DOD Action Needed to Address Long-standing Problems of Management and Oversight of Contractors Supporting Deployed Forces," Government Accountability Office, Washington, D.C., 2006; Katherine Schinasi (Managing Director, Acquisition Source and Management, GAO), *Testimony Before the Subcommittee on Readiness, Management and Support, Committee on Armed Services, U.S. Senate: "Defense Acquisitions: US Needs to Assert Better Management and Oversight to Better Control Acquisition of Services,"* January 17, 2007, http://www.gao.gov/new.items/d07640r.pdf; William Solis (Director, Defense Capabilities and Management, GAO), *Testimony Before the Subcommittee on National Security, Emerging Threats and International Relations, Committee on Government Reform: "Rebuilding Iraq: Actions Still Needed to Improve the Use of Private Security Providers,"* June 13, 2006, http://www.gao.gov/new.items/d06865t.pdf.

86. *Frontline,* "Private Warriors."

87. Isenberg, "A Fistful of Contractors."

88. Philip Carter, "Hired Guns: What to Do About Military Contractors Run Amok," *Slate,* April 9, 2004.

89. Thomas Catan, "Private Armies March into a Legal Vacuum," *Financial Times,* February 10, 2005.

90. The analysis that follows draws from Stanger and Williams, "Private Military Companies: Benefits and Costs of Outsourcing Security."

91. See Deborah Avant, *The Market for Force: The Consequences of Privatizing Security* (New York: Cambridge University Press, 2005), Table 1.1. Since PMCs operate globally, many defy easy classification by country. To resolve this problem, Avant classifies a firm's country of origin with reference to the primary country from which a majority of its employees come.

92. Jonathan Guthrie, "Tim Spicer Finds Security in the World's War Zones," *Financial Times,* April 7, 2006; Debora Spar, *Ruling the Waves: From the Compass to the Internet, a History of Business and Politics Along the Technological Frontier* (New York: Harvest, 2003).

CHAPTER SIX. THE SLOW DEATH OF USAID

1. J. Brian Atwood, M. Peter McPherson, and Andrew Natsios, "Arrested Development," *Foreign Affairs* 87, no. 6 (2008).

2. Greg Behrman, *The Most Noble Adventure: The Marshall Plan and the Time When America Helped Save Europe* (New York: Free Press, 2007).

3. Curt Tarnoff and Larry Nowels, "Foreign Aid: An Introductory Overview of U.S. Programs and Policy," Congressional Research Service, Report for Congress, April 15, 2004, http://fpc.state.gov/documents/organization/31987.pdf.

4. Task Force on Overseas Economic Operations (Henning W. Prentis Jr., chair), "Report on Overseas Economic Operations, Commission on Organization of the

Executive Branch of the Government," March 28, 1955, http://pdf.usaid.gov/pdf_docs/PCAAA435.pdf.

5. Morris K. Udall, "The Foreign Assistance Act of 1961: A Special Report," 1961, http://www.library.arizona.edu/exhibits/udall/special/foreign.html.

6. Steven Radelet, *Challenging Foreign Aid: A Policymaker's Guide to the Millennium Challenge Account* (Washington, D.C.: Center for Global Development, 2003), 4–5.

7. The President's Committee, William H. Draper, chair, "U.S. Military Assistance Program," August 17, 1959, http://pdf.usaid.gov/pdf_docs/PCAAA444.pdf.

8. United States Agency for International Development, "New Directions in Foreign Aid: President Nixon's Message to the Congress," USAID, Washington, D.C., May 28, 1969, http://pdf.usaid.gov/pdf_docs/PCAAA593.pdf.

9. James Grant, "The Pearson Commission Report: A First Look," United States Agency for International Development (USAID), Washington, D.C., October 9, 1969.

10. Ibid.

11. Task Force on International Development, Rudolph Peterson, chair, "U.S. Foreign Assistance in the 1970s: A New Approach," March 4, 1970, http://pdf.usaid.gov/pdf_docs/PNABH264.pdf.

12. Committee to Determine USAID Role in International Assistance, Ernest Stern, chair, "USAID Role in International Assistance (Stern Committee Report)," December 13, 1971, http://pdf.usaid.gov/pdf_docs/PNABR805.pdf (6).

13. President's Task Force on International Private Enterprise and the Agency for International Development, Dwayne O. Andreas, chair, "Report to the President," December 1984, http://pdf.usaid.gov/pdf_docs/PNAAR670.pdf (4).

14. Ibid.

15. The National Bipartisan Commission on Central America, Henry Kissinger, chair, "Report of the National Bipartisan Commission on Central America," January 10, 1984, http://pdf.usaid.gov/pdf_docs/PNABB526.pdf.

16. Ibid., 127.

17. Ibid., 47.

18. Committee on Foreign Affairs, Lee Hamilton, chair, "Report of the Task Force on Foreign Assistance to the Committee on Foreign Affairs," February 1, 1989, http://pdf.usaid.gov/pdf_docs/PNABB596.pdf (26).

19. Ibid., 29–30.

20. George Ingram, in discussion with author, March 26, 2007.

21. U.S. House of Representatives, *Report of the Task Force on Foreign Assistance to the Committee of Foreign Affairs, "Development and the National Interest: U.S. Economic Assistance into the Twenty-first Century (Woods Report),"* February 17, 1989, http://pdf.usaid.gov/pdf_docs/PNABB596.pdf.

22. Walter Bollinger, "Improving Agency Efficiency," internal memorandum, United States Agency for International Development (USAID), December 1989, http://pdf.usaid.gov/pdf_docs/PDABD105.pdf (13).

23. Craig Murphy, *The United Nations Development Programme: A Better Way?* (New York: Cambridge University Press, 2006).

24. Amartya Sen, *Development as Freedom* (New York: Anchor, 2000), 3.

25. William Russell Easterly, *The White Man's Burden: Why the West's Efforts to Aid the Rest Have Done So Much Ill and So Little Good* (New York: Penguin, 2006), 336.

26. Andrew Natsios, in phone discussion with author, June 7, 2008.

27. Michael Cohen, "Poverty, Inequality, and Economic Growth: Challenges for Development," speech presented at the Rohatyn Center for International Affairs, Middlebury College, Middlebury, VT, December 9, 2005.

28. Both the 1989 Hamilton report and the 1993 Wharton report, for example, reached the conclusion that the Foreign Assistance Act had become dysfunctional.

29. United States Agency for International Development, "Tsunami Assistance One Year Later," USAID, http://www.usaid.gov/press/factsheets/2005/fs051221.html.

30. Lael Brainard, "Conclusion and Recommendations," in *Security by Other Means: Foreign Assistance, Global Poverty, and American Leadership*, ed. Lael Brainard (Washington, D.C.: Brookings Institution Press, 2007).

31. Center for Global Prosperity, "Index of Global Philanthropy 2008," Center for Global Prosperity, Hudson Institute, 2008, 17.

32. Tarnoff and Nowels, "Foreign Aid," 32 (footnote 20).

33. Committee on Foreign Affairs, "Report of the Task Force on Foreign Assistance," 2.

34. Ben Barber, "Andrew Natsios: Getting USAID on Its Feet," American Foreign Service Association, Washington, D.C., 2002, 4.

35. Andrew Natsios, in phone discussion with author, June 7, 2008.

36. Rubén Berríos, *Contracting for Development: The Role of for-Profit Contractors in US Development Assistance* (Westport, CT: Praeger, 2000), 128.

37. "Critical Issues/Further Analysis: The President's Commission on the Management of Aid Programs," December 22, 1992, http://pdf.usaid.gov/pdf_docs/PCAAA288.pdf.

38. United States Agency for International Development, "USAID Primer: What We Do and How We Do It," USAID, Washington, D.C., 2005, http://pdf.usaid.gov/pdf_docs/PDACD100.pdf (13). Atwood, McPherson, and Natsios, "Arrested Development."

39. United States Agency for International Development, "A Decade of Change: Profiles of USAID Assistance to Europe and Eurasia," USAID, Washington, D.C., 2000, http://www.usaid.gov/locations/europe_eurasia/ten_year/pdfs/decadeentire.pdf (39).

40. See summary of chapter six in Andrew Natsios, *Foreign Aid in the National Interest: Promoting Freedom, Security, and Opportunity* U.S. Agency for International Development, Washington, D.C., 2003, http://www.usaid.gov/fani/Full_Report—Foreign_Aid_in_the_National_Interest.pdf.

41. Andrew Natsios, "First Principles of Development," Heritage Foundation, Washington, D.C., April 25, 2002, http://pdf.usaid.gov/pdf_docs/PCAAB258.pdf (8).

42. Natsios, *Foreign Aid in the National Interest*, 27; Natsios, "First Principles of Development."

43. Roger Bate, "The Trouble with USAID," American Enterprise Institute for Public Policy Research, Washington, D.C., 2006.

44. Berríos, *Contracting for Development*.

45. Bate, "The Trouble with USAID," 3.

46. Committee on Foreign Affairs, "Report of the Task Force on Foreign Assistance," 27.

47. Perhaps there is some other explanation I don't see. Explore the database yourself at http://www.usaspending.gov/fpds/index.php?reptype=a, and let me know if you can find it!

48. Andrew Natsios, in discussion with author, March 26, 2007.

49. Abby Stoddard, "Trends in U.S. Humanitarian Policy," in *HPG (Humanitarian Policy Group) Briefing*, no. 3, April 2002, http://pdf.usaid.gov/pdf_docs/PCAAB018.pdf (3).

50. Steve Radelet, in discussion with author, March 30, 2007.

51. Roya Wolverson, "Beltway Bandits," *Newsweek*, December 3, 2007.

52. George W. Bush, "Remarks by the President on Global Development," speech presented at the Inter-American Development Bank, March 14, 2002.

53. Barber, "Andrew Natsios: Getting USAID on Its Feet."

54. Stoddard, "Trends in U.S. Humanitarian Policy."

55. United States Agency for International Development, "USAID Primer," 23ff.

56. Barber, "Andrew Natsios: Getting USAID on Its Feet," 3.

57. Radelet, *Challenging Foreign Aid*, 2.

58. United States Agency for International Development, "U.S. Foreign Aid: Meeting the Challenges of the Twenty-first Century," USAID, Washington, D.C., 2004.

59. United States Agency for International Development, "U.S. Agency for International Development Results Report," USAID, Washington, D.C., 2005, 5.

60. United States Agency for International Development, "USAID Primer," 2.

61. United States Agency for International Development, "The Voluntary Foreign Aid Programs: Report of Voluntary Agencies Engaged in Overseas Relief and Development (2006)," USAID, Washington, D.C., 2006.

62. Natsios, *Foreign Aid in the National Interest*, 29.

63. See photo in Daniel Yergin and Joseph Stanislaw, *The Commanding Heights: The Battle for the World Economy* (New York: Simon and Schuster, 2002).

64. United States Agency for International Development, "USAID Primer," 5.

65. Thomas Melia, public lecture, Rohatyn Center for International Affairs, Middlebury College, Middlebury, VT, October 27, 2005.

66. United States Agency for International Development, "USAID Primer," 9.

67. United States Agency for International Development, "U.S. Foreign Aid," 14.

68. Natsios, *Foreign Aid in the National Interest*, 145 (see Table 6.4 on page 146 for summary of estimates).

69. Ibid., 131.

70. Carol Adelman, in discussion with author, June 6, 2007.

71. David Rohde and Carlotta Gall, "Delays Hurting U.S. Rebuilding in Afghanistan," *New York Times*, November 7, 2005.

72. Subcommittee on National Security, Emerging Threats and International Relations of the Committee on Government Reform, "Strategic Workforce Planning at USAID," 108th Congress, 1st sess., September 23, 2003, http://frwebgate.access.gpo.gov/cgi-bin/getdoc.cgi?dbname=108_house_hearings&docid=f:92392.pdf (15).

73. United States Agency for International and Department of State Develop-

ment, "Strategic Plan, Fiscal Years 2004–2009: Aligning Diplomacy and Development Assistance," USAID, Washington, D.C., 2003, http://pdf.usaid.gov/pdf_docs/PDABY700.pdf.

74. United States Agency for International Development, "USAID Primer."

75. Condoleezza Rice, "New Direction for US Foreign Assistance," speech presented at the U.S. Department of State, Washington, D.C., January 19, 2006.

76. Randall Tobias, "Transformational Diplomacy: Sharing the Vision," speech presented to the Society for International Development, Washington, D.C., September 14, 2006; Randall L. Tobias, "Living Up to Our Mission," paper presented at the InterAction Annual Meeting Opening Plenary, L'Enfant Plaza Hotel, Washington, D.C., April 10, 2006.

77. Randall Tobias, "Getting a Better Return on America's Investment in People," remarks at the Initiative for Global Development 2006 National Summit, Washington, D.C., June 15, 2006.

78. United States Agency for International Development, "USAID Administrator Appoints Chief Economic Advisor," press release, June 6, 2006, http://www.usaid.gov/press/releases/2006/pr060606.html.

79. Glenn Kessler, "Rice Deputy Quits After Query over Escort Service," *Washington Post*, April 28, 2007.

80. Eric Postel, in discussion with author, November 19, 2007.

81. Mary K. Bush, "Beyond Assistance (Help Commission Report)," ed. HELP Commission, 2007.

82. David Brooks, "The Education of Robert Gates," *New York Times*, September 19, 2007.

83. David Sanger, "A Handpicked Team for a Sweeping Shift in Foreign Policy," *New York Times*, December 1, 2008.

84. United States Agency for International Development, "USAID History," USAID, http://www.usaid.gov/about_usaid/usaidhist.html.

85. General Accounting Office, "Foreign Assistance: Strategic Workforce Planning Can Help USAID Address Current and Future Challenges," Washington, D.C., August, 2003, http://www.gao.gov/new.items/d03946.pdf.

86. Rohde and Gall, "Delays Hurting U.S. Rebuilding in Afghanistan."

87. Atwood, McPherson, and Natsios, "Arrested Development."

88. Andrew Natsios, in discussion with author, March 26, 2007; Steve Radelet and Jim Boomgard, in discussions with author, March 30, 2007.

89. General Accounting Office, "Foreign Assistance."

90. Andrew Natsios, in discussion with author, March 26, 2007.

91. Stan Soloway, in discussion with author, March 27, 2007.

92. General Accounting Office, "Foreign Assistance."

93. Lael Brainard, ed., *Security by Other Means: Foreign Assistance, Global Poverty, and American Leadership* (Washington, D.C.: Brookings Institution Press, 2007), 47.

94. United States Agency for International Development, "Tanzania: Activity Data Sheet," USAID, http://www1.usaid.gov/pubs/cbj2002/afr/tz/621–005.html.

95. Jason Aplon, in discussion with author, March 29, 2007.

96. Tarnoff and Nowels, "Foreign Aid," 8.

97. Paul Applegarth, in discussion with author, January 19, 2007.

98. Andrew Natsios, in phone discussion with author, June 7, 2008.

99. Brainard, *Security by Other Means.*

CHAPTER SEVEN. LAISSEZ-FAIRE HOMELAND SECURITY

1. Stephen Flynn, "America the Resilient," *Foreign Affairs* (2008).

2. Partnership for Public Service and American University's Institute for the Study of Public Policy Implementation, "The Best Places to Work in the Federal Government," Washington, D.C., 2007, http://bestplacestowork.org/BPTW/rankings/.

3. Stephen Barr, "Morale at Homeland Security Still Shaky After Five Years," *Washington Post,* April 18, 2008. Those worrisome circumstances made this chapter the most difficult to research. Few DHS employees agreed to be interviewed. Some agreed, but only if written questions were submitted in advance and the response to them could be in writing. My experience at the Pentagon was just the opposite. Every interview generated new names for my interview list, and no Pentagon employee declined an interview.

4. Joseph Lieberman, "The Best Defense: Leveraging the Strength of Our Military to Protect the Homeland," speech presented to the Progressive Policy Institute, Washington, D.C, June 26, 2002.

5. Howard Ball, *U.S. Homeland Security: A Reference Handbook,* Contemporary World Issues (Santa Barbara, CA: ABC-CLIO, 2005), 27.

6. Susan B. Glasser and Michael Grunwald, "Department's Mission Was Undermined from Start," *Washington Post,* December 22, 2005.

7. Ball, *U.S. Homeland Security,* 28.

8. Richard Clarke, *Against All Enemies: Inside America's War on Terror* (New York: Free Press, 2004), 250.

9. G. W. Bush, "Remarks by the President in an Address to the Nation," The Cross Hall, Washington, D.C., June 6, 2002.

10. Ball, *U.S. Homeland Security,* 28.

11. Department of Homeland Security, "Homeland Security Act of 2002," Department of Homeland Security, http://www.dhs.gov/xabout/laws/law_regulation_rule_0011.shtm.

12. John Hamre (president and CEO, Center for Strategic and International Studies), *Testimony Before the Committee on Appropriations, U.S. Senate, "9/11 Commission Recommendations,"* September 22, 2004, http://www.csis.org/media/csis/congress/ts040922hamre.pdf.

13. D. F. Kettl, *System Under Stress: Homeland Security and American Politics* (Washington, D.C.: Congressional Quarterly Press, 2004), 35.

14. Those twenty-two agencies and their former assignments are the following: U.S. Customs Service (Treasury), Immigration and Naturalization Service (Justice), Federal Protective Service, Transport Security Administration (Transportation), Federal Law Enforcement Training Center (Treasury), Animal and Plant Health Inspection Service (Agriculture), Office for Domestic Preparedness (Treasury), Federal

Emergency Management Agency (FEMA), Strategic National Stockpile and the National Disaster Medical System (Health and Human Services), Nuclear Incident Response Team (Energy), Domestic Energy Support Teams (Justice), National Domestic Preparedness Office (FBI), CBRN Countermeasures Programs (Energy), Environmental Measurements Laboratory (Energy), National BW Defense Analysis Center (Defense), Plum Island Animal Disease Center (Agriculture), Federal Computer Incident Response Center (GSA), National Communications System (Defense), National Infrastructure Protection Center (FBI), Energy Assistance and Assurance Program (Energy), Secret Service, Coast Guard. Department of Homeland Security, "History: Who Became a Part of the Department?" Department of Homeland Security, www.dhs.gov, 2006.

15. M. E. O'Hanlon et al., *Protecting the American Homeland* (Brookings Institution Press, 2003), 25.

16. G. W. Bush, "Remarks by the President at Swearing-In of Tom Ridge," Cross Hall, Washington, D.C., January 24, 2003.

17. Glasser and Grunwald, "Department's Mission Was Undermined from Start."

18. Juliette N. Kayyem, "The Homeland Security Muddle," *American Prospect* 14, no. 10 (2003); Patricia Dalton (director, Strategic Issues), *Testimony Before the Subcommittee on Government Efficiency, Financial Management, and Intergovernmental Relations, Committee on Government Reform, House of Representatives: "Homeland Security: Effective Intergovernmental Organization Is Key to Success,"* August 20, 2002, http://www.gao.gov/new.items/do21011t.pdf.

19. "John DiIulio's Letter: Your Next Essay on the Bush Administration," *Esquire*, http://www.esquire.com/features/dilulio.

20. Michael Chertoff, "Remarks at the Harvard School of Public Health National Preparedness Leadership Initiative," June 13, 2007.

21. O'Hanlon et al., *Protecting the American Homeland*, 10.

22. Glasser and Grunwald, "Department's Mission Was Undermined from Start."

23. Ibid.

24. Michael A. Wermuth (director, Homeland Security Program, the Rand Corporation), *Testimony Before the Committee on Homeland Security and Governmental Affairs, United States Senate, "The Road Ahead,"* January 26, 2005, http://rand.org/pubs/testimonies/2005/RAND_CT233.pdf (20).

25. Department of Homeland Security, "National Strategy for Homeland Security," Department of Homeland Security, http://www.dhs.gov/xlibrary/assets/nat_strat_hls.pdf.

26. Peter F. Verga, *Testimony Before the National Commission on Terrorist Attacks upon the United States,* Seventh Public Hearing, January 26, 2004, http://www.9-11commission.gov/hearings/hearing7/witness_verga.htm.

27. U.S. Department of Defense, "Strategy for Homeland Defense and Civil Support," Department of Defense, Washington, D.C., 2005.

28. Peter F. Verga, in discussion with author, June 6, 2007.

29. Joseph Cuddihy, in discussion with author, June 5, 2007.

30. Norman J. Rabkin (managing director, Homeland Security and Justice), *Testimony Before the Subcommittee on Management, Integration, and Oversight, Committee on Homeland Security, U.S. House of Representatives: "Overview of Department of Homeland Security Management Challenges,"* April 20, 2005, http://www.gao.gov/new.items/d05573t.pdf.

31. *The 9/11 Commission Report* (New York: Norton, 2004), 399.

32. Ibid., 427.

33. 9/11 Public Discourse Project, "Final Report on 9/11 Commission Recommendations," 9/11 Public Discourse Project, http://www.9-11pdp.org/press/2005-12-05_summary.pdf.

34. Shane Harris and Greta Wodele, "Bureaucracy Hinders 9/11 Commission Recommendations," *National Journal Online,* January 13, 2006, http://www.govexec.com/dailyfed/0106/011306nj1.htm.

35. Ibid.

36. Ibid.

37. Amy Harder, "Panel Warns of DHS Oversight Overkill," *National Journal Online,* November 20, 2008, http://lostintransition.nationaljournal.com/2008/11/dhs-oversight.php; Richard A. Falkenrath (visiting fellow, the Brookings Institution), *Testimony Before the United States Senate Committee on Homeland Security and Governmental Affairs,* January 26, 2005.

38. Amy Zegart, Matthew Hipp, and Seth Jacobson, "Governance Challenges in Port Security: A Case Study of Emergency Response Capabilities at the Ports of Los Angeles and Long Beach," in *Protecting the Nation's Seaports: Balancing Security and Cost,* ed. Jon D. Haveman and Howard J. Shatz (San Francisco: Public Policy Institute of California, 2006).

39. David M. Walker, *Testimony Before the Subcommittee on Technology, Terrorism and Government Information, Senate Committee on the Judiciary, "Homeland Security: Proposal for Cabinet Agency Has Merit but Implementation Will Be Pivotal to Success,"* June 25, 2002, http://www.gao.gov/new.items/d02886t.pdf.

40. Paul Verkuil, *Outsourcing Sovereignty: Why Privatization of Government Function Threatens Democracy and What We Can Do About It* (New York: Cambridge University Press, 2007).

41. Kathleen Kraninger, in discussion with author, June 5, 2007.

42. Paul Verkuil, "The Publicization of Airport Security," *Cardozo Law Review* 27, no. 5 (2006).

43. FOXNews.com, "House Panel Votes to Block Ports Deal," FOXNews.com, http://www.foxnews.com/story/0,2933,187147,00.html.

44. Michael O'Hanlon and Jeremy Shapiro, "Introduction," in *Protecting the Homeland 2006/2007,* ed. Michael O'Hanlon and Jeremy Shapiro (Washington, D.C.: Brookings Institution Press, 2006).

45. U.S. House of Representatives Committee on Oversight and Government Reform, "Dollars, Not Sense: Government Contracting Under the Bush Administration," June 2006, http://oversight.house.gov/Documents/20060711103910-86046.pdf.

46. Lee Hamilton and Thomas Keane, "A Formula for Disaster," *New York Times,* December 5, 2005.

47. Veronica De Rugy, "Are We Ready for the Next 9/11? The Sorry State—and

Stunning Waste—of Homeland Security Spending," *Reason* (2006), http://www.aei. org/include/pub_print.asp?pubID=23956&url=http://www.aei.org/publications/ filter.foreign,pubID.23956/pub_detail.asp.

48. Sarah Posner, "Security for Sale," *American Prospect* 17, no. 1 (2006).

49. Stephen L. Caldwell (acting director of Homeland Security and Justice Issues), *Testimony Before the Subcommittee on Coast Guard and Maritime Transportation, Committee on Transportation and Infrastructure, House of Representatives: "Status of Efforts to Improve Deepwater Program Management and Address Operational Challenges,"* March 8, 2007, http://www.gao.gov/new.items/d07575t.pdf.

50. *60 Minutes,* "The Troubled Waters of Deepwater," CBS News, 2007.

51. Ibid.

52. Eric Lipton, "Failure to Navigate: Billions Later, Plan to Remake the Coast Guard Fleet Stumbles," *New York Times,* December 9, 2006.

53. Michael DeKort, "Please Call Your Congressman and Demand Hearings," YouTube.com, 2006.

54. Lipton, "Failure to Navigate."

55. Eric Lipton, "Coast Guard to Manage Fleet Modernization," *New York Times,* April 18, 2007.

56. John Palguta, in discussion with author, June 6, 2007.

57. Naomi Klein, *The Shock Doctrine: The Rise of Disaster Capitalism* (New York: Metropolitan, 2007), 315.

58. Reuters, "Tom Ridge to Advise Techradium on 'Iris' Technology," January 9, 2008.

59. House Bipartisan Committee, "A Failure of Initiative," February 15, 2006, http://www.gpoaccess.gov/katrinareport/mainreport.pdf (361).

60. Christopher Swope and Zach Patton, "In Disaster's Wake," *Governing,* November 2005.

61. Frances Fragos Townsend (chair), "The Federal Response to Hurricane Katrina: Lessons Learned," White House (review commission), Washington, D.C., February 2006, http://library.stmarytx.edu/acadlib/edocs/katrinawh.pdf (74).

62. Ibid., 74–75.

63. Ibid., 78.

64. Ibid., 62.

65. Paul McHale (assistant secretary of defense for homeland defense), *Testimony Before the Committee on Armed Services, U.S. House of Representatives: "Statement to the House Armed Services Committee,"* May 25, 2006, http://www.globalsecurity.org/security/ library/congress/2006_h/060525-mchale.pdf.

66. Michael Chertoff, "Statement by Secretary Chertoff Regarding White House Katrina Lessons Learned Report," Department of Homeland Security, February 23, 2006, http://www.dhs.gov/xnews/releases/press_release_0866.shtm.

67. House Bipartisan Committee, "A Failure of Initiative," 1.

68. Ibid., 2–3.

69. Ibid., 359.

70. For examples, see Townsend, "The Federal Response to Hurricane Katrina," 136–37, appendix B.

71. House Bipartisan Committee, "A Failure of Initiative," 354.

72. Jeremy Scahill, *Blackwater: The Rise of the World's Most Powerful Mercenary Army* (New York: Nation, 2007), 326–27.

73. Klein, *The Shock Doctrine*, 410–11.

74. Chertoff, "Statement by Secretary Chertoff."

75. House Bipartisan Committee, "A Failure of Initiative," 361.

76. The governor of Louisiana had to call back over a third of her National Guard from service in Iraq (many of whom were due to rotate anyway). This suggests that the personnel crisis in Iraq has an even deeper dimension. If National Guard are demanded back home for other duties (including not only hurricanes but possibly even border patrol), how can they provide half of the personnel in Iraq?

77. G. W. Bush, "Remarks by the President in an Address to the Nation," New Orleans, Louisiana (Jackson Square), September 15, 2005.

78. Amartya Sen, *Development as Freedom* (New York: Anchor, 2000), 128.

79. Michael A. Wermuth (director, Homeland Security Program, Rand Corporation), *Testimony Before the Senate Committee on Homeland Security and Governmental Affairs, "The Road Ahead,"* January 26, 2005, http://rand.org/pubs/testimonies/2005/RAND_CT233.pdf.

80. Thomas P. M. Barnett, *Great Powers: America and the World After Bush* (New York: Putnam, 2009), 400.

81. Stephen Flynn and Daniel B. Prieto, "Neglected Defense: Mobilizing the Private Sector to Support Homeland Security," *Council on Foreign Relations Special Report*, no. 14 (2006): 11.

82. Gary Hart and Warren Rudman, "America: Still Unprepared, Still in Danger," Council on Foreign Relations, 2002, https://secure.www.cfr.org/content/publications/attachments/Homeland_TF.pdf.

83. Flynn and Prieto, "Neglected Defense."

84. Progressive Policy Institute, "America at Risk: A Homeland Security Report Card," 2003, 7.

85. Customs and Border Protection Office of International Affairs, CSI Division, "Container Security Initiative: Strategic Plan 2006–2011," 2006.

86. Savi Technologies, "Smart and Secure Trade Lanes," Savi Technologies, http://www.savi.com/products/casestudies/wp.sst_initiative.pdf.

87. Office of Field Operations and Office of Policy and Planning, "Securing the Global Supply Chain: C-TPAT Strategic Plan," U.S. Customs and Border Protection, November 2004.

88. Bruce V. Bigelow, "High Tech Ideas for Border," *San Diego Union-Tribune*, May 18, 2006.

89. It bears mention that the original statute that created DHS had specifically stipulated the appointment of a special assistant to the secretary for the private sector, an unusual thing to require by law. However, that position in 2005 morphed into an assistant secretary position when Martinez-Fonts assumed it, a clear demotion of the office's authority.

90. Jan W. Mares, in discussion with author, June 5, 2007.

91. See http://www.dhs.gov/xopnbiz/.

92. Stephen Flynn, *America the Vulnerable: How Our Government Is Failing to Protect Us from Terrorism* (New York: Harper Collins, 2004), 50–52.

93. Richard A. Falkenrath (visiting fellow, Brookings Institution), *Testimony Before the United States Senate Committee on Homeland Security and Governmental Affairs*, January 26, 2005.

94. Stephen Goldsmith and William D. Eggers, *Governing by Network: The New Shape of the Public Sector* (Washington, D.C.: Brookings Institution, 2004), 7.

CHAPTER EIGHT. A POSTINDUSTRIAL FOREIGN POLICY

1. Scott Shane and Ron Nixon, "In Washington, Contractors Take on Biggest Role Ever," *New York Times*, February 4, 2007.

2. Stephanie Strom, "Businesses Try to Make Money and Save the World," *New York Times*, May 6, 2007.

3. CBS News, *Sixty Minutes*, "All in the Family," September 21, 2003.

4. Dana Priest, *The Mission: Waging War and Keeping Peace with America's Military* (New York: W. W. Norton, 2004).

5. Lawrence Wilkerson (former State Department chief of staff for Colin Powell), in discussion with author, March 28, 2007.

6. Anthony Zinni, in discussion with author, January 18, 2007.

7. J. Anthony Holmes, "Where Are the Civilians? How to Rebuild the U.S. Foreign Service," *Foreign Affairs* 88, no. 1 (2009).

8. George Packer, "Knowing Thy Enemy," *New Yorker*, December 18, 2006.

9. Thom Shanker, "Proposed Military Spending Is Highest Since WWII," *New York Times*, February 4, 2008.

10. Robert Blackwill, in discussion with author, March 26, 2007.

11. Jacqueline Williams-Bridgers, in discussion with author, March 27, 2007.

12. Stewart Patrick, in discussion with author, March 30, 2007.

13. Robert Gates, "Landon Lecture," speech presented at Kansas State University, November 26, 2007.

14. Department of Defense, "2006 Quadrennial Defense Review," Washington, D.C., 2006; Andrew Natsios, in discussion with author, March 26, 2007.

15. Amy Zegart, "Not So Smart Intelligence," *Los Angeles Times*, September 17, 2006.

16. Wilkerson, in discussion with author, March 28, 2007.

17. William Russell Easterly, *The White Man's Burden: Why the West's Efforts to Aid the Rest Have Done So Much Ill and So Little Good* (New York: Penguin, 2006), 312.

18. Anne-Marie Slaughter, *The Idea That Is America* (New York: Basic, 2007).

19. Figures are from Office of Management and Budget, "Budget of the United States Government (Historical Tables)," and from the Internal Revenue Service, "SOI Tax Stats—Integrated Business Data." Unfortunately, 2002 is the most recent data available. It would obviously be interesting to see how the statistic has changed with wartime spending in full gear.

20. See, for example, Yochi Dreazen, "U.S. Military Becomes Alternate-Fuel Pioneer," *Wall Street Journal*, May 21, 2008; Thomas L. Friedman, *Hot, Flat, and Crowded: Why We Need a Green Revolution—and How It Can Renew America* (New York: Farrar, Straus, and Giroux, 2008).

21. Bernard Wysocki, "Is the U.S. Government Outsourcing Its Brain?," *Wall Street Journal*, March 30, 2007.

22. Strobe Talbott, in discussion with author, March 28, 2007.

23. John Hamre, in discussion with author, March 27, 2007.

24. Williams-Bridgers, in discussion with author, March 27, 2007.

25. Henry A. Waxman, *Testimony Before the Committee on Government Reform, House of Representatives, "Contracting Abuses in Iraq,"* 108th Congress, October 15, 2003, http:// oversight.house.gov/documents/20040624072659–41626.pdf.

26. Ibid.

27. Stan Soloway, in discussion with author, March 27, 2007.

28. Elaine Kamarck, *The End of Government as We Know It: Making Public Policy Work* (Lynne Rienner, 2007).

29. Wilkerson, in discussion with author, March 28, 2007.

30. Walter Russell Mead, *Special Providence: American Foreign Policy and How It Changed the World* (London: Routledge, 2002).

31. Jeffrey E. Garten, *The Politics of Fortune: A New Agenda for Business Leaders* (Boston: Harvard Business School Press, 2002), 22–23.

32. Max Stier, in discussion with author, January 18, 2007.

33. Malcolm Gladwell, *The Tipping Point: How Little Things Can Make a Big Difference* (New York: Little, Brown, 2000).

34. Dov Seidman, *How: Why How We Do Anything Means Everything . . . in Business (and in Life)* (New York: Wiley, 2007).

35. Cullen Murphy, *Are We Rome? The Fall of an Empire and the Fate of America* (New York: Houghton Mifflin, 2007).

36. Nayan Chanda, *Bound Together: How Traders, Adventurers, Preachers, and Warriors Shaped Globalization* (New Haven: Yale University Press, 2007).

37. Karl Polanyi, *The Great Transformation* (Boston: Beacon Press, 2001).

38. David Vogel, *The Market for Virtue: The Potential and Limits of Corporate Social Responsibility* (Washington, D.C.: Brookings Institution, 2006).

39. George Lodge and Craig Wilson, *A Corporate Solution to Global Poverty: How Multinational Corporations Can Help the Poor and Invigorate Their Own Legitimacy* (Princeton, NJ: Princeton University Press, 2006).

40. David Vogel et al., "Corporate Social Responsibility and Government: Creating a Market for Virtue," panel discussion, Brookings Institution, Washington, D.C., November 2, 2005.

41. Bob Fisher, "Corporate Social Responsibility: Where Value and Values Intersect," public lecture, Rohatyn Center for International Affairs, Middlebury College, Middlebury, VT, April 10, 2006.

42. David McCormick, in discussion with author, March 27, 2007; Robin Toner, "For Democrats, New Challenge in Age-Old Rift," *New York Times*, May 8, 2007.

43. David Walker, in discussion with author, June 4, 2007.

44. Quoted in Daniel Yergin and Joseph Stanislaw, *The Commanding Heights: The Battle for the World Economy* (New York: Simon and Schuster, 2002), 187.

45. Eric Schmitt, "What Is Really Different Now?," *New York Times*, December 16, 2007.

46. Change Congress, "Change Congress," http://change-congress.org/.

47. Robert Keohane and Joseph Nye, "Power and Interdependence in the Information Age," *Foreign Affairs* 77, no. 5 (1998).

48. Joseph Stiglitz, *Making Globalization Work* (New York: W. W. Norton, 2006), 132.

49. Wikileaks, "Wikileaks," http://wikileaks.org/.

50. Andrew Ross Sorkin, "What If Watchdogs Got Bonuses?," *New York Times,* February 2, 2009.

51. Cuddihy, in discussion with author, June 5, 2007.

52. Robert C. Pozen, "Reporting for Duty," *New York Times,* March 3, 2007.

53. Sebastian Mallaby, "Good and Bad Capitalists," *Washington Post,* January 28, 2008.

54. United Nations Development Programme, "Growing Inclusive Markets," UNDP Office of the Private Sector, www.growinginclusivemarkets.org.

55. Government Accountability Office, "21st Century Challenges: Reexamining the Base of the Federal Government," Washington, D.C., February 2005, http://www.gao.gov/new.items/d05325sp.pdf (77).

56. Laura Dickinson, *Outsourcing War and Peace,* forthcoming.

57. Jeremy Scahill, *Blackwater: The Rise of the World's Most Powerful Mercenary Army* (New York: Nation, 2007), 363–64.

58. Richard Armitage and Joseph Nye, *A Smarter, More Secure America (Report of the CSIS Commission on Smart Power)* (Washington, D.C.: Center for Strategic and International Studies, 2007).

59. Google, "Google and Four U.S. States Improve Public Access to Government Websites," Google Press Center, http://www.google.com/intl/en/press/pressrel/govt_access.html.

60. Klaus Schwab, "Global Corporate Citizenship: Working with Governments and Civil Society," *Foreign Affairs* 87, no. 1 (2008).

61. Center for American Progress, "Integrated Power," Center for American Progress, http://www.americanprogress.org/issues/2005/06/b742277.html.

62. Ibid.

Bibliography

Acumen. "The Acumen Fund." Acumen, http://www.acumenfund.org/.

Adelman, Carol. In discussion with author, June 6, 2007.

Aplon, Jason. In discussion with author, March 29, 2007.

Applegarth, Paul. In discussion with author, January 19, 2007.

Argyros, George L., Marc Grossman, and Felix G. Rohatyn. "The Embassy of the Future." Washington, D.C.: Center for Strategic and International Studies, 2007.

Armitage, Richard, and Joseph Nye. *A Smarter, More Secure America (Report of the CSIS Commission on Smart Power)*. Washington, D.C.: Center for Strategic and International Studies, 2007.

Ashoka. "What Is a Social Entrepreneur? Ashoka.Org." Ashoka: Innovators for the Public, http://www.ashoka.org/social_entrepreneur.

Associated Press. "180,000 Private Contractors Flood Iraq," *New York Times*, September 19, 2007.

Atwood, J. Brian, M. Peter McPherson, and Andrew Natsios. "Arrested Development." *Foreign Affairs* 87, no. 6 (2008).

Avant, Deborah. *The Market for Force: The Consequences of Privatizing Security*. New York: Cambridge University Press, 2005.

————. "What Are Those Contractors Doing in Iraq?" *Washington Post*, May 9, 2004.

Baker, James, and Lee Hamilton. *Iraq Study Group Report*. New York: Random House, 2006.

Ball, Howard. *U.S. Homeland Security: A Reference Handbook*. Santa Barbara, Calif.: ABC-CLIO, 2005.

Barbaro, Michael. "Wal-Mart Chief Offers a Social Manifesto." *New York Times*, January 24, 2008.

Barber, Ben. "Andrew Natsios: Getting USAID on Its Feet." Washington, D.C., American Foreign Service Association, 2002.

Barnett, Thomas P. M. *Great Powers: America and the World After Bush*. New York: Putnam, 2009.

Barr, Stephen. "Morale at Homeland Security Still Shaky After Five Years." *Washington Post*, April 18, 2008.

Barton, Rick. In discussion with author, January 16, 2007.

Bass, Gary. E-mail message to author, May 19, 2008.

Bate, Roger. "The Trouble with USAID." *American Enterprise Institute for Public Policy Research*, 2006.

Bauman, Zygmunt. *Globalization: The Human Consequences.* New York: Columbia University Press, 2000.

Behrman, Greg. *The Most Noble Adventure: The Marshall Plan and the Time When America Helped Save Europe.* New York: Free Press, 2007.

Beinart, Peter. *The Good Fight: Why Liberals—and Only Liberals—Can Win the War on Terror and Make America Great Again.* New York: Harper Collins, 2006.

Berríos, Rubén. *Contracting for Development: The Role of for-Profit Contractors in US Development Assistance.* Westport, CT: Praeger, 2000.

Bianco, Anthony, and Stephanie Anderson Forest. "Outsourcing War." *Business Week,* September 15, 2003.

Bigelow, Bruce V. "High Tech Ideas for Border." *San Diego Union-Tribune,* May 18, 2006.

Blackwill, Robert. In discussion with author, March 26, 2007.

Blair, Tony. "A Battle for Global Values." *Foreign Affairs* 86, no. 1 (2007).

———. "Check Against Delivery," Speech at Georgetown University. Washington D.C., May 26, 2006.

Bollinger, Walter. "Improving Agency Efficiency." USAID internal memorandum, December 1989, http://pdf.usaid.gov/pdf_docs/PDABD105.pdf.

Boomgard, Jim. In discussion with author, March 30, 2007.

Borger, Julian, Ewen MacAskill, and Jonathan Watts. "Special Report: How the Balance of Power and Influence Is Changing: New Diplomatic Priorities Offer Snapshot of Changing World Order: US Moves Resources from Europe to Asian Giants: Global Context Changed, Says Foreign Office." *The Guardian,* March 4, 2006.

Bornstein, David. *How to Change the World: Social Entrepreneurs and the Power of New Ideas.* New York: Oxford University Press, 2004.

Boxell, James. "Competition Hits Security Groups in Iraq." *Financial Times,* November 5, 2005.

Boyatt, Thomas D. "Managing Secretary Rice's State Department: An Independent Assessment." Foreign Affairs Council Task Force, Washington, D.C., 2007.

Brainard, Lael. "Conclusion and Recommendations." In *Security by Other Means: Foreign Assistance, Global Poverty, and American Leadership.* Edited by Lael Brainard, 321–33. Washington, D.C.: Brookings Institution Press, 2007.

———. In discussion with author, March 28, 2007.

———. "Organizing US Foreign Assistance to Meet Twenty-First Century Challenges." In *Security by Other Means: Foreign Assistance, Global Poverty, and American Leadership.* Edited by Lael Brainard, 33–66. Washington, D.C.: Brookings Institution Press, 2007.

Brinkley, Joel, and Eric Schmitt. "Halliburton Will Repay U.S. Excess Charges for Troops' Meals." *The New York Times,* February 3, 2004.

Broder, John, and James Risen. "Death Toll for Contractors Reaches New High in Iraq." *New York Times,* May 19, 2007.

Broder, John, and David Rohde. "State Department Use of Contractors Leaps in 4 Years." *New York Times,* October 24, 2007.

Brooks, David. "The Education of Robert Gates." *New York Times,* September 19, 2007.

Brooks, Doug. In discussion with author, January 16, 2007.

Bush, George W. "Remarks Delivered at the Swearing-In Ceremony of the CEO for Millennium Challenge Corporation." Washington D.C., December 20, 2005.

———. "Remarks by the President in an Address to the Nation." New Orleans, LA (Jackson Square), September 15, 2005.

———. "Remarks by the President in an Address to the Nation." Washington D.C. (The Cross Hall), June 6, 2002.

———. "Remarks by the President at Swearing-In of Tom Ridge." Washington, D.C. (The Cross Hall), January 24, 2003.

———. Speech to the Inter-American Development Bank. March 14, 2002.

Bush, Mary K. "Beyond Assistance (Help Commission Report)." Edited by HELP Commission, 2007.

Business for Diplomatic Action. "America's Role in the World: A Business Perspective on Public Diplomacy." Business for Diplomatic Action, 2007.

Caldwell, Stephen L. (Acting Director of Homeland Security and Justice Issues). *Testimony Before the Subcommittee on Coast Guard and Maritime Transportation, Committee on Transportation and Infrastructure, House of Representatives: "Status of Efforts to Improve Deepwater Program Management and Address Operational Challenges,"* March 8, 2007, http://www.gao.gov/new.items/d07575t.pdf.

Center for American Progress. "Integrated Power." Center for American Progress, http://www.americanprogress.org/issues/2005/06/b742277.html.

Center for Global Prosperity. "Index of Global Philanthropy 2008." Center for Global Prosperity, Hudson Institute, 2008.

Center for Public Integrity. "Making a Killing: The Business of War." Washington, D.C., 2002.

Chanda, Nayan. *Bound Together: How Traders, Adventurers, Preachers, and Warriors Shaped Globalization.* New Haven: Yale University Press, 2007.

Chandrasekaran, Rajiv. *Imperial Life in the Emerald City: Inside Iraq's Green Zone.* New York: Knopf, 2006.

Change Congress. "Change Congress." http://change-congress.org/.

Chaterjee, Pratap. "Private Contractors and Torture at Abu Ghraib, Iraq." Democracy Now, http://www.democracynow.org/2004/5/12/private_contractors_and_torture_at_abu.

Chertoff, Michael. "Remarks at the Harvard School of Public Health National Preparedness Leadership Initiative," June 13, 2007.

Chollet, Derek, and James M. Goldgeier. "The Faulty Premises of the Next Marshall Plan." *The Washington Quarterly* 29, no. 1 (2005–2006): 7–19.

Clarke, Richard. *Against All Enemies: Inside America's War on Terror.* New York: Free Press, 2004.

CNN News. "Contractor for Military Committed Serious Violations." Special Investigations Unit, CNN News, November 24, 2008.

Coase, Ronald. "The Nature of the Firm." *Economica* 4 (1937): 386–405.

Cohen, Michael. "Poverty, Inequality, and Economic Growth: Challenges for Development." Speech delivered at the Rohatyn Center for International Affairs, Middlebury College, Middlebury, VT, December 9, 2005.

Cohen, Roger. "The MacArthur Lunch." *New York Times,* August 27, 2007.

Cohen, William. "Speech to the Business Executives for National Security Eisenhower Awards Dinner." Washington D.C., May 6, 1997.

Committee to Determine USAID role in International Assistance (Ernest Stern, Chair). *USAID Role in International Assistance (Stern Committee Report),* December 13, 1971, http://pdf.usaid.gov/pdf_docs/PNABR805.pdf.

"Contractors' Support of Us Operations in Iraq." Washington D.C.: Congressional Budget Office, 2008.

Cooper, Helene. "U.S. Is Urging Blair to Be Lead Mideast Envoy." *New York Times*, June 21, 2007.

Craner, Lorne, Bill Frist, Kenneth Hackett, and Alan Patricoff. "U.S. Aid Should Be Earned." *New York Times*, December 20, 2008.

Cuddihy, Joseph. In discussion with author, June 5, 2007.

Customs and Border Protection (CBP) Office of International Affairs, CSI Division, Washington, D.C. "Container Security Initiative: Strategic Plan 2006–2011," 2006.

Daalder, Ivo and James Lindsay. "American Empire: Not 'If' but 'What Kind.'" *New York Times*, May 10, 2003, 9.

Dalton, Patricia (Director, Strategic Issues). *Testimony Before the Subcommittee on Government Efficiency, Financial Management, and Intergovernmental Relations, Committee on Government Reform, House of Representatives "Homeland Security: Effective Intergovernmental Organization Is Key to Success,"* August 20, 2002, http://www.gao.gov/new.items/d021011t.pdf.

Danilovich, John. "Remarks by MCC CEO John Danilovich at a Center for Global Development Conversation with Steve Radelet," January 13, 2009.

Daragahi, Borzou. "In Iraq, Private Contractors Lighten Load on U.S. Troops." *Pittsburgh Post-Gazette*, September 28, 2003.

De Rugy, Veronica. "Are We Ready for the Next 9/11? The Sorry State—and Stunning Waste—of Homeland Security Spending." *Reason* (2006), http://www.aei.org/include/pub_print.asp?pubID=23956&url=http://www.aei.org/publications/filter.foreign,pubID.23956/pub_detail.asp.

DeKort, Michael. "Please Call Your Congressman and Demand Hearings." YouTube.com, 2006.

Department of Defense. "Strategy for Homeland Defense and Civil Support." Washington, D.C., Department of Defense, 2005.

———. "2006 Quadrennial Defense Review." Department of Defense, Washington, D.C., 2006.

Department of Homeland Security. "Homeland Security Act of 2002." Department of Homeland Security, http://www.dhs.gov/xabout/laws/law_regulation_rule_0011.shtm.

———. "National Strategy for Homeland Security." Department of Homeland Security, http://www.dhs.gov/xlibrary/assets/nat_strat_hls.pdf.

———. "Statement by Secretary Chertoff Regarding White House Katrina Lessons Learned Report," Department of Homeland Security, Washington, D.C., 2006.

Dickinson, Laura. *Outsourcing War and Peace*. New Haven: Yale University Press, forthcoming.

Dilulio, John. "John Dilulio's Letter: Your Next Essay on the Bush Administration." *Esquire*, http://www.esquire.com/features/dilulio.

Discover America Partnership. "Discover America Partnership—the Power of Travel." Discover America Partnership Online, http://www.poweroftravel.org/default.aspx.

Dory, Amanda. In discussion with author, March 26, 2007.

Dreazen, Yochi. "U.S. Military Becomes Alternate-Fuel Pioneer." *Wall Street Journal*, May 21, 2008.

Drummond, Jamie. In discussion with author, June 23, 2008.

Easterly, William Russell. *The White Man's Burden: Why the West's Efforts to Aid the Rest Have Done So Much Ill and So Little Good*. New York: Penguin, 2006.

Eckholm, Erik. "Excess Billing by Halliburton Is Put at $108 Million in Audit." *New York Times*, March 15, 2005.

Eisenhower, Dwight D. "Farewell Address," January 17, 1961.

Falkenrath, Richard A. (Visiting Fellow, Brookings Institution). *Testimony Before the United States Senate Committee on Homeland Security and Governmental Affairs*. January 26, 2005.

Farrar, Jay. In discussion with author, March 28, 2007.

Fenster, Herb. In discussion with author, March 28, 2007.

Ferris, George M., Jr. (Chair, President's Commission on the Management of A.I.D. Programs). *Critical Underlying Issues—Further Analysis* (Ferris Report). United States Agency for International Development, Washington, D.C. December 22, 1992, PC-AAA-288.

Fidler, Stephen. "Private Security: Operating in a Troubling Legal Vacuum." *Financial Times*, May 6, 2005.

Fisher, Bob. "Corporate Social Responsibility: Where Value and Values Intersect." Public lecture, Rohatyn Center for International Affairs, Middlebury College, Middlebury, VT, April 10, 2006.

Flynn, Stephen. "America the Resilient." *Foreign Affairs* (2008).

———. *America the Vulnerable: How Our Government Is Failing to Protect Us from Terrorism*. New York: Harper Collins, 2004.

Flynn, Stephen, and Daniel B. Prieto. "Neglected Defense: Mobilizing the Private Sector to Support Homeland Security." *Council Special Report*, no. 14 (2006).

FOXNews.com. "House Panel Votes to Block Ports Deal." FOXNews.com, http://www.foxnews.com/story/0,2933,187147,00.html.

Friedman, Milton. *Why Government Is the Problem*. Palo Alto, CA: Hoover Institution Press, 1993.

Friedman, Thomas L. *Hot, Flat, and Crowded: Why We Need a Green Revolution—and How It Can Renew America*. New York: Farrar, Straus, and Giroux, 2008.

———. *The Lexus and the Olive Tree: Understanding Globalization*. New York: Anchor, 2000.

———. *The World Is Flat: A Brief History of the Twenty-First Century*. New York: Farrar, Straus, Giroux, 2006.

Fukuyama, Francis. "After Neoconservatism." *New York Times Magazine*, February 19, 2006, 62ff.

———. *America at the Crossroads: Democracy, Power, and the Neoconservative Legacy*. New Haven: Yale University Press, 2007.

Garten, Jeffrey E. *The Politics of Fortune: A New Agenda for Business Leaders*. Boston: Harvard Business School Press, 2002.

Gates, Bill. "Creative Capitalism." Speech at World Economic Forum, Davos, Switzerland, January 24, 2008.

Gates, Robert. "Landon Lecture." Speech delivered at Kansas State University, Manhattan, Kansas, November 26, 2007.

———. "Remarks Delivered to the Association of the United States Army," Washington, D.C., October 10, 2007.

General Accounting Office. "Contingency Operations: Army Should Do More to Control Contract Costs in the Balkans." General Accounting Office, Washington, D.C., 2000.

———. "Defense Acquisitions: Tailored Approach Needed to Improve Service Acquisition Outcomes." Government Accountability Office, Washington, D.C., 2006.

———. "Foreign Assistance: Strategic Workforce Planning Can Help USAID Address

Current and Future Challenges." General Accounting Office, Washington, D.C., 2003.

———. "High-Risk Series: An Update." Government Accountability Office, Washington, D.C., 2007.

———. "Implementation of O.M.B Circular Number A-76 at Science Agencies." Briefing for Congressional Staff. Government Accountability Office, Washington, D.C., 2007.

———. "Improvements Needed to F.P.D.S.-N.G." Government Accountability Office, Washington, D.C., 2005.

———. "Military Operations: High Level DOD Action Needed to Address Long-standing Problems of Management and Oversight of Contractors Supporting Deployed Forces." Government Accountability Office, Washington, D.C., 2006.

———. "21st Century Challenges: Reexamining the Base of the Federal Government." Government Accountability Office, Washington, D.C., 2005.

General Services Administration. "Electronic Subcontracting Reporting System (E-Srs)." http://www.esrs.gov/index?cck=1.

———. "Federal Procurement Data System-Next Generation [F.P.D.S.-N.G.]." https://www.fpds.gov/.

Gladwell, Malcolm. *The Tipping Point: How Little Things Can Make a Big Difference.* New York: Little, Brown, 2000.

Glanz, James. "Iraq Spending Ignored Rules, Pentagon Says." *New York Times*, May 23, 2008.

———. "Official at Saudi Company and Ex-Employee at Halliburton Unit Accused in Kickback Inquiry." *New York Times*, March 24, 2006.

Glanz, James, and Riyadh Mohammed. "Premier of Iraq Is Quietly Firing Fraud Monitors." *New York Times*, November 17, 2008.

Glasser, Susan B., and Michael Grunwald. "Department's Mission Was Undermined from Start." *Washington Post*, December 22 2005.

GlobalGiving. "Global Giving: Donate to Grassroots Projects, Education, Health, Microfinance." GlobalGiving, http://www.globalgiving.com/index.html.

Goldsmith, Stephen, and William D. Eggers. *Governing by Network: The New Shape of the Public Sector.* Washington, D.C.: Brookings Institution Press, 2004.

Goodwin, Doris Kearns. *Team of Rivals: The Political Genius of Abraham Lincoln.* New York: Simon and Schuster, 2005.

Google. "Google and Four U.S. States Improve Public Access to Government Websites." Google Press Center, http://www.google.com/intl/en/press/pressrel/govt_access.html.

Gorman, Siobhan. "CIA Likely Let Contractors Perform Waterboarding." *Wall Street Journal*, February 8, 2008.

Gramsci, Antonio. *The Antonio Gramsci Reader: Selected Writings, 1916–1935.* New York: New York University Press, 2000.

Grant, James. "The Pearson Commission Report: A First Look." United States Agency for International Development (USAID), Washington, D.C., October 9, 1969.

Grossman, Marc. "Are We Ready for 21st Century Diplomacy?" Paper presented at "A New American Diplomacy: Requirements for the 21st Century," Belmont Conference Center, Elkridge, Maryland, October 2, 2000.

———. In discussion with author, March 29, 2007.

Guthrie, Jonathan. "Tim Spicer Finds Security in the World's War Zones." *Financial Times*, April 7, 2006.

Guttman, Dan. "The Shadow Pentagon: Private Contractors Play a Huge Role in

Basic Government Work—Mostly out of View." Center for Public Integrity, Washington, D.C., 2004.

Hacker, Jacob. *The Great Risk Shift: The Assault on American Jobs, Families, Health Care, and Retirement—and How You Can Fight Back.* New York: Oxford University Press, 2006.

——— (Professor of Political Science, Yale University). *Testimony Before the Committee on Education and Labor, U.S. House of Representatives,* January 31, 2007, http://edlabor.house.gov/testimony/013107JacobHackertestimony.pdf

Hafner, Katie. "Philanthropy Google's Way: Not the Usual." *New York Times,* September 14, 2006.

Hamilton, Lee, and Thomas Keane. "A Formula for Disaster." *New York Times,* December 5, 2005.

Hamre, John. In discussion with author, March 27, 2007.

———. "The Privatization of National Security: Remarks by John Hamre at the Rohatyn Center for International Affairs," Middlebury College. Middlebury, VT, October 9, 2004.

——— (President and CEO, Center for Strategic and International Studies). *Testimony Before the Committee on Appropriations, U.S. Senate, "9/11 Commission Recommendations,"* September 22, 2004, http://www.csis.org/media/csis/congress/ts040922hamre.pdf.

Harder, Amy. "Panel Warns of DHS Oversight Overkill." *National Journal Online,* November 20, 2008, http://lostintransition.nationaljournal.com/2008/11/dhs-oversight.php.

Hardy, Michael. "Defense Bill Would Halt A-76 Competition." *Federal Computer Weekly* (May 15, 2008), http://www.fcw.com/online/news/152543-1.html.

Harris, Shane, and Greta Wodele. "Bureaucracy Hinders 9/11 Commission Recommendations." *National Journal Online,* January 13, 2006, http://www.govexec.com/dailyfed/0106/011306nj1.htm.

Hart, Gary, and Warren Rudman. "America: Still Unprepared, Still in Danger." Council on Foreign Relations, 2002, https://secure.www.cfr.org/content/publications/attachments/Homeland_TF.pdf.

Hauser, Christine, and Taghreed El-Khodary. "Blair Is Appointed Mideast Envoy." *New York Times,* June 27, 2007.

Herrling, Sheila, and Sarah Rose. "Will the Millennium Challenge Account Be Caught in the Crosshairs? A Critical Year for Funding." Center for Global Development (March 30, 2007), http://www.cgdev.org/content/publications/detail/13398.

Hewko, John. In discussion with author, January 17, 2007.

———. E-mail message to author, January 5, 2009.

———. E-mail message to author, June 4, 2008.

Hirsh, Michael. "Watchdogs Are Warning That Corruption in Iraq Is out of Control." *Newsweek,* October 16, 2007.

Hocking, Brian. "Privatizing Diplomacy." *International Studies Perspectives* 5 (2004): 147–52.

Holmes, J. Anthony. "Where Are the Civilians? How to Rebuild the U.S. Foreign Service." *Foreign Affairs* 88, no. 1 (2009): 148–60.

Hormats, Robert D. *The Price of Liberty: Paying for America's Wars.* New York: Times Books, 2007.

House Bipartisan Committee. "A Failure of Initiative." February 15, 2006. http://www.gpoaccess.gov/katrinareport/mainreport.pdf.

House of Commons. "Private Military Companies: Options for Regulation." House of Commons, London, U.K., 2002.

Hughes, Adam. In discussion with author, April 9, 2008.

Hughes, Karen, and Office of Private Sector Outreach. "Public Diplomacy Update." U.S. State Department, Washington, D.C., October 2006.

Hull, Edmund. In discussion with author, January 15, 2007.

Hurst, Lynda. "The Privatization of Abu Ghraib." *Toronto Star,* May 16, 2004.

Ikenberry, John. "Illusions of Empire: Defining the New American Order." *Foreign Affairs* 83, no. 2 (2004).

Ikenberry, John, and Anne-Marie Slaughter. "Forging a World of Liberty Under Law: US National Security in the Twenty-First Century (Final Report of the Princeton Project on National Security)." Woodrow Wilson School of Public and International Affairs, Princeton, NJ, 2006.

Ingram, George. In discussion with author, March 26, 2007.

Internal Revenue Service. "SOI Tax Stats—Integrated Business Data." Department of the Treasury, Washington, D.C., http://www.irs.gov/taxstats/bustaxstats/article/0,,id=152029,00.html.

International Campaign to Ban Landmines (ICBL). "International Campaign to Ban Landmines," http://www.icbl.org/.

Isenberg, David. "A Fistful of Contractors: The Case for a Pragmatic Assessment of Private Military Companies in Iraq." In *British American Security International Council (BASIC) Research Report.* BASIC, Washington, D.C., 2004.

Jacobs, Lawrence R., and Benjamin I. Page. "Who Influences US Foreign Policy?" *American Political Science Review* 99, no. 1 (2005): 107–23.

Jennings, Ray. In discussion with author, March 29, 2007.

Kamarck, Elaine. *The End of Government as We Know It: Making Public Policy Work.* Boulder, CO: Lynne Rienner, 2007.

Kaul, Inge, and Pedro Conceição, eds. *The New Public Finance: Responding to Global Challenges.* New York: Oxford University Press, 2006.

Kayyem, Juliette N. "The Homeland Security Muddle." *The American Prospect* 14, no. 10 (2003).

Kennan, George F. "Diplomacy Without Diplomats? (75th Anniversary Issue)." *Foreign Affairs (75th Anniversary Issue)* 76, no. 5 (1997): 198(15).

Keohane, Robert, and Joseph Nye. "Globalization: What's New? What's Not? (and So What?)." *Foreign Policy,* no. 118 (2000): 104–19.

———. *Power and Interdependence.* 3d ed. New York: Longman, 2000.

———. "Power and Interdependence in the Information Age." In *Democracy.Com? Governance in a Networked World.* Edited by Elaine Kamarck and Joseph Nye, 197–214. Hollis, NH: Hollis, 1999.

———. "Power and Interdependence in the Information Age." *Foreign Affairs* (1998).

Kessler, Glenn. "Iraq Embassy Cost Rises $144 Million Amid Project Delays." *Washington Post,* October 7, 2007.

———. "Rice Deputy Quits After Query over Escort Service." *Washington Post,* April 28, 2007.

Kettl, D. F. *System Under Stress: Homeland Security and American Politics.* Washington, D.C.: Congressional Quarterly Press, 2004.

Kettl, Donald. *Sharing Power: Public Governance and Private Markets.* Washington, D.C.: Brookings Institution, 1993.

King, Neil Jr. "Pentagon Questions Halliburton on $1.8 Billion in Work." *Wall Street Journal,* August 11, 2004.

Kissinger, Henry. *Does America Need a Foreign Policy?* New York: Simon and Schuster, 2001.

————. *A World Restored: Metternich, Castlereagh and the Problems of Peace, 1812–1822:* London: Weidenfeld and Nicholson, 2000.

Kiva. "Kiva: Loans That Change Lives." http://www.kiva.org/.

Klein, Naomi. *The Shock Doctrine: The Rise of Disaster Capitalism.* New York: Metropolitan Books, 2007.

Korb, Lawrence. In discussion with author, January 18, 2007.

Kozaryn, Linda D. "Gore Lauds DOD Reforms." American Forces Press Service, Washington D.C., 1997.

Kraninger, Kathleen. In discussion with author, June 5, 2007.

Kristof, Nicholas D. "Do-gooders with Spread Sheets." *New York Times,* January 30, 2007.

Lake, Anthony. In discussion with author by phone, June 14, 2007.

Langewiesche, William. "The Mega-Bunker of Baghdad." *Vanity Fair* (2007): 200–8.

Lieberman, Joseph. "The Best Defense: Leveraging the Strength of Our Military to Protect the Homeland." Speech to the Progressive Policy Institute. Washington D.C., June 26, 2002.

Lieven, Anatol, and John Hulsman. *Ethical Realism: A Vision for America's Role in the World.* New York: Pantheon, 2006.

Light, Paul. *The New Public Service.* Washington, D.C.: Brookings Institution, 1999.

————. "The Real New Size of Government." *Organizational Performance Initiative, Research Brief,* no. 2 (2006).

————. *The True Size of Government.* Washington, D.C.: Brookings Institution, 1999.

Lipton, Eric. "Coast Guard to Manage Fleet Modernization." *New York Times,* April 18, 2007.

————. "Failure to Navigate: Billions Later, Plan to Remake the Coast Guard Fleet Stumbles." *New York Times,* December 9, 2006.

Livy. *Livy, with an English Translation.* Translated by B. O. Foster. 13 vols. Vol. 4, The Loeb Classical Library. London: Heinemann; New York, Putnam, 1919.

Lodge, George, and Craig Wilson. *A Corporate Solution to Global Poverty: How Multinational Corporations Can Help the Poor and Invigorate Their Own Legitimacy:* Princeton, NJ: Princeton University Press, 2006.

Lundestad, Geir. *The United States and Western Europe Since 1945: From 'Empire' by Invitation to Transatlantic Drift.* Oxford: Oxford University Press, 2003.

Lunstead, Jeffrey. In discussion with author, January 28, 2007.

Lynn, Barry C. *End of the Line: The Rise and Coming Fall of the Global Corporation.* New York: Doubleday, 2005.

MacCormack, Charles. In discussion with author, April 7, 2006.

Maier, Charles S. *Among Empires: American Ascendancy and Its Predecessors.* Cambridge, MA: Harvard University Press, 2006.

Mallaby, Sebastian. "Good and Bad Capitalists." *Washington Post,* January 28, 2008, A21.

————. "The Slate 60." *Slate* (2006).

Mares, Jan W. In discussion with author, June 5, 2007.

Matthews, Jessica. In discussion with author, January 17, 2007.

————. "Power Shift." *Foreign Affairs* 76, no. 1 (1997): 50–67.

McCormick, David. In discussion with author, March 27, 2007.

McGarvey, Ayelish. "Outsourcing Private Ryan (an interview with Peter Singer)," 2004, http://www.prospect.org/cs/articles?article=outsourcing_private_ryan.

McHale, Paul (Assistant Secretary of Defense for Homeland Defense). *Testimony Before the Committee on Armed Services, U.S. House of Representatives: "Statement to the House*

Armed Services Committee," May 25, 2006, http://www.globalsecurity.org/security/
library/congress/2006_h/060525-mchale.pdf.

Mead, Walter Russell. *Special Providence: American Foreign Policy and How It Changed the
World.* London: Routledge, 2002.

Melia, Thomas. Public lecture, Rohatyn Center for International Affairs, Middlebury
College, Middlebury, VT, October 27, 2005.

Merle, Renae. "Census Counts 100,000 Contractors in Iraq." *Washington Post,* December 5, 2006.

Miller, T. Christian. "Private Contractors Outnumber U.S. Troops in Iraq." *Los Angeles
Times,* July 3, 2007.

Morse, Jodie. "Charity Without the Checks." *Time,* October 28, 2001, http://www.
time.com/time/magazine/article/0,9171,181571,00.html.

Motyl, Alexander. "Empire Falls: Washington May Be Imperious but It Is Not
Imperial." *Foreign Affairs* 85, no. 4 (2006): 190–94.

Murphy, Craig. *The United Nations Development Programme: A Better Way?* New York:
Cambridge University Press, 2006.

Murphy, Cullen. *Are We Rome? The Fall of an Empire and the Fate of America.* New York:
Houghton Mifflin, 2007.

Murray, Royce. In discussion with author, March 29, 2007.

National Bipartisan Commission on Central America (Henry Kissinger, Chair). *Report
of the National Bipartisan Commission on Central America,* January 10, 1984, http://pdf.
usaid.gov/pdf_docs/PNABB526.pdf.

Natsios, Andrew. "American Fortresses." *Weekly Standard,* May 15, 2006.

———. In discussion with author, March 26, 2007, and by phone June 7, 2008.

———. "First Principles of Development." Heritage Foundation, Washington, D.C.,
2002, 8.

———. *Foreign Aid in the National Interest: Promoting Freedom, Security, and Opportunity.*
Washington, D.C.: United States Agency for International Development, 2003.

9/11 Commission. *The 9/11 Commission Report.* New York: W. W. Norton, 2004.

9/11 Public Discourse Project. "Final Report on 9/11 Commission Recommendations." 9/11 Public Discourse Project, http://www.9-11pdp.org/
press/2005-12-05_summary.pdf.

Nye, Joseph. "The Dependent Colossus." *Foreign Policy* (March–April 2002): 74–76.

Oakley, Robert. In discussion with author, January 15, 2007.

Odom, William E., and Robert Dujarric. *America's Inadvertent Empire.* New Haven: Yale
University Press, 2004.

Office of Field Operations and Office of Policy and Planning. "Securing the Global
Supply Chain: C-TPAT Strategic Plan." U.S. Customs and Border Protection,
Washington, D.C.

Office of Management and Budget. "Budget of the United States Government
(Historical Tables)." White House, Washington, D.C., 2008, http://www.
whitehouse.gov/omb/budget/fy2008/pdf/hist.pdf.

———. "Circular Number A-76: Performance of Commercial Activities." OMB,
http://www.whitehouse.gov/omb/circulars/a076/a076.html.

———. "Fedspending.Org." http://www.fedspending.org/.

O'Hanlon, M. E., et. al. *Protecting the American Homeland.* Washington, D.C.: Brookings
Institution Press, 2003.

O'Hanlon, Michael, and Jeremy Shapiro. "Introduction." In *Protecting the Homeland
2006/2007.* Edited by Michael O'Hanlon and Jeremy Shapiro. Washington, D.C.:
Brookings Institution Press, 2006.

"Omidyar Network." Omidyar Network, http://www.omidyar.net/.

One Laptop Per Child. "One Laptop Per Child: A Low Cost Connected Laptop for the Worlds' Childrens' Education." OLPC, http://laptop.org/.

Packer, George. *The Assassin's Gate: America in Iraq.* New York: Farrar, Straus, and Giroux, 2005.

———. "Knowing Thy Enemy." *New Yorker,* December 18, 2006.

Palguta, John. In discussion with author, June 6, 2007.

Palmisano, Samuel. "The Globally Integrated Enterprise." *Foreign Affairs* 85, no. 3 (2006): 127–36.

Partnership for Public Service and American University's Institute for the Study of Public Policy Implementation. "The Best Places to Work in the Federal Government." Washington, D.C., 2007, http://bestplacestowork.org/BPTW/rankings/.

Patrick, Stewart. In discussion with author, March 30, 2007.

———. "The U.S. Response to Precarious States: Tentative Progress and Remaining Obstacles to Coherence," 2007, http://www.cgdev.org/content/publications/detail/14093/.

Patton, James. In discussion with author, March 30, 2007.

Peckenpaugh, Jason. "Definition of 'Inherently Governmental' Could Change." *Government Executive Daily News Service,* June 8, 2001, http://www.govexec.com/dailyfed/0601/060801p1.htm.

Peterson, Laura. "Privatizing Conflict: The New World Order." Center for Public Integrity, Washington, D.C., 2002.

Peterson, Peter G. "Privatizing U.S. Public Diplomacy." *Financial Times,* January 21, 2004.

———. "Public Diplomacy and the War on Terrorism." *Foreign Affairs* 81, no. 5 (2002).

Pincus, Walter. "Increase in Contracting Intelligence Jobs Raises Concerns" *Washington Post,* March 19, 2006.

———. "U.S. Cannot Manage Contractors in Wars, Officials Testify on Hill." *Washington Post,* January 5, 2008.

Pogue, David. "Laptop with a Mission That Widens Its Audience." *New York Times,* October 4, 2007.

Polanyi, Karl. *The Great Transformation.* Boston: Beacon Press, 2001.

Polmateer, Cathy. In discussion with author, June 5, 2007.

Posner, Sarah. "Security for Sale." *American Prospect* 17, no. 1 (2006).

Postel, Eric. In discussion with author, November 19, 2007.

Pozen, Robert C. "Reporting for Duty." *New York Times,* March 3, 2007.

President's Committee to Study the United States Military Assistance Program (William H. Draper, Chair). "U.S. Military Assistance Program," August 17, 1959, http://pdf.usaid.gov/pdf_docs/PCAAA444.pdf.

President's Task Force on International Private Enterprise and the Agency for International Development (Dwayne O. Andreas, Chair). "Report to the President," December 1984, http://pdf.usaid.gov/pdf_docs/PNAAR670.pdf.

Priest, Dana. *The Mission: Waging War and Keeping Peace with America's Military.* New York: W. W. Norton, 2004.

Private Sector Council. "Creating Momentum in Contract Management: The Acquisition Innovation Pilot Handbook." Partnership for Public Service, Washington, D.C., November 2006, http://ourpublicservice.org/OPS/publications/viewcontentdetails.php?id=46.

Progressive Policy Institute. "America at Risk: A Homeland Security Report Card." Progressive Policy Institute, Washington, D.C., 2003.

Quainton, Anthony. "Diplomacy for the Twenty-First Century." In *Global Challenges in the Twenty-first Century*. Chesterton, MD: Literary House Press, 2000.

———. In discussion with author, January 15, 2007.

Quirk, Matthew. "Private Military Contractors." *Atlantic Monthly*, September 2004.

Rabkin, Norman J. (Managing Director, Homeland Security and Justice, GAO). *Testimony Before the Subcommittee on Management, Integration, and Oversight, Committee on Homeland Security, U.S. House of Representatives: "Overview of Department of Homeland Security Management Challenges,"* April 20, 2005, http://www.gao.gov/new.items/d05573t.pdf.

Rabkin, Norm. In discussion with author, March 27, 2007.

Radelet, Steven. In discussion with author, March 30, 2007.

———. *Challenging Foreign Aid: A Policymaker's Guide to the Millennium Challenge Account*. Washington, D.C.: Center for Global Development, 2003.

Randall, Tobias. "Advancing the Message That Foreign Assistance Works." Remarks at the U.S. Global Leadership Campaign, Washington D.C., June 26, 2006.

Reinhard, Keith. In discussion with author, September 13, 2007.

———. Letter to Karen Hughes, December 5, 2005.

——— (President, Business for Diplomatic Action). *Testimony Before the House Subcommittee on National Security, Emerging Threats, and International Relations*, August 23, 2004, http://www.businessfordiplomaticaction.org/action/written_testimony.pdf.

Report of the Defense Science Board Task Force on Outsourcing and Privatization. Defense Science Board, Washington, D.C., 1996, http://www.dtic.mil/cgi-bin/GetTRDoc?AD=ADA316936&Location=U2&doc=GetTRDoc.pdf.

Reuters. "Tom Ridge to Advise Techradium on 'IRIS' Technology," January 9, 2008.

Rice, Condoleezza. "New Direction for US Foreign Assistance." Speech given to the U.S. Department of State, Washington D.C., January 19, 2006.

———. Remarks at the 2006 Awards for Corporate Excellence Ceremony, Washington D.C., November 6, 2006.

———. "Tenure of Paul Applegarth at the Millennium Challenge Corporation." Speech on the occasion of Paul Applegarth's resignation, Washington D.C., June 17, 2005.

———. "Transformational Diplomacy," Speech at Georgetown University, Washington D.C., January 18, 2006.

Rieffel, Lex, and James Fox. "The Brookings Institution Policy Brief #145." Brookings Institution, Washington, D.C., 2005.

———. "The Millennium Challenge Corporation: An Opportunity for the Next President (Working Paper 30)." Edited by Center for Global Economy and Development. Brookings Institution, Washington, D.C., 2008.

Risen, James. "2005 Use of Gas by Blackwater Leaves Questions." *New York Times*, January 10, 2008.

———. "Use of Iraq Contractors Costs Billions, Report Says." *New York Times*, August 11, 2008.

Robb, John. *Brave New War: The Next State of Terrorism and the End of Globalization*. New York: Wiley, 2007.

Robinson, Linda, and Douglas Pasternak. "America's Secret Armies." *U.S. News and World Report*, November 4, 2002.

Rohatyn, Felix. In discussion with author, November 4, 2007.

Rohde, David, and Carlotta Gall. "Delays Hurting U.S. Rebuilding in Afghanistan." *New York Times*, November 7, 2005, 1.

Ross, Carne. *Independent Diplomat: Dispatches from an Unaccountable Elite.* Ithaca, NY: Cornell University Press, 2007.

Rothkopf, David. In discussion with author, June 6, 2007.

———. *Running the World: The Inside Story of the National Security Council and the Architects of American Power.* New York: Public Affairs, 2005.

———. *Superclass: The Global Power Elite and the World They Are Making.* New York: Farrar, Straus and Giroux, 2008.

Rubin, Harriet. "Google Offers a Map for Its Philanthropy." *New York Times,* January 18, 2008.

Rumsfeld, Donald. *Budget Testimony Before the Senate-House Armed Services Committee,* February 17, 2005, http://www.defenselink.mil/speeches/speech. aspx?speechid=56.

———. "Bureaucracy to Battlefield." Speech given to the Pentagon, Washington D.C., September 10, 2001.

———. Speech on the future of Iraq, Johns Hopkins School of Advanced International Studies. Baltimore, MD, December 5, 2005.

———. Tribute to Milton Friedman, May 9, 2002.

———. "Twenty-First Century Transformation." Remarks at the National Defense University, Fort McNair, Washington D.C., January 31, 2002.

Sandel, Michael J. *Liberalism and the Limits of Justice.* New York: Cambridge University Press, 1998.

Sanger, David. "A Handpicked Team for a Sweeping Shift in Foreign Policy." *New York Times,* December 1, 2008.

———. "The Reach of War: News Analysis." *New York Times,* April 12, 2007.

———. "The Reach of War: News Analysis; Amid Hints Bush Will Change Policy, Clues That He Won't." *New York Times,* December 4, 2006.

Savi Technologies. "Smart and Secure Trade Lanes." Savi Technologies, http://www. savi.com/products/casestudies/wp.sst_initiative.pdf.

Scahill, Jeremy. *Blackwater: The Rise of the World's Most Powerful Mercenary Army.* New York: Nation, 2007.

Schinasi, Katherine. In discussion with author, June 4, 2007.

——— (Managing Director, Acquisition and Sourcing Management, GAO). *Testimony Before the Subcommittee on Readiness, Management and Support, Committee on Armed Services, U.S. Senate: "Defense Acquisitions: US Needs to Assert Better Management and Oversight to Better Control Acquisition of Services,"* January 17, 2007, http://www.gao.gov/new. items/d07640r.pdf.

Schmitt, Eric. "What Is Really Different Now?" *New York Times,* December 16, 2007.

Schmitt, Eric, and David Rohde. "Reports Assail State Dept. On Iraq Security." *New York Times,* October 23, 2007.

Schmitt, Eric, and Ginger Thompson. "Top Air Force Official Dies in Apparent Suicide." *New York Times,* October 16, 2007.

Schwab, Klaus. "Global Corporate Citizenship: Working with Governments and Civil Society." *Foreign Affairs* 87, no. 1 (2008).

Schwab Foundation. "Schwab Foundation for Social Entrepreneurship." Schwab Foundation, http://www.schwabfound.org/.

Scully, Megan. "Bill Would Bar Contractors from Running Defense Programs." *Government Executive.com* (May 16, 2007), http://www.govexec.com/story_page. cfm?articleid=36940.

Seidman, Dov. *How: Why How We Do Anything Means Everything . . . In Business (and in Life).* New York: Wiley, 2007.

Sen, Amartya. *Development as Freedom.* New York: Anchor, 2000.

Shane, Scott, and Ron Nixon. "In Washington, Contractors Take on Biggest Role Ever." *New York Times,* February 4, 2007.

Shanker, Thom. "Proposed Military Spending Is Highest Since W.W.I.I." *New York Times,* February 4, 2008.

Shea, Robert. E-mail message to author, May 21, 2008.

Shearer, David. "Private Military Force and Challenges for the Future." *Cambridge Review of International Affairs* 13, no. 1 (1999): 80–104.

Shenon, Philip. "Army Says It Will Withhold $19.6 Million from Halliburton, Citing Potential Contract Breach." *New York Times,* February 8, 2007.

Singer, P. W. "The Law Catches Up to Private Military and Embeds," http://www.defensetech.org/archives/003123.html.

———. "Lessons Not Learned: Contracting Out Iraqi Army Advising." Brookings Institution, Washington, D.C., 2008.

———. "Nation Builders and Low Bidders in Iraq." *New York Times,* June 15, 2004.

Singer, Peter W. *Corporate Warriors: The Rise of the Privatized Military Industry.* Ithaca: Cornell University Press, 2003.

60 Minutes. "All in the Family." September 21, 2003.

———. "The Troubled Waters of Deepwater" (interview with Captain Kevin Jarvis). August 19, 2007.

Slaughter, Anne-Marie. "America's Edge in a Networked World." *Foreign Affairs* 88, no. 1 (2009): 94–113.

———. *The Idea That Is America.* New York: Basic, 2007.

———. *A New World Order.* Princeton, NJ: Princeton University Press, 2004.

Solis, William (Director, Defense Capabilities and Management, GAO). *Testimony Before the Subcommittee on National Security, Emerging Threats and International Relations, Committee on Government Reform: "Rebuilding Iraq: Actions Still Needed to Improve the Use of Private Security Providers,"* June 13, 2006, http://www.gao.gov/new.items/d06865t.pdf.

Soloway, Stan. In discussion with author, March 27, 2007.

Sorkin, Andrew Ross. "What If Watchdogs Got Bonuses?" *New York Times,* February 2, 2009.

Source Watch. "Erinys International Ltd.—Source Watch." Source Watch: A project of the Center for Media and Democracy, http://www.sourcewatch.org/index.php?title=Erinys_International_Ltd.

South Asia Earthquake Relief Fund. "South Asia Earthquake Relief." South Asia Earthquake Relief Fund, https://www.southasiaearthquakerelief.org/.

Soyster, Ed. In discussion with author, January 16, 2007.

Spar, Debora. *Ruling the Waves: From the Compass to the Internet, a History of Business and Politics Along the Technological Frontier.* New York: Harvest, 2003.

Spicer, Tim. *An Unorthodox Soldier: Peace and War and the Sandline Affair.* Edinburgh, U.K.: Mainstream, 1999.

Stanger, Allison. "Your Tax Dollars at Work—If You Can Find Them." *Washington Post,* May 18, 2008.

Stanger, Allison, and Omnivore. "Foreign Policy, Privatized." *New York Times,* October 5, 2007.

Stanger, Allison, and Mark E. Williams. "Private Military Companies: Benefits and Costs of Outsourcing Security." *Yale Journal of International Affairs* 2, no. 1 (2006).

Stark, Betsy, Lara Setrakian, and Teri Whitcraft. "Peace Through Paypal?" http://abcnews.go.com/print?id=3244120.

Starr, Paul. "The Meaning of Privatization." *Yale Law and Policy Review* 6 (1988): 6–41.

———. "The New Life of the Liberal State: Privatization and the Restructuring of State-Society Relations." In *Public Enterprise and Privatization.* Edited by John Waterbury and Ezra Suleiman. Boulder, CO: Westview, 1990, 22–54.

Steuerle, Eugene. "'Creative Capitalism': Can It Meet the Needs of the World's Poor?" Hudson Institute Center for Global Prosperity, Washington, D.C., 2008.

Stier, Max. In discussion with author, January 18 and June 6, 2007.

Stiglitz, Joseph. *Making Globalization Work.* New York: W. W. Norton, 2006.

Stoddard, Abby. "Trends in U.S. Humanitarian Policy." *HPG (Humanitarian Policy Group) Briefing,* no. 3, April 2002, http://pdf.usaid.gov/pdf_docs/PCAAB018.pdf.

Strom, Stephanie. "Businesses Try to Make Money and Save the World." *New York Times,* May 6, 2007.

Surowiecki, James. "Army, Inc." *New Yorker,* January 12, 2004.

Swope, Christopher, and Zach Patton. "In Disaster's Wake." *Governing,* November 2005, 48–58.

Tabarrok, Alexander. "The Rise, Fall, and Rise Again of Privateers." *Independent Review* 11, no. 4 (2007): 565–77.

Talbott, Strobe. In discussion with author, March 28, 2007.

Tarnoff, Curt, and Larry Nowels. "Foreign Aid: An Introductory Overview of U.S. Programs and Policy." Congressional Research Service, Report for Congress, April 15, 2004, http://fpc.state.gov/documents/organization/31987.pdf.

Task Force on International Development (Rudolph Peterson, Chair). "U.S. Foreign Assistance in the 1970s: A New Approach," March 4, 1970, http://pdf.usaid.gov/pdf_docs/PNABH264.pdf.

Task Force on Overseas Economic Operations (Henning W. Prentis Jr., Chair). *Report on Overseas Economic Operations, Commission on Organization of the Executive Branch of the Government,* March 28, 1955, http://pdf.usaid.gov/pdf_docs/PCAAA435.pdf.

Tepperman, Jonathan D. "Can Mercenaries Protect Hamid Karzai?" *New Republic,* November 18, 2002.

Thommessen, Christian. In discussion with author, September 14, 2007.

Tobias, Randall. "Getting a Better Return on America's Investment in People." Remarks at the Initiative for Global Development 2006 National Summit, Washington, D.C., June 15, 2006.

———. "Living Up to Our Mission." Paper presented at the InterAction Annual Meeting Opening Plenary, L'Enfant Plaza Hotel, Washington, D.C., April 10, 2006.

———. "Transformational Diplomacy: Sharing the Vision." Speech to the Society for International Development, Washington D.C., September 14, 2006.

Tocqueville, Alexis. *Democracy in America.* Edited by J. P. Mayer. Translated by George Lawrence. New York: HarperPerennial, 1988.

Toner, Robin. "For Democrats, New Challenge in Age-Old Rift." *New York Times,* May 8, 2007.

Townsend, Frances Fragos (Chair). *The Federal Response to Hurricane Katrina: Lessons Learned.* White House (review commission), Washington, D.C., February 2006, http://library.stmarytx.edu/acadlib/edocs/katrinawh.pdf.

Trice, Stanley. In discussion with author, June 5, 2007.

Tucker, Neely. "A Web of Truth." *Washington Post,* October 9, 2005.

Udall, Morris K. "The Foreign Assistance Act of 1961: A Special Report," 1961, http://www.library.arizona.edu/exhibits/udall/special/foreign.html.

United Nations Development Programme. "Growing Inclusive Markets." UNDP Office of the Private Sector, www.growinginclusivemarkets.org

U.S. Advisory Commission on Public Diplomacy. "The New Diplomacy: Utilizing Innovative Communication Concepts That Recognize Resource Constraints." United States Advisory Commission on Public Diplomacy, 2003.

U.S. Agency for International Development. "A Decade of Change: Profiles of USAID Assistance to Europe and Eurasia." USAID, Washington, D.C., 2000.

———. "New Directions in Foreign Aid: President Nixon's Message to the Congress." 11. USAID, Washington, D.C., May 28, 1969.

———. "Press Release: USAID Administrator Appoints Chief Economic Advisor." USAID, Washington D.C., 2006.

———. "Press Release: USAID Announces Partnership with Procter & Gamble for Pakistan Earthquake Survivors." USAID, Washington D.C., 2005.

———. "Tanzania: Activity Data Sheet." USAID, http://www.usaid.gov/pubs/ cbj2002/afr/tz/621–005.html.

———. "Tsunami Assistance One Year Later." USAID, http://www.usaid.gov/press/ factsheets/2005/fs051221.html.

———. "U.S. Foreign Aid: Meeting the Challenges of the Twenty-First Century." USAID, Washington, D.C., 2004.

———. "USAID History." USAID, http://www.usaid.gov/about_usaid/usaidhist. html.

———. "USAID Primer: What We Do and How We Do It." USAID, Washington, D.C., 2005.

U.S. Agency for International Development and Department of State. "Strategic Plan, Fiscal Years 2004–2009: Aligning Diplomacy and Development Assistance." Washington, D.C., USAID, Department of State, 2003.

U.S. Congress. House. *Report of the Task Force on Foreign Assistance to the Committee of Foreign Affairs, "Development and the National Interest: U.S. Economic Assistance into the Twenty-first Century (Woods Report)*," February 17, 1989, http://pdf.usaid.gov/pdf_docs/ PNABB596.pdf.

U.S. Congress. House. Committee on Foreign Affairs (Lee Hamilton, Chair). "Report of the Task Force on Foreign Assistance to the Committee on Foreign Affairs," February 1, 1989, http://pdf.usaid.gov/pdf_docs/PNABB596.pdf.

U.S. Congress. House. Committee on Government Reform. "Dollars, Not Sense: Government Contracting under the Bush Administration," June 2006, http:// oversight.house.gov/Documents/20060711103910–86046.pdf.

U.S. Congress. House. Committee on Oversight and Government Reform. "More Dollars, Less Sense: Worsening Contracting Trends Under the Bush Administration," June 2007, http://oversight.house.gov/features/moredollars/.

U.S. Congress. House. Subcommittee on National Security, Emerging Threats and International Relations of the Committee on Government Reform. *Strategic Workforce Planning at USAID.* 108th Cong., 1st sess., September 23, 2003, http:// frwebgate.access.gpo.gov/cgi-bin/getdoc.cgi?dbname=108_house_ hearings&docid=f:92392.pdf.

U.S. Department of Defense. "Improving the Combat Edge Through Outsourcing." U.S. Department of Defense, Washington, D.C., March 1996.

U.S. Department of State. "Middle East Partnership Initiative—Outreach." http:// mepi.state.gov/outreach/index.htm.

———. "Private Sector Summit on Public Diplomacy: Models for Action." U.S. State Department and the PR Coalition, Washington, D.C., 2007.

———. "U.S.-Lebanon Partnership." Bureau of Public Affairs, Washington, D.C., http://www.state.gov/documents/organization/79536.pdf.

———. "U.S.-Palestinian Partnership." Bureau of Public Affairs, Washington, D.C., January 14, 2008, http://www.state.gov/documents/organization/99505.pdf.

"U.S. Foreign Policy: Missteps, Mistakes, and Broken Promises (an Interview with Tom Daschle)." *Harvard International Review* 28, no. 1 (2006): 74(4).

Verga, Peter F. In discussion with author, June 6, 2007.

———. *Testimony Before the National Commission on Terrorist Attacks upon the United States, Seventh Public Hearing,* January 26, 2004, http://www.9-11commission.gov/hearings/hearing7/witness_verga.htm.

Verkuil, Paul. In discussion with author, June 8, 2007.

———. *Outsourcing Sovereignty: Why Privatization of Government Function Threatens Democracy and What We Can Do About It.* New York: Cambridge University Press, 2007.

———. "The Publicization of Airport Security." *Cardoza Law Review* 27, no. 5 (2006): 2243–54.

Vermillion, Jim. In discussion with author, June 6, 2007.

Vest, Jason. "Dyncorp's Drug Problem." *Nation,* July 11, 2001.

———. "State Outsources Secret War." *Nation,* May 23, 2001.

Vogel, David. *The Market for Virtue: The Potential and Limits of Corporate Social Responsibility.* Washington, D.C.: The Brookings Institution, 2006.

Vogel, David, et. al. "Corporate Social Responsibility and Government: Creating a Market for Virtue." Brookings Institution, Washington, D.C., 2005.

Vogel, Steve. *The Pentagon: A History.* New York: Random House, 2007.

Walker, David. In discussion with author, June 4, 2007.

——— (Comptroller General of the United States). *Testimony Before the Committee on Government Oversight and Reform, House of Representatives, "Rebuilding Iraq: Reconstruction Progress Hindered by Contracting, Security, and Capacity Challenges,"* February 15, 2007, http://www.gao.gov/new.items/d07426t.pdf.

——— (Comptroller General of the United States). *Testimony Before the Subcommittee on Defense, Committee on Appropriations, House of Representatives, "D.O.D. Acquisitions: Contracting for Better Outcomes,"* September 7, 2006, http://www.gao.gov/new.items/d0680ot.pdf.

——— (Comptroller General of the United States). *Testimony Before the Subcommittee on Technology, Terrorism and Government Information, Senate Committee on the Judiciary, "Homeland Security: Proposal for Cabinet Agency Has Merit but Implementation Will Be Pivotal to Success,"* June 25, 2002, http://www.gao.gov/new.items/d02886t.pdf.

Walker, Martin. "America's Virtual Empire." *World Policy Journal* 19, no. 2 (2002): 13–21.

Waltz, Kenneth. "Globalization and American Power." *National Interest* (Spring 2000).

Walzer, Michael. "Is There an American Empire?" *Dissent* (Fall 2003).

Waxman, Henry. *Testimony Before the Committee on Government Reform, House of Representatives, 108th Congress, "Contracting Abuses in Iraq,"* October 15, 2003, http://oversight.house.gov/documents/20040624072659-41626.pdf.

Wayne, Leslie. "A Growing Military Contract Scandal." *New York Times,* October 8, 2004.

Weber, Max. "Politics as a Vocation." In *From Max Weber: Essays in Sociology.* Edited by H. H. Gerth and C. Wright Mills, 77–78. New York: Oxford University Press, 1958.

Weiner, Tim. "Lockheed and the Future of Warfare." *New York Times,* November 28, 2004.

Wermuth, Michael A. (Director, Homeland Security Program, Rand Corporation).

Testimony Before the Committee on Homeland Security and Governmental Affairs, United States Senate, "The Road Ahead," January 26, 2005, http://rand.org/pubs/testimonies/2005/RAND_CT233.pdf.

West, Owen. "Private Contractors Aren't the Answer to the Army's Problems." http://slate.msn.com/id/2104305/entry/2104507/.

WGBH Boston. *Frontline,* "Private Warriors." First aired June 21, 2005.

Whelan, Theresa. In discussion with author, January 17, 2007.

White House, "National Security Presidential Directive/NSPD-44," December 7, 2005, http://www.fas.org/irp/offdocs/nspd/nspd-44.html.

Wikileaks. "Wikileaks." http://wikileaks.org/.

Wilkerson, Lawrence. In discussion with author, March 28, 2007.

Williams-Bridgers, Jacqueline. In discussion with author, March 27, 2007.

Wolverson, Roya. "Beltway Bandits." *Newsweek,* December 3, 2007.

Wood, Nicholas. "Rebellious Diplomat Finds Work as Envoy of the Voiceless." *New York Times,* March 3, 2007.

Wysocki, Bernard. "Is the U.S. Government Outsourcing Its Brain?" *Wall Street Journal,* March 30, 2007, A1.

Yarwood, Susan. In discussion with author, June 10, 2007.

Yergin, Daniel, and Joseph Stanislaw. *The Commanding Heights: The Battle for the World Economy.* New York: Simon and Schuster, 2002.

Yunus, Muhammed. *Creating a World Without Poverty: Social Business and the Future of Capitalism.* New York: Public Affairs, 2008.

———. "Grameen: Banking for the Poor." Grameen, http://www.grameen-info.org/index.html.

Zakaria, Fareed. *The Future of Freedom.* New York: W. W. Norton, 2003.

Zegart, Amy. "Not So Smart Intelligence." *Los Angeles Times,* September 17, 2006.

Zegart, Amy, Matthew Hipp, and Seth Jacobson. "Governance Challenges in Port Security: A Case Study of Emergency Response Capabilities at the Ports of Los Angeles and Long Beach." In *Protecting the Nation's Seaports: Balancing Security and Cost.* Edited by Jon D. Haveman and Howard J. Shatz. San Francisco: Public Policy Institute of California, 2006.

Zelikow, Philip. E-mail messages to author, October 6 and 8, 2007.

Zinni, Anthony. In discussion with author, January 18, 2007.

Index

Abu Ghraib, 4, 92, 99, 100

Accountability: and congressional oversight, 16, 18, 28, 91, 95, 104, 147–48, 166, 177; of contractors, 18–19, 90–93, 104–5, 168; and elections, 177; internal, 90–91; lack of, 9, 18–21, 33, 81, 82, 91–93, 104–5, 123, 166; and sovereignty, 16; and transparency, 21–25, 105, 123, 168, 177

Acumen Fund, 36

Adjudication, 27, 28

Aegis Defense Services, 90, 100, 171

Afghanistan: contractors in, 2, 3, 27, 63, 87, 89, 128, 162; diplomatic staffing in, 60, 69; imperial U.S. intervention in, 9, 51, 83; peace failures in, 54; reconstruction of, 61, 82, 128, 165; schools in, 4

Africa: contracts for logistical support in, 94; contracts for training in, 87, 94, 98; development in, 77; HIV/AIDS in, 1–2

Aftergood, Steven, 91

AirScan, 89

Allbaugh, Joe, 105, 153

Allen, Thad W., 152

Al Qaeda, 35, 54

Applegarth, Paul, 77, 78, 79, 133

Arab Women's Legal Network, 71

ArmorGroup, 105

Army, U.S.: contractors used by, 89, 97; recruitment difficulties of, 93

Asali, Ziad, 6

Ashcroft, John, 141, 152

Ashoka: Innovators for the Public, 36

Atwood, Brian, 121, 123

Avant, Deborah, 107

Aviation and Transportation Security Act (2001), 147

Baker, Mike, 105

BearingPoint, 2, 68

Bechtel, 81, 156, 168

Beinart, Peter, 42

Biden, Joseph, 60–61

Bin Laden, Osama, 57, 63, 182

Bismarck, Otto von, 62, 64, 68

Blackwater USA, 3, 4, 11, 57, 62, 82, 89, 97, 99; contractors hanged in Iraq, 100, 106; and Hurricane Katrina, 136, 155–56

Blackwill, Robert, 63, 74

Blair, Tony, 7, 41, 47, 57, 60, 69

Boeing Corporation, 3, 12

Bollinger, Walter, 116

Bolten, Joshua, 22

Bono, 1, 63, 75, 79, 176

Booz Allen Hamilton, 87, 113, 153

Bosnia: Dayton Peace Accords, 66; sex slave ring in, 92; U.S. intervention in, 40

Bowen, Stuart W. Jr., 19

Brainard, Lael, 79

Branson, Sir Richard, 5

Bremer, Paul, 99

Brennan, John O., 96

Brin, Sergey, 37

Brookings Institution, 168

Brooks, David, 130

Brown, Michael D., 153

Brown and Root, 95

Buffet, Warren, 34, 35, 36, 53, 119

Burt, Richard, 105

Bush, George H. W., 44, 105, 120

Bush, George W., 136, 153, 156

Bush administration: antigovernment, 150; contract spending by, 10, 12–13, 23–24, 87–90, 168–69, 170; contradictions within, 57, 133, 139–40; and DHS (*see* Homeland Security); and fast-track FDA approval, 5–6; foreign aid in, 125–26, 128–29, 131; foreign policy in, 11, 51, 52, 60, 74–80, 81, 163; and international education, 71–72; leadership failures of, 3, 143–45, 154, 156–58, 164, 168, 170; National Security Strategy of, 125, 129; outsourcing defense, 86–90; outsourcing oversight, 168; and private/public initiatives, 6–7, 34, 36, 73, 156–57; and transformational diplomacy, 69, 71–72, 73–74, 104, 131; unilateralism of, 164, 166; and war, 33. *See also* Afghanistan; Iraq

Business: antitrust litigation, 158; bottom line in, 9; and charitable giving, 37–39; in Cold War, 35; collaboration of government and, 54–55, 125, 176–77, 183; competition in, 33, 122, 163; consultants used by, 84, 86, 89–90; corporate model, 86; government rendered superfluous by, 129, 163; revolving door from government to, 105–6, 170, 180; short-term goals of, 171, 174, 181–82. *See also* Corporations

Business for Diplomatic Action (BDA), 70

Buy American Act (*1933*), 122

CACI International, 4, 99

Capitalism, varieties of, 51

Card, Andrew H. Jr., 126, 138

Carlyle Group, 105

Carter, Phillip, 106

Case, Jean, 6

Case, Steve, 37

Castlereagh, Robert Stewart, Viscount, 56, 57

Castro, Fidel, 112

Center for Public Integrity, 87

Central American Development Organization, 115

CGI (Clinton Global Initiative), 4–5

Chalabi, Ahmed, 101

Chanda, Nayam, 174

Chandrasekaran, Rajiv, 99, 100

Change Congress, 178

Charitable contributions, 8, 35–39, 44, 53, 54, 119

Cheney, Dick, 163, 169

Chertoff, Michael, 140, 155, 156

China: capitalism in, 49, 51; in Cold War, 111; U.S. embassy in, 69

CH2M Hill, 156

CIA (Central Intelligence Agency): contracts awarded by, 91; creation of, 58–59; interrogation program of, 4; jurisdiction of, 139; and turf protection, 144

Clarke, Richard, 152

Clinton, Bill: and philanthropy, 44; unofficial diplomatic agenda of, 63

Clinton administration: and ACE, 72; American "presence posts" (APPs), 72; and armed security contractors, 15; budget cuts by, 59; Commission on Critical Infrastructure Protection, 157–58; National Performance Review, 120–21; outsourcing by, 15, 29, 59, 86, 163; reinvention of government by, 15, 59, 120, 123, 162; roles of military in, 164; and USAID, 127, 129

Coalition Provisional Authority (CPA), 99, 106

Coast Guard: and Deepwater, 28, 150–52, 168; and port security, 147

Coburn, Tom, 21

Cohen, Roger, 103

Cohen, William, 86, 164

Cold War: anti-Communism in, 112; diplomatic service in, 58; end of, 44, 59, 85, 93, 110; information security as priority in, 62, 144; matching Soviet capability in, 85; media in, 69–70; national security in, 172, 182; nuclear threat in, 34; and peace dividend, 85–86,

87; postwar foreign aid, 117–20; three sectors in, 35, 43; U.S. foreign aid in, 53, 58, 109, 110–17

Colombia: contractors abducted in, 92; corporate awards in, 72; and drugs, 92, 94; third-party military personnel in, 15

Commission on Critical Infrastructure Protection, 157–58

Congress, U.S.: and accountability, 16, 18, 28, 91, 95, 104, 147–48, 166, 177; and appropriations, 120, 166; and budget cuts, 131–32; and change, 28, 144; and homeland security, 138, 139, 140, 145, 146–47; and Hurricane Katrina, 155; and Iraq, 102; and Millennium Challenge Account, 75, 76, 77, 78, 79; no-bid contracts in, 33; powers of, 26, 144; Senate Foreign Relations Committee, 61, 72, 110; shrinking government, 131; and special interests, 144, 150, 152, 167, 177, 178, 180

Congress of Vienna, 39, 56

Constitution, U.S.: checks and balances in, 26; Marque and Reprisal Clause of, 26; president's responsibility for, 170; on sovereignty, 16

Consular service, 57–58

Container Security Initiative (CSI), 158–59

Contractors: accountability of, 18–19, 90–93, 104–5, 168; armed, 15, 27, 28, 105, 106, 183; benefits of, 93–94, 96–98; bipartisan use of, 162–63; coordination of, 100, 134; corruption of, 3, 9, 18, 89, 94–95, 105, 133, 157, 163, 169; costs of, 12–13, 90–93, 94–98, 170; death and danger to, 9, 100, 106; diplomatic scandals caused by, 4, 62, 92; and ethics, 16, 95; fatal errors by, 62, 92; and foreign aid, 121, 134; and foreign policy, 32–33, 162–63; government ceding responsibility to, 9–10, 17, 28, 29, 32–33, 156, 161, 163, 168, 170; hybrid organizations, 162, 172; inadequate record-keeping on, 19, 22, 84, 87; Iraqis not used as, 101–4, 106, 169; language skills of, 100, 101; legal jurisdiction in question with, 3, 4, 92, 106; monitoring results of, 170; no-bid awards to, 33, 91, 95, 97, 122–23, 155–56, 168–69;

170, 182; overseas, 29–33, 97; oversight evaded by, 91–92, 182; physical security handed to, 62–63, 68; profits of, 12; security clearances for, 102; and subcontractors, 2, 3, 9, 18, 84, 91, 96, 104, 122, 168; for surge capacity, 93, 98; time saved, 97–98

Corporations: competition of, 33, 122; income of, 12, 47, 167; mergers of, 141; as model for government, 20, 129–30; and network security, 160–61; power of, 9, 172; social responsibility of, 54, 176; vertically integrated, 46. *See also* Business

Council on Foreign Relations, 158

Creative capitalism, 5–6, 35–39, 54

Croatia: army training in, 93–94; and Dayton Peace Accords, 94

Crocker, Ryan, 3

Crown, Lester, 6

Cuba, Communism in, 112

Custer Battles, 3

Customs-Trade Partnership Against Terrorism (C-TPAT), 159

Czechoslovakia, dismemberment of, 45

Danilovich, John, 78

Dayton Peace Accords, 66, 94

Declaration of Independence, 50

Deepwater scandal, 28, 150–52, 168

Defense Advanced Research Projects Agency (DARPANET), 167

Defense Department, U.S. (DOD): and accountability, 22, 92; contracting by, 86–90, 91, 180; creation of, 14, 57, 58, 85, 140; cuts in workforce by, 28, 91; and foreign aid, 130; and homeland security, 142, 145, 154–55; inadequate record-keeping in, 87; and interagency competition, 58, 60–62, 83, 85, 143, 144, 165; military aid administered in, 111; no-bid contracts awarded by, 33, 91, 95, 97; reorganization of, 85, 140, 161, 184; ships and planes no longer built by, 85; spending by, 22–24, 33, 164–65. *See also* Pentagon

DeKort, Michael, 152

Democratization, 80, 125

Deng Xiaoping, 177

DiIulio, John, 139–40

Diligence LLC, 105–6

Diplomacy: in advancing state interests, 65–66; American presence posts (APPs), 72, 73; "crisis," 74; and embassy staffing, 65; of the future, 63–68; and information revolution, 64–65; multilateral, 64; privatization of, 63–64, 66–68; public-private partnerships for, 70–71; traditional definition of, 62; traditional vs. global, 65–68, 81; transformational (*see* Transformational diplomacy); underfunding of, 82; virtual presence posts, 73

Diplomatic corps: accountability of, 62; ambassadorial posts in, 58, 59, 62, 65; attrition of, 132; in Cold War, 58; creation of, 57, 58; and encryption technology, 59; militarization of, 63; outsourcing diplomacy by, 60; politicization of, 58; security guards for, 62, 89; special envoys, 59–60; zero-risk mentality in, 63

Discover America Partnership, 70–71

DonorsChoose, 37

Drummond, Jamie, 75

Druyun, Darleen A., 3

Dubai Ports World, 147

DynCorp, 57, 82, 92, 94, 99, 136

Easterly, Bill, 118

East India Company, 50

eBay, 37

Edson, Gary, 75

Education: collaborative initiatives in, 181; international, 71–72

Eggers, William, 18–19

Eisenhower, Dwight D., on military-industrial complex, 14, 166–67, 176–77

Eisenhower administration, and shadow government, 13–15, 16

Empire of the willing, 8–9, 48–53; ideals of, 9, 178

Endeavor Global, 36, 37

Equality of opportunity, 8, 9, 55

Erinys International, 99, 101

ESS Support Services, 3

Europe: capitalism in, 51; and colonialism, 40, 50; and Marshall Plan, 109; national

interest in, 43; and Thirty Years' War, 39, 56; and Treaty of Westphalia, 39, 45, 56

European Union: and Mideast peace process, 7, 60; and Ottawa Convention, 6

FAIR (Federal Activities Inventory Reform) Act (*1998*), 15

FAR (Federal Acquisition Regulation), 16, 169

FBI (Federal Bureau of Investigation), 144

FEMA (Federal Emergency Management Agency), 136, 153–54, 156

Ferris Commission, 120

FFATA (Federal Funding Accountability and Transparency Act), 21–22, 32, 179

Finance, democratization of, 43, 174

First Kuwaiti General Trade and Contracting, 2–3

Fluor, 156

Foreign Affairs Department, U.S., 57

Foreign Affairs Reorganization (*1998*), 123

Foreign aid: bottom-up initiatives in, 133–35; in Cold War, 53, 58, 109, 110–17; and congressional cuts, 131–32; corporate model for, 2, 129–30; for development, 110, 112–19, 121, 125–35, 171; and enlightened national interest, 113; and globalization, 117, 119–20, 121, 133–34; Hamilton report on, 116; HELP Commission, 130; humanitarian, 109–10, 117, 125; investment approach to, 77, 80; Kissinger Commission, 115; legislative barriers to, 117, 118, 126; Millennium Challenge Account, 74–80, 125–26; moral purposes of, 113; multilateral programs of, 114; needs-based, 77, 78; overseas direct assistance, 74, 110, 128–29; partnership approach to, 114, 118–19; Pearson Commission on, 113–14; performance-based, 77; Peterson Commission on, 114; policymaking separated from implementation in, 133–34; in post–Cold War period, 117–20; privatization of, 113, 115, 121, 125, 127–28, 131, 133; Stern Report on, 114; Task Force on Foreign Assistance, 115; Task Force on Private Enterprise, 114–15; transformational development,

127–30, 131, 132–33, 171; and USAID (*see* USAID)

Foreign Assistance Act (*1961*), 110, 111–12, 115, 118, 122, 126, 130

Foreign policy: bottom-up initiatives in, 7; demilitarization of, 182–83; market for virtue in, 175–76, 177, 178, 180; militarization of, 9, 10, 83, 164–67; opacity of, 18, 32, 60; outdated design of, 143; postindustrial, 163; privatization of, 9, 15, 29–33, 53, 66–68, 134, 163, 171–74; traditional view of, 62; transparency in, 178–79

Foreign Service, U.S., creation of, 58

FPDS (Federal Procurement Data Service), 21–25, 123

Freedom of Information Act, 91, 158

Free markets: competition in, 122; faith in, 13, 14, 19–20, 51, 157; government intervention in, 170, 175; limitations of, 173, 175; power of, 8, 118; rewards of, 174; self-enforcing norms in, 108

French Revolution, 52–53

Friedman, Milton, 26–27

Friedman, Thomas, 43

Fukuyama, Francis, 41, 42

GAO (General Accounting Office), 120

GAO (Government Accountability Office), 22, 33; and Deepwater, 151; and fiscal policy, 182; and homeland security, 143; on human capital, 132; on Iraq, 32

Gates, Bill, 5–6, 36, 44, 54

Gates, Robert, 60, 130

Gates Foundation, 53, 119

Geldof, Bob, 75

General Dynamics, 12

General Motors, 72

Geneva Convention, 92, 106

Germany: military of, 45; unification of, 64; U.S. diplomatic posts in, 69

Ghani, Ashraf, 2

Giuliani, Rudy, 152

Glasser, Susan, 141

Global Development Alliance (GDA), 126

GlobalGiving, 37

Globalization: Bin Laden's war on, 182; and changing nature of power, 43–48, 172;

common values needed in, 10, 41; and democratization of finance, 43, 174; and democratization of information, 43, 174; and democratization of technology, 43, 174; disaggregated states in, 4, 40–41; and Fast World vs. Slow World, 43; and foreign aid, 117, 119–20, 121, 133–34; interdependence in, 41, 69; and philanthropy, 119; and privatization, 33, 43, 46, 165; and U.S. embassies, 65

Global Threat Reduction Initiative, 35–36

Golden, James L., 3

Goldman Sachs, 12, 72

Goldsmith, Stephen, 18–19

Goldwater-Nichols Defense Reorganization Act (*1986*), 85, 140, 161, 184

Google, 1, 37–38, 54

Gore, Al, 63, 86

Government: acquisition workforce of, 17–18, 28; advisory councils of, 170; aid between governments, 74; antiquated sense of purpose, 176, 183; basic functions of, 26; and bottom-up solutions, 170–71; bureaucracy of, 61, 144–45, 165, 171–72; checks and balances in, 26, 91, 170; in Cold War, 35; and common good, 8, 10, 157, 160, 175; core and peripheral functions of, 15–16, 27; cost of, 17; departing employees of, 180; distrust of, 14, 19–20, 28, 98, 138, 150, 163, 171; fiscal irresponsibility in, 9, 20; good, loss of, 11; hollowed-out, 9, 16, 17–21, 28; human capital crisis in, 17, 18, 27, 28, 181; inherently governmental (necessary) roles of, 8, 14, 15–16, 20, 26–29, 146–48, 171, 172, 173; interagency competition in, 58, 59–62, 85, 91, 111–12, 143, 144–45, 165, 184; market interventions by, 170, 175; misguided priorities of, 167; oversight responsibility of, 28–29, 32–33, 170, 171, 173, 180–81; partisan politics in, 170; pay rates in, 17–18, 19, 85, 96; privatization of, 2, 7, 8, 20, 163; reinvention of, 15, 59, 86, 120–23, 138, 162; responsibility ceded to contractors by, 9–10, 17, 28, 29, 32–33, 156, 161, 163, 168, 170; security as basic function of, 174, 175; shadow, 13–17, 173;

Government *(continued)*
  talented employees needed in, 173, 181;
  and think tanks, 168; undermining, 8, 26,
  98, 131, 132, 144–45
Grameen Bank, 36, 37
Gramsci, Antonio, 49
Great Britain: and Empire, 50; Foreign
  Office, 69; Ministry of International
  Development, 110; and privatization, 107
Grossman, Marc, 68, 73
Grunwald, Michael, 141
GSA (General Services Administration), 22

Hacker, Jacob, 32
Hadley, Stephen, 60
Haiti, U.S. intervention in, 40
Halliburton, 3, 54, 81, 87, 95, 156, 162–63,
  168, 169
Hamilton, Lee, 115
Hamilton Task Force on Foreign Assistance,
  115–16, 126
Hammes, Thomas, 98
Hamre, John, 138, 168
Hart-Rudman Commission, 158
Hegemony, 49, 174
Helms, Jesse, 72, 110
HELP Commission, 130
Homeland Security, U.S. Department of:
  accountability in, 145, 146, 148, 150;
  beyond the Beltway, 145–48; bottom-up
  process of, 161; branding, 140–45;
  bureaucracy of, 139, 140–41, 143, 145, 150,
  154, 157, 160; and business interests,
  152–53; cooperation with foreign
  governments, 158–59; creation of, 137–40,
  146; employee morale in, 136–37; and
  failure of leadership, 143–45, 156–58;
  funding shortfall of, 159–60; and
  Hurricane Katrina, 136, 153–56; identity
  confusion of, 142–45, 146; lack of
  oversight, 148–53, 156–57, 160; limited
  authority of, 139–40, 141–42, 143, 145;
  and national security, 134, 146, 147,
  160–61, 184; and network security,
  160–61; no-bid contracts awarded by, 33;
  outsourcing by, 25, 137, 148, 150;
  overlapping functions of, 142–43, 160;
  performance of, 148, 150–53; private-

public cooperation on, 158–59, 160–61;
  spending by, 22–24, 148, 149, 150; in
  wartime, 140–41, 143; Web sites, 159
Honduras, MCA-Honduras, 76, 77, 78
Horberger, Arnold, 130
Hughes, Karen, 70
Hu Jintao, 68
Hull, Edmund, 83
Hulsman, John, 42
Hurricane Katrina, 136, 153–56
Hussein, Saddam, 40, 102
Hybrid organizations, 162, 172

IAEA (International Atomic Energy
  Agency), 34
ICBL (International Campaign to Ban
  Landmines), 6
Idealism, 39, 41
Ikenberry, John, 49
Immelt, Jeff, 71
Immigration policy, revamping, 181
Independent Diplomat, 63–64
India, U.S. embassy in, 69
Indian Ocean tsunami, 44, 118–19
Information: democratization of, 43, 174; in
  emergencies, 155; instant, 178; as power,
  44, 64; revolution in, 64–65, 69;
  stovepiping, 64–65; transformed cost of,
  44; velocity of exchange, 44, 64
Integrated Coast Guard Systems (ICGS),
  151, 152
Internet: impact of, 44, 59, 64; microfinance
  via, 133; origins of, 167; and virtual
  presence posts, 73; as weapon of the
  weak, 178; whistleblowers on, 179
Iran-Contra scandal, 15
Iraq: accountability absent in, 19, 82, 104–5;
  army trained by contractors, 87, 99–100;
  civilian deaths in, 62; civil war in, 61, 80,
  105; contractors in, 2, 3–4, 9, 10, 11, 18,
  19, 27, 32, 53, 62, 63, 68, 82, 84, 87, 89,
  95, 97, 99–104, 156, 162, 168–69, 182;
  Free Forces of, 101; hiring Iraqis in, 101–4;
  imperial U.S. intervention in, 9, 40, 51,
  81, 83; insurgency in, 47; interrogation
  services outsourced in, 99, 100; lack of
  oversight in, 32, 82; lessons learned in,
  104–8; microlending in, 66; mistakes and

abuses in, 19, 60, 81, 82, 83, 95; oil
pipeline security in, 99, 101, 169; peace
failures in, 54; police training in, 99;
privatization in, 81, 84, 133; reconstruction of, 4, 9, 19, 53, 60, 61, 81, 82, 83, 99,
101–3, 105, 132–33, 165, 168–69; regime
change in, 102; shifting responsibility in,
32, 60, 82; transformational development
in, 132–33; U.S. Assistance to Iraq
program, 133; U.S. embassy in, 2–3,
80–81; U.S. military in, 84; and weapons
of mass destruction, 65
Isaacson, Walter, 6
Israeli-Palestinian peace process, 7

Jackson, Michael P., 159
Jakarta, Indonesia, U.S. embassy in, 69
Japan: military of, 45; overseas remittances
to, 121
Jarvis, Kevin, 151
Jefferson, Thomas, 52, 57
Joint Chiefs of Staff, 85, 140
Jolie, Angelina, 63
Justice Department, U.S.: and contractor
crimes, 106; and homeland security, 139,
145

Kellogg, Brown & Root (KBR), 3, 87, 90,
95, 96, 101, 102, 156, 169
Kelly, Jim, 71
Kennan, George, 42, 58
Kennedy, John F., 131
Kennedy administration, 110
Keohane, Robert, 41
Kettl, Donald, 42, 139
Khrushchev, Nikita, 110
Kissinger, Henry A., 39–40, 115
Kissinger Commission on Central America,
115
Kiva, 4, 37, 66
Klein, Naomi, 103, 152–53, 155
Kosovo, U.S. intervention in, 40
Kristof, Nicholas, 37

Lake, Anthony, 60
Law, international, 42
Law enforcement, 27, 28
Lead Systems Integrator (LSI), 28

League of Nations, 39
Lebanon: overseas remittances to, 121;
reconstruction of, 71
Lessig, Lawrence, 178
Liberal internationalism, 39–43
Liberalism, appeal of, 51
Lieberman, Joseph, 137, 138
Lieven, Anatol, 42
Light, Paul, 18, 23
LoBiondo, Frank, 152
Lockheed Martin, 3, 12, 151–52
Los Angeles/Long Beach port, 146
Louis Berger Group, 2
Lugar, Richard, 60, 61
Lute, Douglas E., 60

Madagascar, and Millennium Challenge
Corporation, 77, 78, 79
Maddox, David M., 17
Major, John, 105
Malaria No More, 134–35
Market for virtue, 175–76, 177; demilitarization of foreign policy, 182–83; in
departing government employees, 180;
human capital strategy for, 181; long-term
goals for, 181–82; national security
discussions for, 182; regulation and
oversight in, 180–81; restriction of no-bid
contracts in, 182; and special interests,
180; streamlining government in, 183–84;
technological advantage utilized in, 183;
and transparency, 178–79, 180; Wikileaks,
179–80, 181
Marshall, George C., 109
Marshall Plan (1948–1951), 109, 110, 111, 115,
116, 127, 133, 168, 172–73
Martinez-Fonts, Alfonso, 159
Mathias, Ed, 105
McKinnell, Hank Jr., 71
McNamara, Robert S., 113
McPherson, M. Peter, 133
MEET US (Middle East Entrepreneur
Training), 71
Melville, Andy, 101
MEPI (Middle East Partnership Initiative),
71, 82
Metternich, Klemens von, 56, 57, 62, 65, 68
Mexico, U.S. embassy in, 65

Microfinance, 5, 36, 66, 133
Middle East, failure of democracy in, 80, 166
Military: aerial surveillance, 89; all-volunteer, 85, 93; contractors outside chain of command, 90–91; court-martial system of, 92–93; and domestic law enforcement, 142, 156; draft, 10, 33, 98; "jointness" as goal of, 85; and patriotic duty, 98; president's use of, 142; private military companies (PMCs), 15, 89–94, 97, 107–8; recruitment shortfalls of, 27; secrecy in, 32, 91; support functions outsourced by, 86, 87, 89, 90; surge capacity of, 93, 98; training to be a soldier, 98
Military Extraterritorial Jurisdiction Act (2000), 106
Military-industrial complex, 14, 166–67, 176–77
Millennium Challenge Account (MCA), 74–80, 125–26
Millennium Challenge Corporation (MCC), 75–80, 119, 131, 133, 170–71; and civil wars, 83; creation of, 77; expectations for, 77–78; funding for, 78; local input to, 76, 78–79, 80; measurable results required by, 76; multiplier effect of, 76; resistance to, 77–78, 79–80; in threshold countries, 76
Monnet, Jean, 36
Monterrey Consensus, 74, 77, 125
Morgenthau, Hans, 42
MPRI (Military Professional Resources Incorporated), 90, 93, 94
Mulcahy, Anne, 71
Murphy, Cullen, 174
Musharraf, Pervez, 71

Napoleon Bonaparte, 56
National defense, 27, 28, 143
National Defense Authorization Act (2009), 16
National Geographic Society, 37
National Guard, and Hurricane Katrina, 156
National Intelligence Center, 139
National Performance Review, 120–21
National security, 27, 40, 134, 146, 160–61, 182, 184

National Security Act (1947), 14, 57, 58–59, 85
National Security Council (NSC): creation of, 57, 58; and interagency competition, 59–60, 85; and Millennium Challenge Account, 75
National Security Strategy (2002), 125, 129
NATO, 52
Natsios, Andrew, 63, 121, 126, 127–28, 129, 131, 132, 133
Navy Department, U.S., 58, 85
Negroponte, Nicholas, 6
New Bridge Strategies, 153
NGOs (nongovernmental organizations): in Cold War, 35; power of, 1, 45, 134–35, 172
Nicaragua, Sandinistas in, 115
Niebuhr, Reinhold, 42
Nihilists, 56
9/11 Commission, 82, 142, 143–44, 145
9/11 Public Discourse Project, 143
Nixon, Richard M., 113
North, Oliver, 15
Northrop Grumman, 12, 87, 92, 151, 152
Nuclear threat, 10, 34, 35–36, 46
Nunn, Sam, 34, 35
Nye, Joseph, 41

Obama, Barack, 21, 123, 178, 179, 180
Obama administration, 60
Official Development Assistance (ODA), 119, 121
OLPC (One Laptop Per Child), 6
OMB (Office of Management and Budget): and accountability, 21–25; public-private competition promoted by, 14, 15; and think tanks, 168
OMB Watch, 21, 23, 181
Omidyar, Pierre, 37
Omidyar Network, 36–37
Omnibus Anti-Red Tape Law (2002), 158
Omnibus Appropriations bill (2008), 34
Ottawa Convention, on landmines, 6
Outsourcing: annual inventories of, 15; and budget cuts, 132; corruption and mismanagement in, 89, 94–95, 151–52, 170; of defense, 86–90, 91; defined, 7, 13; and disaggregated states, 40; labor costs of, 96–97; laissez-faire, 9, 150, 163, 166,

170; limitations on, 28–29; of oversight, 8, 32, 82, 91–92, 123, 133, 166, 168–69, 171, 177; of peripheral functions, 15–16; and power shift, 47–48; reasons for, 25, 93–94, 165; short-term political benefits of, 93, 98

Overseas Private Investment Corporation (OPIC), 113

Packer, George, 57, 81
Page, Larry, 37
Palestinian-Israeli peace process, 7
Palmisano, Samuel, 46
Parsons, 156
Partnership for Public Service, 17–18
Patriot Act, 150
Paulson, Henry, 20
Pearson Commission, 113–14
Pentagon: acquisition workforce of, 17, 89, 91; and all-volunteer military, 85, 93; budget of, 10, 70, 85–86, 165, 166; bureaucracy of, 86; court-martial system of, 92; creation of, 14, 182; Defense Acquisition Regulation Supplement (DFARS), 105, 106; and development aid, 165; Foreign Military Sales program of, 91; and homeland security, 139, 142, 155, 156; inadequate record-keeping in, 19, 22, 84, 87, 89, 91–92, 95, 105; "inherently governmental" functions in, 27; intelligence activities of, 165; and interagency competition, 60–62, 91, 111, 144, 165; and Iraq, 19, 83; and militarization of foreign policy, 10, 83, 164–67; outsourcing by, 3, 25, 27, 85–90, 91, 93–94, 165; pay scales of, 85; and privatization, 85–90; Quadrennial Defense Review, 165; resistance to change, 144; September 11 attack on, 144; and State Department, 164; and supplemental funding, 166; taking up the slack, 61, 62, 63; and tsunami relief, 119
Persian Gulf War, contractors in, 84, 89
Peterson, Peter G., 70
Peterson Commission, 114
Philanthropreneurs, 35–39, 44, 53, 54, 119
Polanyi, Karl, 174–75
Posse Comitatus Act, 142
Postel, Eric, 130

Powell, Colin, 61, 73, 75, 102, 103, 126, 164
Powell, Dina Habib, 71
Powell, Lord Charles, 105
Power: abuse of, 18; changing nature of, 8, 43–48; corporate, 9, 172; and globalization, 43–48
Pozen, Robert, 181–82
PR Coalition, 73
Prentis, Henning W. Jr., 111
President's Emergency Plan for AIDS Relief, 125, 131
Princeton Project on National Security, 42
Private sector: best practices of, 20; business as usual for, 157; in Cold War, 35; comparative advantage of, 12; empowerment of, 43–45; foreign policy influence of, 32, 35, 74; in Hurricane Katrina, 136, 155–56; and opacity, 32; power shift to, 47–48; revolving door from government to, 105–6, 170, 180; use of term, 7. See also Corporations
Private security companies, 47
Privatization: benefits of, 27–28, 33, 93–94; costs of, 90–93, 94–98; of foreign policy, 9, 15, 29–33, 53, 66–68, 134, 163, 171–74; and globalization, 33, 43, 46, 165; of governance, 2, 7, 8, 20, 163; of high-tech systems, 93; limitations on, 25–29; and the military, 86–94, 97, 107–8; outsourcing, 7, 8, 86; as revolt against bureaucracy, 171–72; scope of, 8, 20, 170; and sovereignty, 16; thought experiment on, 95–96
Project (Red), 1–2

Quainton, Anthony, 59, 63
"Quartet," 7, 60

Radelet, Steve, 79, 126
Rangel, Charles, 176
Raytheon, 12
Reagan, Ronald, 171
Reagan administration, 15, 114–15
Realism: ethical, 42; state emphasized in, 40, 41, 65–66; and Truman administration, 42; and Westphalia, 39, 42; and Wilsonianism, 41, 42; zero-sum thinking in, 40

Reinhard, Keith, 70
Rice, Condoleezza, 60, 62, 68, 70, 73, 75, 129, 138
Ridge, Tom, 137, 139, 140, 141, 143, 145, 150, 152, 153
Riechers, Charles D., 3
Rifkind, Sir Malcolm, 105
Risk, outsourcing of, 32–33
Rogers, Ed, 105
Rogers Act (*1924*), 58
Rohatyn, Felix, 72
Roman Empire, 174
Ross, Carne, 63–64
Rothkopf, David, 7, 46, 73
Rottenberg, Linda, 37
Rumsfeld, Donald, 26, 60, 62, 86, 87, 93, 95, 164
Russia: authoritarian governance of, 172; foreign aid to, 120; gangster capitalism in, 49; and Mideast peace process, 7, 60; U.S. diplomatic positions in, 69

Sandel, Michael, 51
Sandinistas, 115
Sandline International, 90
Schinasi, Katherine, 22
Schooner, Steven, 89, 91
Schwab, Klaus, 36
Scott, H. Lee Jr., 1
Secure Border Initiative, 159
Self-interest, enlightened, 10, 175–76
Sen, Amartya, 117–18, 119, 157
September *11* attacks, 56, 69, 86, 87, 137, 143, 144
Serbia, vs. Croatia, 93–94
Shaw, 156
Shriver, Bobby, 1
Singer, Peter, 89
Slaughter, Anne-Marie, 40, 51
Smart and Secure Trade Lanes Initiative, 159
Smith, Adam, 38
Social entrepreneurship, 36–39
Solis, William M., 19
Soloway, Stan, 132
Somalia, U.S. intervention in, 40
Soros, George, 54, 63
South Asia Earthquake Relief Fund, 71
Sovereignty: of the people vs. states, 16; and

universal human rights, 45; and Westphalia, 39, 45, 56
Soviet Union: in Cold War, 34, 51, 85, 110–12, 116–17; dismemberment of, 45, 53, 59, 87, 110, 117, 118, 121
Soviet Union, former, foreign aid to, 120, 121
Spicer, Tim, 90, 100, 103
Sri Lanka, civil war in, 83
Starbucks, 54
State Department, U.S.: abdication of responsibility by, 82, 91–92; and ACE, 72; budget cuts in, 59, 66, 69, 70, 72, 83; bureaucracy of, 61; careers in, 61–62; creation of, 57; and diplomacy (*see* Diplomacy; Diplomatic corps); and embassy staffing, 65; inadequate record-keeping in, 92; increased expectations for, 62, 70; and interagency competition, 58, 59–62, 83, 91, 111, 165; jurisdiction in, 65; military aid administered by, 111; and Millennium Challenge Account, 75–79; outsourcing by, 25, 31, 33, 57, 59, 62, 66–68, 82, 91–92, 97; and peace dividend, 29; and Pentagon, 164; and public-private partnerships, 7, 73–74; rise and decline of, 57–63, 64; security for personnel of, 89; and special envoys, 59–60; spending by, 24, 29, 31, 165; and transformational diplomacy, 68–70, 129–30; underfunded, 62, 69, 165; and underlying policy, 83; and USAID, 110, 118, 120, 123, 129
States: definition of, 45; disaggregated, 40–41, 42; failed, 93; financial leverage of, 44–45; information monopoly of, 44; and legitimate use of force, 44, 45–46; sovereignty of, 39–40, 41, 45
Stern Report (*1971*), 114
Stier, Max, 173
Stiglitz, Joseph, 104
Stovepiping, 64–65
Summers, Larry, 118
Sunlight Network, 181

Tanzania, USAID in, 132
Task Force on Foreign Assistance, 115–16
Task Force on Private Enterprise, 114–15

Taylor, Gene, 152

Technology: democratization of, 43, 174; U.S. advantage in, 183

Terrorism: and developing countries, 74; by global guerillas, 47; and homeland security, 137, 138, 142, 145–46, 157, 160; Internet connections of, 56; suicide bombers, 45, 56; systems disruption as aim of, 47; targets for, 63; threat of, 10, 125; war on, 125, 143

Thatcher, Margaret, 105

Thirty Years' War, 39, 56

Titan International, 4, 99

Tobias, Randall, 129–30

Tocqueville, Alexis de (*Democracy in America*), 10, 12, 175–76, 177

Townsend Commission, 154–55

Trade: mutual gain in, 40; promotion of, 14, 58

Tragedy of the commons, 157

Transformational diplomacy, 68–83, 104, 129–30; awards in, 72; implementation as policy in, 171; limits of, 80–83; and Millennium Challenge Account, 74–80; private sector in, 70–71, 73, 74

Transparency: and accountability, 21–25, 105, 123, 168, 177; commitment to, 178; lack of, 8, 32, 81, 122, 168; and market for virtue, 178–79, 180

Transparency International, 3

Treasury Department, U.S.: and Millennium Challenge Account, 75; multilateral aid administered in, 111

Trice, Stanley, 22

Trippi, Joe, 178

Truman administration, 42

TSA (Transportation Security Agency), 146–47

Tsunami relief, funds raised for, 44, 118–19

Turner, Ted, 34, 35, 38, 44, 54

Udall, Morris, 111

Uniform Code of Military Justice, 92, 106

United Nations: and former Yugoslavia, 93; and Iraq, 40; and Mideast peace process, 7, 60; and Ottawa Convention, 6; and Westphalia, 39

United States: anti-American sentiment, 54;

capitalism in, 51; core values of, 8, 10, 14, 50–51, 55; economic risk transferred to families in, 32; and empire of the willing, 48–53, 174; foreign perceptions of, 144; hegemony of, 49, 174; hypocrisy of, 82–83; interventions by, 9, 40, 83; and Mideast peace process, 7, 60; militarized foreign policy of, 9, 10, 54, 83, 164–67; military budget of, 14, 45–46; unilateralism of, 54

Universalism, 56

USAID (United States Agency for International Development), 2, 53, 109–35; accountability problems in, 123; Bollinger report on, 116; bureaucracy of, 123, 130, 134; in Cold War, 58, 110–17; collaborative agreement in, 127; and competitive sourcing, 127, 128; as contract clearinghouse, 63, 110, 119, 125, 131, 132, 133; creation of, 109–12; development aid via, 110, 111, 112, 113, 116, 118, 120, 121, 122, 125–30; and domestic economic interests, 122; Ferris Commission report on, 120; goals of, 126, 127, 134; and Hamilton task force, 115–16, 126; human capital vulnerabilities of, 132; humanitarian aid via, 109–10, 126; and Information Age, 130–35; and interagency competition, 111–12, 165; and Kissinger Commission, 115; lack of support for, 120–23, 129–30, 131; and Millennium Challenge Account, 75, 76, 77; needs-based aid from, 77; no-bid contracts awarded by, 33, 122; oversight cut in, 125, 132; partners in development, 112, 118, 126, 127; and Peterson Commission, 114; political opposition to, 110, 116, 126; in post–Cold War period, 117–20; procurement data from, 123, 124; project-based aid in, 125; and public-private partnerships, 7, 113, 118–19, 121, 122, 127–30; reinventing, 120–23, 126–29, 134; secrecy in, 122; spending by, 24, 165; staff reductions in, 19, 63, 119, 125, 131–32; and State Department, 110, 118, 120, 123, 129; Stern Report on, 114; and Task Force on Foreign Assistance, 115; and transformational development, 127–30, 131, 132–33

USAspending.gov, 21–24, 33, 123, 179
U.S. Central Command, 102
USIA (United States Information Agency), 58, 130
U.S.-Lebanon Partnership, 71
U.S.-Palestinian Public-Private Partnership, 6–7
U.S. Project Management Office, 100

Verga, Peter, 142
Verkuil, Paul, 16, 26
Vietnam War, 84, 93, 114
Vinca nuclear reactor, Belgrade, 35
Vinnell Corporation, 99
Virgin Group, 5
Virtue: meanings of term, 175. *See also* Market for virtue
Vogel, David, 175

Walker, David A., 27, 28, 146, 177
Wal-Mart, 1, 136, 155
Walzer, Michael, 49
War: extrabudgetary financing of, 166; of the future, 56–57; high-tech weapons in, 93; and legitimate use of force, 45–46; mercenaries in, 84, 106; and military power, 46; "open source," 47; privatization of, 27, 33, 84–108
War Department, U.S., 58, 85
Waxman, Henry, 33, 89, 168–69
Wealth gap, 10, 117, 118
Weber, Max, 45
Webster, William, 105

Weill, Sandy, 6, 71
Welfare state, emergence of, 175
Wempen, Rex, 100
Westphalia, Treaty of: overturning of, 40, 42, 43, 56; and realism, 39, 42; state sovereignty in, 39, 45, 56
Whelan, Theresa, 87, 98
Why We Fight (film), 166–67
Wikileaks, 179–80, 181
Wilkerson, Lawrence, 102, 164, 166
Williams, Jody, 6
Williams-Bridgers, Jacquelyn, 32
Wilson, James, 16
Women: status of, 118; voting rights for, 52
Wood, Gordon, 16
Woods, Alan, 116
Woolsey, James, 153
World Bank, and development aid, 113
World Economic Forum, Davos, 5, 36
World Trade Center, attacks on, 56, 86, 144

Yarwood, Susan, 87
Yugoslavia, former: army training in, 93–94; and Dayton Peace Accords, 94; dismemberment of, 45; sex slavery ring in, 92; third-party military personnel in, 15
Yunus, Mohammed, 36

Zakaria, Fareed, 48, 54
Zelikow, Philip, 82
Zero-sum thinking, 40
Zinni, Anthony, 29, 164